Air Wars

Air Wars

TELEVISION ADVERTISING IN
ELECTION CAMPAIGNS, 1952-1992

Darrell M. West
Brown University

Congressional Quarterly Inc.
Washington, D.C.

Printed in the United States of America

Second Printing

Cover design: Ed Atkeson/Berg Design, Albany, New York

Library of Congress Cataloging-in-Publication Data

West, Darrell M., 1954-
    Air wars : television advertising in election campaigns, 1952-1992 / Darrell M. West.
        p.   cm.
    Includes index.
    ISBN 0-87187-757-0 (cloth) - - ISBN 0-87187-756-2 (pbk.)
    1. Advertising, Political- -United States.   2. Television in politics- -United States.
3. Electioneering- -United States.   4. United States- -Politics and government- -1989-1993.
I. Title.
    JF2112.A4W47   1993
    659.2' 932- -dc20   93-14231
                                                                                             CIP

To Annie Schmitt, for her
constant encouragement and support

————————————

Contents

Tables and Figures

Tables

Figures

Preface

Few topics have generated greater interest among observers of the media recently than the widespread use of television advertising in election campaigns. Commercials have become one of the dominant means of communication in contemporary races. Citizens are bombarded with millions of dollars' worth of ads during the political season.[1] In today's world, it is nearly impossible to imagine campaigns without political commercials.

Air Wars: Television Advertising in Election Campaigns, 1952-1992 addresses two central questions about television advertisements. First, how much influence do ads have on viewers? Much has been made about the presumed ability of campaign commercials to alter public opinion, but there have been few detailed historical studies of this subject.[2] Aside from analyses of ad content, which have addressed changes in the television spots themselves, not many projects have examined the effects of political commercials over several decades. This omission makes it difficult to know whether particular results are limited to the election under consideration or represent a more general feature.

Second, are campaign ads good for democracy? Many observers have voiced complaints about democracy in the United States—for example, that citizens lack knowledge and that the nation's representative institutions are weak.[3] However, few developments have prompted more concern about the overall health of democracy than the reliance by candidates for public office on paid television advertisements. Critics charge that campaign commercials undermine democracy by shortening public discourse to thirty-second segments. Moreover, advertisements are said to distort citizens' assessments of the candidates because of the tendency of individuals to engage in "information grazing." If people only periodically tune in to the campaign, there is a potential danger to decision making.[4]

The research reported in this book adopts a fundamentally different perspective than is found elsewhere in the media studies field. To explore the impact of the media, scholars have used psychological models linked to citizens' exposure to and processing of information provided by the media.[5] The assumption is that individual attributes, such as background qualities and personal orientations, are the primary explanations of viewers' responses. Although these models have been useful for general analysis, they cannot be used for gauging the impact of campaign commercials. Psychological perspectives common in news studies need to be supplemented with material from the broader fabric of campaign politics. Spot advertising is inherently a political phenomenon in which the context of ad development, broadcasting, and response is quite important. The same type of commercial can have remarkably different consequences depending on the electoral setting and behavior of the candidates. Therefore, I develop a contextual model of advertising that looks at the structure of the campaign system, the strategic behavior of candidates, and coverage by the news media. Paid advertisements cannot be understood without considering these vital features of the political context.

Chapter 1 introduces the framework upon which the book rests. Chapter 2 reviews the methodology of advertising research. The analysis of campaign advertisements poses a number of challenges, including how best to study ads, how to measure viewers' reactions, and how to disentangle the effects of advertising from their possible influences on citizens. In Chapter 2 I discuss how I addressed these challenges.

Chapter 3 investigates the strategic aspects of advertising by looking at the content of ads from 1952 to 1992. I demonstrate that candidates' appeals have varied considerably over the years but that the level of specificity increased in the 1980s and 1990s. Commercials have become quite negative in style of presentation, although this trend is not without precedent in the period immediately after World War II.

Chapter 4 studies changes in media coverage of campaign advertisements since 1952. No aspect of political spots has undergone more dramatic development than this one. Journalistic attention to ads has increased substantially over the past forty years. However, much of the coverage of advertising emphasizes strategic rationales behind the commercials and the electoral consequences for candidates, rather than the content of the commercials.

Chapters 5 through 7 investigate voters' reactions to television spots. Chapter 5 relies on models of learning to examine the effects of advertising on views about the candidates. What do citizens learn about the contestants based on exposure to television ads? Briefly, I show that ads contribute to citizens' impressions of candidates' prospects and images.

Agenda setting is the subject of Chapter 6. How do ads influence voters' feelings regarding public priorities? Using citizens' assessments of the most important problems facing the country and the most significant events of the campaign, I investigate how ads influence and reflect voters' feelings regarding public priorities. Leaders are able to shift citizens' impressions through the ephemeral and media-dominated world of campaign events as well as through public policy.

Chapter 7 examines priming in election campaigns: Can political commercials change the standards by which candidates are evaluated? I distinguish priming from defusing and show that at various times television advertising can either elevate (prime) or weaken (defuse) the importance of particular factors in vote choice. Candidates can have considerable success by defusing matters that are problematic for themselves or by playing the blame game so that their opponent is seen as responsible for turning the tone of the campaign negative.

Chapter 8 discusses the significance for democratic elections of the results obtained in this study. Elections are the lifeblood of democratic political systems. They are a means by which ordinary people acting together determine who leads the country. However, the heavy reliance on television advertising at a time when the political system places great emphasis on personal popularity has raised doubts about the quality of the information presented during election campaigns and about how voters make decisions. Chapter 8 reviews these concerns and assesses the contexts in which ads are most problematic.

Acknowledgments

Many people deserve thanks for their assistance with this project. Steven Ansolabehere, Richard Brody, Doris A. Graber, Kathleen Jamieson, Dorothy Nesbit, and Michael Traugott gave careful readings to earlier versions of this manuscript. Their comments were quite helpful, and I owe them a lot. In addition, Thomas Anton, Kathleen Dolan, Ellen Hume, Shanto Iyengar, Tom James, Lynda Lee Kaid, Marvin Kalb, Patrick Kenney, Margaret Latimer, Richard Marshall, Robert McClure, Jonathan Nagler, Eric Nordlinger, Victor Ottati, Thomas Patterson, Nancy Rosenblum, Annie Schmitt, John Zaller, and Alan Zuckerman made valuable comments on papers drawn from this manuscript. Dean Alger, Tim Cook, Ann Crigler, Marion Just, and Montague Kern shared their reactions with me during our collaboration on the 1992 media project.

Outstanding research assistance was provided by a number of undergraduate and graduate students at Brown University: Rima Alaily, Christopher Goodwin, Leslyn Hall, Jonathan Klarfeld, Sara Leppo, Nancy Lublin, Dan Miller, Cristina Munoz-Fazakes, Martin Sabarsky, Daryl Wiesen, Matthew Woods, and Jonathan Wyche. This book could not have been written without them. I am deeply grateful to the scores of students who have taken my "Campaigns and Elections," and "Politics and the Mass Media" courses in recent years. The chance to bounce preliminary ideas off bright and engaging students was invaluable.

Videotapes of commercials of past races were provided by Julian Kanter of the Political Commercial Archive at the University of Oklahoma. Patrick Devlin of the University of Rhode Island also made available selected ads from previous elections. Marilyn Fancher of the Broadcast Division at the Republican National Committee helped arrange permission to use the 1988 Bush ads in this research. Frank Greer and Alexa Suma provided access to Clinton's and Bush's 1992 ads, respectively. Video Plus provided copies of Perot's thirty-minute infomercials. In addition, I benefited enormously from a number of lengthy interviews conducted with prominent journalists in 1992: Brooks Jackson of the Cable News Network, Elizabeth Kolbert of the *New York Times,* Howard Kurtz of the *Washington Post,* Mara Liasson of National Public Radio, Renee Loth of the *Boston Globe,* and Tom Rosenstiel of the *Los Angeles Times.* My thanks to these individuals for sharing their impressions with me. Conversations over the years with journalists in Rhode Island also have sharpened my understanding of campaigns and elections. A thank you to M. Charles Bakst, Russ Garland, Katherine Gregg, Scott MacKay, John Martin, and Mark

Patinkin of the *Providence Journal;* Dyana Koelsch, Jim Taricani, Doug White, and Patrice Wood at WJAR-TV; Sean Daly, David Layman, and Barbara Meagher of WLNE-TV; Walter Cryan of WPRI-TV; Paul Zangari of WSBE-TV; Steve Kass and Arlene Violet of WHJJ Radio; and Mary Ann Sorrentino of WPRO Radio.

Jeanne Ferris of Congressional Quarterly deserves kudos for her assistance on my manuscript. She made a number of helpful suggestions, which strengthened the arguments developed in this book. Nola Healy Lynch improved the manuscript considerably through a superb job of copy editing, and Laura Carter performed admirably as production editor despite the difficulties of intercontinental communication. Every author should be fortunate enough to have editors like these.

The John Hazen White, Sr., Public Opinion Laboratory of the A. Alfred Taubman Center for Public Policy and American Institutions at Brown University, the Institute for Research in Social Science at the University of North Carolina, the Inter-University Consortium for Political and Social Research at the University of Michigan, and the CBS/*New York Times* survey operation facilitated this analysis by making available data from a number of public opinion surveys. Jack Combs, research administrator at the Taubman Center, and Matthew Woods deserve a big thank you for making sure that our 1992 surveys ran smoothly. A sabbatical leave at Nuffield College of Oxford University provided a stimulating environment as I was wrapping up this project. My thanks to Byron Shafer for helping to arrange the time for writing.

A special debt of gratitude is owed to John Hazen White, Sr., president of Taco, Inc., of Cranston, Rhode Island, and his wife, Happy White. At a time of great crisis within the state, the White family provided a generous endowment for the Public Opinion Laboratory at Brown. This timely contribution helped make possible the analysis presented in this book.

Finally, I would like to acknowledge the financial support of the National Science Foundation (SES-9122729), MacArthur Foundation, Ford Foundation, Twentieth Century Fund, Joan Shorenstein Barone Center on Press, Politics and Public Policy at Harvard University, Everett McKinley Dirksen Congressional Leadership Research Center, and the following units at Brown University: the Department of Political Science, the A. Alfred Taubman Center for

Preface

Public Policy and American Institutions, the Undergraduate Teaching and Research Assistantship program of the Dean of the College, and the Small Grants program of the Graduate School. None of these individuals or organizations bears any responsibility for the interpretations presented here.

Chapter 1

Rethinking Ads

Erotic images filled TV screens in Georgia before that state's March 3, 1992, primary. Television commentator Patrick Buchanan was challenging President George Bush's renomination with a hard-hitting commercial claiming the president had betrayed the conservative cause by supporting federal funds for homoerotic art. As scenes of scantily clad, dancing, gay men filled the screen, an announcer intoned: "In the last three years, the Bush Administration has invested our tax dollars in pornographic and blasphemous art too shocking to show. This so-called art has glorified homosexuality, exploited children, and perverted the image of Jesus Christ. Even after good people protested, Bush continued to fund this kind of art. Send Bush a message. We need a leader who will fight for what we believe in." [1] Despite this appeal, Buchanan lost the Georgia primary to Bush by almost 30 points.

The fall campaign was no less eventful. Viewers were saturated with debates, lengthy interviews by Larry King, Phil Donahue, and Arsenio Hall, short commercials, and thirty-minute "infomercials"—the program-length commercials favored by Ross Perot. The three-way battle between Bush, Bill Clinton, and Perot stimulated volatility in the preelection polls. Throughout the race, Bush used ads to attack Clinton's character and record as governor of Arkansas. But in 1992 Bush could not prevail. Between the poor economy, Bush's personal unpopularity, and the backlash that developed against Bush's advertising attacks, Clinton won by 43 to 38 percent over Bush. Perot finished in third place with 19 percent, the best showing for a third party candidate since Theodore Roosevelt in 1912. [2]

The election of 1988 had been different. Early in the summer, Michael Dukakis was riding high. Gallup had just released a poll in which the Massachusetts governor had a 17 percentage point lead over his Republican rival, Vice President Bush. Even more impressive were the less publicized numbers. Women preferred Dukakis over Bush by a large margin, and the governor was doing well among blacks, the elderly, and Democrats who previously had supported Ronald Reagan. Campaign officials began to talk openly about a Dukakis presidency.

Meanwhile, Republicans were test marketing some new advertising material. Over Memorial Day weekend in Paramus, New Jersey, Bush aides Jim Baker, Lee Atwater, Roger Ailes, Robert Teeter, and Nicholas Brady stood behind a one-way mirror observing a small group of Reagan Democrats. Information concerning William Horton, a convicted black man who—while on furlough from a Massachusetts prison—brutally raped a white woman, was being presented. The audience seemed quite disturbed. Atwater later boasted to party operatives, "By the time this election is over, Willie Horton will be a household name." [3] The words were eerily prophetic, and Bush went on to beat Dukakis by 53 to 46 percent.

Studying Ads in Context

From the earliest days of the Republic, communications devices have been essential to presidential campaigns. In 1828, for example, John Quincy Adams was portrayed in a handbill distributed by supporters of Andrew Jackson as "driving off with a horsewhip a crippled old soldier who dared to speak to him, to ask an alms." A circular distributed by Adams's forces meanwhile attacked Jackson for "ordering other executions, massacring Indians, stabbing a Samuel Jackson in the back, murdering one soldier who disobeyed his commands, and hanging three Indians." [4]

The method, though perhaps not the tone, of communicating with the electorate has changed dramatically since 1828. Handbills have disappeared. Newspapers have become less overtly partisan. Radio became the popular medium, then was supplanted by television. Throughout these upheavals (or maybe because of them), the media have remained a compelling topic of interest to observers of the political scene.

Those who study the media have two main reasons for their fascination. The first is curiosity about how the media wield influence. People are not equally susceptible to the media, and scholars have tried to find out how media power actually operates. The second relates to normative concerns about this power: If the media are influential, what is their effect on the political system?

Early studies of propaganda attributed great importance to organized information campaigns.[5] German propaganda efforts in the 1930s were seen as very threatening because of the ability of the Nazis to use radio and motion pictures to inflame public passions. Countless movie reels from that period showed German leaders inciting huge crowds with Nazi appeals. This was profoundly disturbing to observers who feared that mass media would become vehicles for totalitarianism.

Yet these fears receded when later research showed significant limits on the power of political leaders to manipulate citizens. The rise of the "minimal effects" model after World War II disputed earlier results regarding the power of propaganda. The pioneering work of Paul Lazarsfeld, Bernard Berelson, and others suggested that candidates faced clear limits on their persuasive abilities.[6] Evidence from American general elections in the 1940s and 1950s demonstrated that voters often made up their minds early in the race and stuck with their choices despite the fervent appeals of opposition candidates.

The conflicting findings on the influence of the media generated a wide range of explanations to account for the differences. A number of studies found that citizens' knowledge and sophistication were longstanding barriers to media influence. Generally, less knowledge-able people were seen as more susceptible to influence than those who closely followed public affairs. Preexisting beliefs and values were also instrumental in determining media influence. The media are most persuasive when firmly held convictions are absent. Cognitive consistency theories meanwhile pointed out that it is painful for average people to be presented with information that runs contrary to cherished beliefs. Therefore, to avoid this pain, they expose themselves selectively to the media and screen out information they do not like.

But each of these explanations—political sophistication, prior beliefs, and selective perceptions—emphasizes individual attributes as the primary determinants of viewers' response. If television has modest effects and thus poses little danger, it is because viewers are sophisticated, engage in "counterarguing," or screen information. If agenda-setting research shows much stronger media effects, then either strong opinions must be lacking or underlying values must have been activated.

It is no accident that individual-level explanations have dominated media studies. The research is based on psychological models and is conducted in standard ways. Typically, viewers are brought into a laboratory setting, randomly assigned to groups, and shown different versions of the evening news. Some designs, such as those of Shanto Iyengar and Donald Kinder, aim for greater realism by inviting participants to bring family members and friends and by providing snacks for those assembled.[7] But even advanced designs have the goal of testing propositions derived from political psychology.

Psychological models have been crucial to our understanding of the news media. For example, research has found that television can prime voters by altering standards of evaluation. Heavy television coverage of personal qualities, such as that seen in the 1992 presidential campaign, leads voters to weigh character more heavily in their assessments of candidates. Furthermore, important new work has been done on framing, which shows the importance of interpretation. Viewers blame individual poor people for their poverty if the coverage emphasizes episodic events, such as welfare cheating, but society in general is blamed if stories stress thematic points, such as the number of people living below the poverty line.[8]

But there are dangers to relying exclusively on psychological models. These approaches take respondents out of their social and political environments, and therefore run the risk of removing viewers' judgments from their context. A growing body of literature emphasizes the crucial role of leaders in structuring public responses.[9] Viewers operate within systems defined by elites, and they relate to information on the basis of broadly defined cultural and political imperatives.

Raymond Williams argues that not just particular programs, but the cultural setting and sequence of "information flows," influence viewers. A vivid example is found in Kathleen Jamieson's study of the 1988 presidential campaign. The effectiveness of Bush's "Revolving Door" ad on Dukakis's crime record was enhanced by cultural fears about black men raping white women and from earlier news stories that had sensationalized Horton's crime spree. Bush did not have to mention Horton in this ad for viewers to make the connection between Dukakis and heinous crimes.[10] The constructionist framework developed by William Gamson, and by Russell

Neuman, Marion Just, and Ann Crigler, also suggests that one cannot look only at isolated events but instead must be aware of how storytelling devices are used to encapsulate political developments.[11]

A study of the 1992 presidential nominating process by Montague Kern, Dean Alger, and me illustrates the importance of visually conveyed narratives to the storage and recall of messages.[12] As students of rhetoric long have known, narratives that include elements of conflict, surprise, or suspense are often used to generate audience response. Visual symbols that convey emotion and that relate to voters' experience are combined with narrative forms. For example, soft-sell pitches in 1992 emphasized light colors, humor, self-deprecation, and unexpected images to create positive feelings toward candidates. Attack messages in 1988 used dark colors, threatening sounds (drums, metal stairs, and voices), and scary symbols (a guard with a rifle, a barbed-wire fence, and close-ups of prisoners escaping) to tell the tale of a presidential candidate (Dukakis) who seemingly cared more for criminals than for the common person.

These ideas are central to understanding campaign advertisements. Commercials cannot be explored in isolation from leadership behavior and the flow of information. Nor can they be examined apart from the narratives of political campaigns. The analysis of thirty-second spots requires a keen awareness of electoral context, advertising strategies, and media coverage.[13]

The nature of the campaign system has enormous consequences for advertising. An electoral structure that leaves far more decisions to voters has fundamentally altered the dynamics of elite competition. It has brought unknown candidates to the forefront and has given them powerful new electronic tools for communicating with voters. Since past psychological research has demonstrated that the effects of media vary considerably with voters' retention of information and cues from competing sources, one can hypothesize that low-visibility elections and candidates will be most likely to benefit from advertising.[14]

There are other factors that affect the impact of advertising. First, a campaign's overall strategy dictates the timing and content of ads. Campaigns have become a blitz of competing ads, quick responses, and attacks on the opposition. Election campaigns feature strategic interactions that are as important as any individual ads.[15] Second, to study advertising one must also look at the news media as an influence on effectiveness. Media coverage has consequences for advertising because reporters incorporate narrative information about ads in their news stories. The most effective ads are those whose basic message is reinforced by the news media.

The Nature of the Electoral System

The structure of an election defines the opportunities available to candidates. Campaigners have very different prospects for advertising depending on how the game is set up. According to Samuel Kernell, the most common systems in the United States are those based on institutionalized and individualized pluralism.[16] In the former, politics is an elite bargaining game. Candidates must appeal to other political leaders and build support through elite endorsements. Citizens participate sporadically, and their interests are represented largely through intermediary organizations, such as political parties and interest groups. Individualized pluralism, on the other hand, involves mass politics in which candidates must demonstrate public popularity. "Going public" is the watchword as campaigners travel extensively, address countless rallies, and use television to communicate their views to the electorate.

A number of observers have outlined how American elections in recent decades have moved from institutionalized to individualized pluralism. Structural changes have opened up the electoral process to an extent unprecedented in American history. The most important development at the presidential level has been the dramatic change in how convention delegates are selected. Once controlled by party leaders in small-scale caucus settings thought to be immune from media influence, nominations have become open and lengthy affairs that are significantly shaped by the mass media. As shown in Figure 1-1, the percentage of delegates to national nominating conventions selected through primaries increased significantly after 1968. From the 1920s to the 1960s, about 40 percent of delegates were selected in primaries, with the remainder chosen in caucus settings dominated by party leaders. However, after rules changes set in motion by the McGovern-Fraser Commission of the Democratic party following the 1968 election, about 65 to 70 percent of convention delegates were chosen directly by voters in presidential primaries.

Nominating reforms have required candidates to appeal directly to voters for support and in the eyes of many observers have altered the

Figure 1-1 Percentage of Nominating Convention Delegates Chosen Through Primaries, 1912-1992

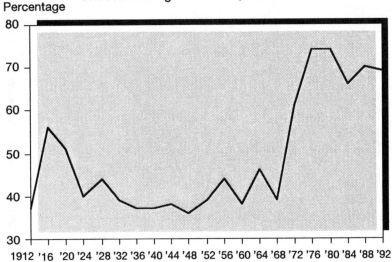

Percentage

Sources: For 1912-1988: Stephen Wayne, *The Road to the White House*, 3d ed. (New York: St. Martin's, 1988),12; for 1992: *Congressional Quarterly Weekly Report*, "Nominating Season at a Glance," February 1, 1992, 259.

character of the electoral system.[17] No longer are candidates dependent on negotiations with a handful of party leaders. Instead, they must demonstrate public appeal and run campaigns that win media attention. Campaigns have become longer and have come to depend increasingly on television as a means of attracting public support.

Television advertisements now represent the biggest expenditure of most campaigns. Figure 1-2 charts the percentage of overall expenditures devoted to radio and television advertising in presidential general election campaigns from 1952 to 1992. Generally speaking, advertising costs have risen to about two-thirds of overall spending. For example, Bush and Clinton devoted about 60 percent of their general election budgets to campaign spots in 1992. Perot was less forthcoming about his ad expenditures, but estimates range from about 70 to 75 percent of his fall budget. This heavy emphasis on commercials led Massachusetts senator Paul Tsongas to describe ads as the "nuclear weapon" of the campaign business.[18]

Some campaigns get far more attention than others. Citizens are most interested in and knowledgeable about presidential general

Figure 1-2 Percentage of Presidential Campaign Budget Spent
on Radio and Television Ads, 1952-1992

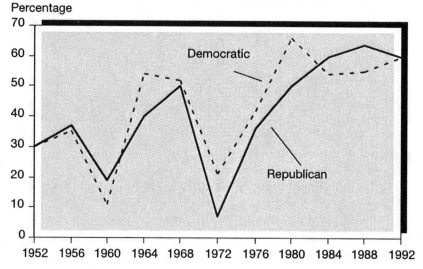

Sources: For 1952-1980, Herbert Alexander, *Financing Politics* (Washington,
D.C.: CQ Press, 1984), 4-12; for 1984, Stephen Wayne, *The Road to
the White House* 3d ed. (New York: St. Martin's, 1988), 28-31; for 1988,
Patrick Devlin, *"Contrasts in Presidential Campaign Commercials,"*
American Behavioral Scientist, 32 (1989): 389-414; for 1992, *Newsweek,*
"How He Won," November/December 1992 (special issue).

election campaigns, and media coverage is thorough. Voters pay
attention to these contests. Presidential nominating contests and
Senate campaigns, on the other hand, are less visible. Although there
is a fair amount of variation in individual contests depending on the
particular candidates involved, these races generate less citizen
interest and less media coverage. It is much more common for
candidates who are not well known to run in these contests. Not
surprisingly, it takes citizens longer to get to know the contestants.

Differences in electoral settings and individual candidates are
important for the study of television advertisements. Because presidential nominations often feature six or seven candidates who are not
well known, ad effects on citizens' familiarity with and opinion of
the candidates can be significant. Changes in the electoral process
have also pushed new types of effects, such as campaign momentum,
to the forefront as crucial forces in voters' decision making. Short-
term strategic factors have become more important as the electoral
system has become more open and the electorate has become less

dependent on political parties and other traditional sources of stability. In the chapters that follow I demonstrate that ads have the most influence in less visible settings and with candidates who are not well known by the public.

Just as television has emerged as the most important force in elections, a new era has arisen in campaign finance, with major consequences for federal contests. Finance regulations adopted in 1974 placed limits of $1,000 per election stage (nominating or general election) on large contributors. In the nominating process, candidates must raise money directly from small contributors, which then are matched by public subsidies. Direct contributions from individuals to the candidates are banned in the general election, but indirect contributions—through political action committees, for example—and independent expenditures—which are not under the control of the candidate—are still allowed.

These changes have fundamentally altered the dynamics of electoral contests. Campaigners who do well in primaries are able to raise money, while those who fare poorly see their funds dry up almost immediately. According to former Kennedy staffer Richard Stearns, "One of the consequences of the campaign finance laws [was that] . . . we made the news media the most powerful actor in the nomination process. . . . You cannot raise the money nor can you spend it under these laws to carry your own message directly to the voters. So you have to begin thinking of ways to influence the press to carry the message for you. You have to somehow beguile or trap the media into doing for you what you can't pay for yourselves." [19]

In this situation of limited money, expenditures by organizations independent of the candidate have become increasingly important in election campaigns. At the presidential level, Republican groups historically have outspent Democratic groups, although this was not the case in 1992. The Democratic National Committee that year devoted considerable effort to fund raising, and Democrats were able to air several independently produced ads, such as spots featuring young people worrying about their economic future. These ads were widely viewed as effective in helping Clinton mobilize the youth vote. However, according to Republican operative Eddie Mahe, independent expenditures are a double-edged sword. Speaking about his 1980 experience with John Connally, Mahe said, "There was one thing that was missed. Nobody ever wrote a great deal about the vast volume of independent advertising that was done for John

Connally in Iowa, a vast majority of which was very counterproductive. I mean they were running those four-page newspaper ads out there—just outrageous, and you could do nothing about it." [20]

Public opinion and voting behavior furthermore have undergone significant changes in ways that are obviously relevant for advertising. Voters are less trusting of government officials and more independent of political parties today than they were thirty years ago. Whereas 23 percent in 1958 agreed that you cannot trust the government to do what is right most of the time, 75 percent were untrusting in 1990. Citizens are also less likely to identify with one of the major parties. Thirty years ago, about 75 percent identified with either the Republican or Democratic party. Today, less than 60 percent identify with a major party. [21]

All of these developments have altered the tenor of electoral campaigns and have led to extensive efforts to appeal to independent-minded voters. Writing in the 1830s, Alexis de Tocqueville worried that the great masses would make "hasty judgments" based on the "charlatans of every sort [who] so well understand the secret of pleasing them." [22] The prominence today of an open electoral system has done nothing to alleviate this concern. [23] It therefore is not surprising that contemporary campaigns try to influence voters through television appeals. [24]

Advertising and Strategic Politicians

Candidates in this new electoral system operate in a situation that is both highly uncertain and subject to external forces. They need to demonstrate popularity in a variety of settings. Studies have shown how crucial strategic decisions are in this type of structure. Gary Jacobson and Samuel Kernell investigated the strategic aspects of the decision to challenge an incumbent in congressional elections and the way in which candidates deploy resources. [25] Basically, they argue that these decisions are among the most decisive for congressional races. The ebb and flow of partisan fortunes depend not just on the state of the economy and presidential popularity, as is often claimed, but also on the decisions of strong challengers to run. Years when a party has recruited high-quality challengers, measured by successful fund raising and past elective office, are better for the party than periods when such individuals choose not to run.

It is not as well recognized, though, how important strategic reasoning has become in other areas. Television ads provide an interesting arena in which to look at strategic behavior because they are directly under the control of candidates and their staffs. Many other aspects of election campaigns, such as campaign finance and media coverage, are not solely controlled by the organization.[26]

Spot ads have attracted much less attention from scholars than other short-term electoral forces.[27] Early research downplayed the power of ads to mold public images of candidates. The pioneering study was the innovative effort of Thomas Patterson and Robert McClure, *The Unseeing Eye*.[28] Looking at both content and effects, they sought to dispel the concerns of the public and journalists regarding political commercials. Using a cognitive model of psychological reasoning based on voters' knowledge about candidates, these researchers examined whether television ads enabled voters to learn more about the policy views or personal qualities of campaigners. Basically, they found that voters learned more from the candidates' ads than from the news, because ads addressed some issues whereas the news was dominated by coverage of the "horse race"—who is ahead at a given time. The results of Patterson and McClure's study were reprinted in leading textbooks.[29] Popular concerns about the strategic dangers of ads were minimized as uninformed hand-wringing. Once again, social scientists appeared to have proven conventional wisdom wrong.

The study's results also fit with the general view among election experts of the 1960s and 1970s that political strategies were not very decisive in determining election results. The era following the 1960 publication of the classic work on voting behavior, *The American Voter*, proclaimed long-term forces, such as party identification, as the most important. Although a few scholars disputed this interpretation, many argued that short-term factors related to media coverage, candidates' advertisements, and campaign spending simply were not crucial to vote choice. For example, Harold Mendelsohn and Irving Crespi claimed in 1970 that the "injection of high doses of political information during the frenetic periods of national campaigns does very little to alter the deeply rooted, tightly held political attitudes of most voters." [30] Even the later emergence of retrospective voting models did little to change this interpretation. Paid ads were thought to have limited capacity to shape citizens' impressions of the performance of government and the competence of candidates.

Recent decades, though, have begun to see some cracks in the previous consensus. Candidates have started to use commercials more aggressively, and reporters have devoted more attention to paid advertising. It now is recognized that voters' assessments of issues are not dependent just on education and that candidates have the power to sway voters' opinions of them. Accumulating evidence from elections around the country suggests that ads are quite successful in helping candidates develop particular impressions of themselves and that ads alter the dynamics of elections.[31] This is particularly true in multicandidate nominating contests because there are more strategic options available with more candidates involved.

Scholarly research furthermore has been able to discover more about ads. Donald Cundy, for example, argues that candidates can use ads for image making.[32] Not simply a means of educating the public, political commercials can be a potent tactic in the hands of clever strategists. The reality of undecided voters, open electoral arenas, and dynamic campaigns often means that short-term decisions made within campaign organizations can spell the difference between winning and losing.

Because paid ads are so important in contemporary campaigns, candidates take the development of advertising strategies quite seriously. Commercials often are pretested through focus groups and/or public opinion surveys.[33] Themes as well as styles of presentation are tried out before likely voters. What messages are most appealing? When should particular ads be aired? Who should be targeted? How should ads convey information? Only spots that are judged favorably and that meet the strategic needs of the campaign are put on the air.

The content and timing of ads are crucial for candidates because of their link to overall success. In the fast-changing dynamics of election campaigns, decisions to advance or delay particular messages can be quite important. Quick-response strategies require candidates to respond immediately when negative ads appear or political conditions seem favorable for certain messages. In recent races, strategic interactions have been a major factor in election outcomes. Candidates often play off each other's ads in an effort to gain the advantage with voters.

Strategic considerations also play an important role in targeting decisions. It is well recognized that not everyone views politics through the same lens. People differ significantly in their personal circumstances and political perspective. Candidates often develop certain messages with particular constituencies in mind. This is especially true in regard to negative advertisements.

Attack commercials have attracted public criticism lately as a strategic device. Negative appeals, of course, are not a new tactic.[34] They have been around since the founding of the country. A quick review of recent history also reveals a number of races, such as the Lyndon Johnson-Barry Goldwater contest in 1964, in which attack advertisements predominated.

However, the strategic thinking behind the use of negative ads has changed considerably. The conventional wisdom used to be that candidates should wait until the waning days of the campaign before going negative in order to avoid the inevitable voter backlash. Today, in contrast, campaigners have figured out that as long as both sides go negative, there is much less risk of a backlash. Voters cannot easily punish either candidate for negative ads if both are running them. It is riskier to go negative in three- or four-way races because of the possibility that one campaigner will benefit if the others are seen as more negative. But it has become quite common to go negative early and often in two-person races.[35]

Advertising and the News Media

Campaign ads have begun to attract great attention from the news media. One of the most striking developments of the contemporary period, in fact, has been the increasing coverage of political advertising by reporters. Network news executive William Small described this as the most important news trend of recent years: "Commercials are now expected as part of news stories." [36] Many news outlets have even launched "Ad Watch" features. These segments, aired during the news and showed in newspapers, present the ad, along with commentary on its accuracy and effectiveness.

Scholars traditionally have distinguished the free from the paid media. Free media meant reports from newspapers, magazines, radio, and television that were not billed to candidates. The paid media encompassed commercials purchased by the candidate on behalf of the campaign effort. The two avenues of communication were thought to be independent in terms of effects on viewers.

But the increase in news coverage of advertising has blurred or even eliminated this earlier division between the free and paid

media. Traditionalists who separate the effects of these communication channels need to recognize how intertwined the free and paid
media have become. It is now quite common for network news
programs to rebroadcast ads that are entertaining, provocative, or
controversial. Journalists also have begun to evaluate the effects of
campaign commercials, sometimes to the detriment of the candidate
who purchased the ad. It has become clear that the evening news and
the print media are significant audiences for television ads.

Ads that are broadcast for free during the news or discussed in
major newspapers generally have several advantages over those aired
purely as commercials. One strength is that viewers traditionally
have trusted the news media—far more than paid ads—for fairness
and objectivity. William McGuire has shown that the credibility of
the source is one determinant of whether the message is believed.[37]
The high credibility of the media gives ads aired during the news an
important advantage over those seen as plain ads. Roger Ailes
explained it this way: "You get a 30 or 40 percent bump out of [an
ad] by getting it on the news. You get more viewers, you get
credibility, you get it in a framework." [38]

Ads in the news guarantee campaigners a large audience and free
air time. Opinion polls have documented that nearly two-thirds of
Americans cite television as their primary source of news.[39] This is
particularly true for what Michael Robinson refers to as the
"inadvertent audience," those who are least interested in politics and
also among the most volatile in their opinions.[40]

There can be disadvantages to having ads aired during newscasts.
When ads are described as unfair to the opposition, media coverage
undermines the sponsor's message. The advantages of airing the ad
during the news can also be lost if reporters challenge the ad's
accuracy. Since favorable coverage cannot be counted on, how
reporters cover ads affects how people interpret commercials.

Comparing Elections

The importance of contextual factors to the analysis of advertisements necessitates the study of more than one election at a time.
Advertising research has been handicapped by a tendency to
investigate single elections. It is difficult with a single-election design
to know how far to generalize the results. It is well known that no
election is typical; every race has its own combination of candidate

strategies, media reports, and campaign dynamics. Comparing elections helps researchers produce more general conclusions about advertisements.

For this reason, the research presented in this book examines television advertising from 1952 to 1992 in several different types of elections (presidential general elections, presidential nominations, and senatorial general elections).[41] The period covered here is ideal for the study of political commercials because it includes the entire era since campaign spots emerged as an important factor in presidential races. Dwight Eisenhower pioneered the use of video clips featuring celebrity endorsements and scenes from press conferences.[42] With television viewership encompassing virtually the entire population, it now would be unthinkable to run a national campaign without paid television advertisements.

Several categories of advertising effects are addressed in this analysis. They include the subtle but powerful possibilities of learning, agenda setting, priming, and what I call defusing. Learning encompasses the variety of information citizens pick up during the course of election campaigns. While knowledge concerning candidates' issue positions and personal traits is part of this process, citizens also form impressions concerning candidates' likability and prospects for winning.

Agenda setting refers to the political priorities of the nation.[43] Do commercials alter citizens' perceptions of the most important problem and the most notable campaign event? Campaigners can set the agenda in many ways, and advertising therefore needs to be analyzed to determine how it influences viewers' priorities.

Priming and defusing are new theoretical approaches that look at the standards of evaluation used by viewers. Priming refers to efforts to elevate particular standards, such as character traits or issue positions; defusing represents activities that lower the relevance of these standards. Both concepts are far more subtle than what is generally explored, but candidates have clear incentives to use campaign advertising to prime or defuse the electorate. If campaigners cannot influence voters directly, they often attempt to alter the standards in ways that work to their advantage. One therefore must determine how ads influence citizens' standards of evaluating candidates.

Chapter 2

The Study of Campaign Ads

When Eisenhower ran for president, one of his advisers said, "You sell your candidates and your programs the way a business sells its products." [1] This reference to marketing politicians like soap has often been cited to illustrate the similarities between product and campaign advertising. In reality, though, political commercials have little in common with product ads. [2]

One big difference is the memorability of campaign spots. According to Nicholas O'Shaughnessy, 79 percent of television viewers can recall political ads, whereas only 20 percent can recall product commercials. [3] In general, viewers are adept at remembering campaign spots. Unlike product ads, which ceaselessly bombard television watchers, political commercials are novel events. They come only in election years, and they are often attractive to viewers. As shown in Figure 2-1, in the year of general election, ad exposure starts out low but quickly reaches a saturation point of about 80 percent.

Senate elections are less noticed than presidential general elections. In 1974, for example, only 68 percent of those queried said they had seen campaign ads. However, more than 80 percent of this group reported that they had paid at least some attention to the ads. There is extensive variation among individual Senate races. Among larger states represented in the 1974 National Election Study, 74 percent reported seeing ads in the New York campaign that featured Jacob Javits, Ramsey Clark, and Barbara Keating. Ad visibility also was high in California (71 percent) and Arkansas (71 percent). The lowest visibility occurred in Illinois (53 percent), Georgia (56 percent), and North Carolina (56 percent). During a 1990 Rhode Island Senate campaign between Claiborne Pell and Claudine

Figure 2-1 Percentage of Voters Who Saw Ads During Presidential Campaign, Selected Years

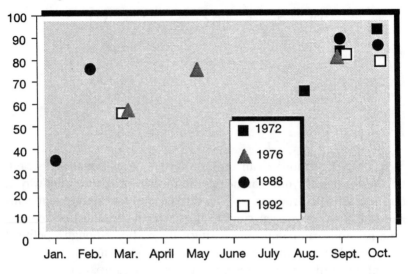

Sources: 1972 Patterson and McClure surveys, 1976 Patterson surveys, 1988 *CBS News/New York Times* surveys, 1992 surveys.

Schneider, 79 percent reported seeing ads in September.

Campaign commercials furthermore have a unique goal: in two-person races, ads must persuade at least 50 percent of voters to "buy" the candidate. Very few private organizations demand a 50 percent "market share" from particular products. Commercial ad pitches that double market share from 5 to 10 percent are considered wild successes. Numbers of that sort for a politician would be grounds for firing the consultant!

The context in which people view ads also differs considerably between political and product advertising. General election campaigns last roughly ten weeks and have a fixed endpoint, while the battles between Pepsi and Coca-Cola are long-term struggles over market share. Private corporations monitor the spots of major rivals and make adjustments from time to time, but they do not need to respond daily to opposition moves. The strategic nature of electoral battles, the defined length of the contests, and the extraordinary amount of press attention generated by campaign events make political races different.

To study campaign commercials one must use a multifaceted approach. Past research often has looked at only one aspect of advertisements without recognizing the interrelatedness of different dimensions. For example, a number of books on the analysis of campaign commercials have limited discussions of the effects of ads on voters or the implications of advertising for democracy.[4] Others deal only with single election years or particular types of campaigns, such as the presidential general election campaign.

Since many aspects of the electoral context are important for advertising, a number of different data sources were used in the study reported here. Twenty surveys from a number of elections (including Senate, presidential nominating, and presidential general elections) were employed to measure citizens' reactions to television ads between 1972 and 1992 (see Appendix for details). For an analysis of media coverage of advertising, I examined *New York Times, Washington Post,* and "CBS Evening News" stories about campaign ads from 1952 to 1992.[5] A study of spot commercials was used in the analysis of the strategic use of ads from 1952 to 1992. Interviews with campaign managers, media consultants, and political strategists conducted at the Harvard University Institute of Politics since 1972 provided further material on strategic thinking within each campaign.[6]

The Problem of Causality

Determining how to isolate the effects of paid commercials from the contributions of all the other forces that influence voters is at the center of political communications research. Political consultants judge the effectiveness of ads by the ultimate results—who wins. This type of test, however, is never possible to complete until after the election. It leads invariably to the immutable law of advertising: winners have great ads and losers do not.

The media often evaluate ads by asking voters to rate them or to indicate whether commercials influenced them. When voters are asked directly whether television commercials helped them decide how to vote, most say ads did not influence them. For example, a CBS News/*New York Times* postelection survey in November 1988 found that 80 percent of those who remembered seeing commercials claimed that ads had had no effect on them. But this is not a meaningful way of looking at the effects of advertising. Direct responses undoubtedly reflect an unwillingness to admit that external agents have an effect. Many people firmly believe that they make up their minds independently of the campaign.[7] Much in the same way teenagers do not like to concede parental influence, few voters are willing to admit that they are influenced by television.

Asking voters about the effects of ads adopts an unduly narrow definition of those effects. Campaign commercials are seen as effective if they alter voting behavior. Certainly this is one way of demonstrating the power of advertising, but it is by no means the most likely avenue of influence. Even if voters do not recognize the link, ads can be quite effective if they alter underlying views about the candidates or the campaign. Commercials also can be powerful agents for legitimating particular interpretations of political events.

Owing to the limitations of direct questions, it is more valid to probe advertising effects indirectly. Citizens are asked whether they have seen ads as well as a series of questions tapping their views about the candidates, how they evaluate candidates, and the most important problems facing the country. In conjunction with information on the content of media coverage and the strategic goals of candidates, responses are compared to determine whether ad viewing is associated with particular impressions that develop.[8] Since ads are merely one source of information for voters during campaigns, each model must include measures for a number of forces generally thought to structure people's reactions to political matters (see Appendix for the wording of the questions).[9]

One thing that clearly makes a difference is the beliefs citizens hold before the campaign. It is well established that television viewers filter political information through the selective lens of partisanship and ideology. Liberals and conservatives bring different values and beliefs to the political arena and therefore are likely to interpret the same event in very different ways. In fact, consultants often advise candidates to focus on their advertising on topics that are salient with the public. This allows ads to attract people who are already interested in the subject and to capture the support of those with established opinions.

In addition, a citizen's television exposure and political sophistication modify the impact of the media. Advertising effects may be linked to the different types of people most likely to see television ads. Media exposure often varies with race, age, and sex, while level of political knowledge is influenced by educational attainment.

Finally, a person's interest in politics and general exposure to the media make a difference. Even if a person's views of the candidates seem to be influenced by ads, one must make sure that the effects are not merely an artifact of general political awareness. This step was particularly relevant in 1992 because the campaigns found new media outlets. Since voters' impressions can be altered in ways that are independent of campaign ads, advertising studies must examine all political and media factors to make sure that attributions of effects to political commercials are not spurious.[10]

Contextual materials are incorporated in the analysis through comparisons of campaigns over time and in various types of races: Senate contests for 1974 nationally, 1990 in Rhode Island and North Carolina, and 1992 in California; presidential nominating races for 1976, 1988, and 1992; and presidential general elections for 1972, 1976, 1984, 1988, and 1992.[11] Strategic interactions are examined through elite interviews and by looking at exposure to the ads of multiple candidates. For example, in 1992 people saw the advertisements of several candidates for president, and one must include exposure to the spots of all leading candidates in order to simulate the actual campaign. Media coverage of ads is assessed throughout the campaign.

Other matters that complicate the study of causality include the so-called projection effect. This model views exposure to paid ads as a function of voters' projection based on their preferences in candidates. That is, viewers display an egocentric bias by projecting personal views onto their memory of advertising. Checks were run to ensure that the analysis was not hopelessly contaminated by projection effects. Correlations between choice of candidate and the ad exposure scales for various races from 1972 to 1992 reveal that viewers do not merely project their personal preferences onto the exposure measures. In general, the correlations were quite small. In fact, of the candidates whose ads had the highest associations (Carter in October 1976, Bush in March and early November 1988, Schneider in 1990, and Helms in 1990), three actually were at odds with voters' preferences. The only exception was Carter in October 1976, but the connection was not very strong.

Models that had the strongest results for commercials were reestimated with a control for choice of candidate to make sure ad effects were not merely projections of voters' preferences. I looked at the impact of advertisements on views about Dukakis's electability in the 1988 Democratic nominating process and on two key 1988 general election agenda items: citing taxation/spending or crime as the most important problem facing the country. Furthermore, I examined ad effects on views about the electability of Buchanan, Bush, and Clinton in 1992 and the crucial 1992 agenda items of unemployment and the creation of jobs as the most important problems facing the country. The coefficients for ad exposure were significant in each model, and this remained true even after the preferred candidate was included in the equation.

Media analyses are muddied by the fact that some relations in the advertising area can be nonrecursive in nature. That is, the causal arrows can point in both directions at once, which leads to problems in the research. Roy Behr and Shanto Iyengar examined this issue in their study of agenda setting through television news. They concluded that the assumption of recursivity in agenda setting is on "solid ground," but this matter continues to be of concern in the media studies area.[12]

Since it is important to be clear about causal sequencing, I repeated the most important results using techniques developed specifically to explore the underlying causal processes of theoretical models.[13] As demonstrated in Chapters 5 through 7, these techniques have the advantage of specifying indirect effects. This step is particularly relevant to the study of political commercials—their influence can come through effects on views about the agenda or attributions of responsibility for negative campaigning.

Surveys versus Experiments

There is a long-running controversy regarding the respective merits of survey approaches and experimental approaches to studying advertising. Experiments are clearer research designs for isolating specific causal linkages. Because of the existence of control groups, which are not subject to experimental treatments, this approach is able to identify precise effects.

However, experiments ignore the political context and are limited in terms of generalizability. Experimental designs cannot readily capture the interactive quality of candidates' strategies, media coverage, and electoral context. Because experiments isolate particular features of advertisements, it is nearly impossible to examine the joint impact of these factors in an experimental design. It is also difficult to apply conclusions reached in laboratory settings to broader audiences in the field. Not only is it impossible to know whether experimental participants represent the full range of relevant voter characteristics, it is not apparent that participants in experiments follow the same decisional processes as voters do in real life.

There is no way with experimental designs to reconstruct earlier viewers' reactions to the ads they saw. Researchers cannot return to the 1970s and 1980s with "retrospective experiments" and determine the impact of ads on the voters of that time. More so than with media studies in general, advertising research must take place during the campaign period in which the ads are aired. Because so much of the behavior of voters depends on the strategic decisions of candidates and coverage by the media, it is hard to imagine that a research strategy relying upon experiments could realistically go back and simulate voters' assessments of the 1972 Richard Nixon-George McGovern race, the 1976 Jimmy Carter nomination surge, or the 1988 Bush-Dukakis campaign.

Surveys have some advantages as a research tool. They are based on random samples of likely voters. This means they can be broadly representative of the overall electorate. Unlike other approaches, which are not easily applied to a broader population, surveys are generalizable. In addition, surveys are based on sample sizes that are large enough to facilitate subgroup analysis. This characteristic is particularly valuable for the study of paid ads because targeting is such an important advertising tactic. The study of advertising through surveys can uncover shifts in the assessments of key voting blocs, such as eighteen-to-twenty-five-year-olds, Reagan Democrats, women, or senior citizens.

Two types of surveys were used in the analysis reported in this book: cross-sectional and panel designs. Cross-sectional polls provide snapshots of voters' assessments at particular times. This type allows researchers to compare voters who see and pay close attention to television spots with those who do not. Through the study of both open- and closed-ended questions, scholars can determine what effects are associated with varying levels of media usage. Panel surveys are based on interviews with the same people at two or more points during the campaign. They are particularly useful for identifying changes in attitudes as electoral developments unfold.

Measuring Ad Viewing

In past studies, it was common to measure viewers' reactions to television ads through simple exposure data (seeing versus not seeing ads). For example, one prevalent technique in experimental research is to expose viewers to particular commercials and then see how viewers contrast with nonviewers in their political beliefs. However, this approach does not incorporate the frequency or attentiveness of viewing in the analysis. The frequency of ad viewing is important. Frequent exposure increases the odds of hearing candidates' messages, which improves the power of ads to influence viewers. How attentive viewers are to television advertisements also needs to be taken into account. Individuals can rank high on television exposure merely by being in the same room with a television set that is turned on, but they may score low on the degree of attention paid to the medium. Attentiveness is particularly salient for television ads that are brief and sandwiched between half-hour programs.

In this project, I used two different techniques for examining advertisements: four-point scales of general ad attentiveness and a dichotomous (yes or no) variable measuring exposure to specific ads, such as Bush's "Revolving Door" or Reagan's "Bear in the Woods." Statistical models were developed to explore the effects of four-point ad viewing scales on learning, agenda setting, priming, and defusing. The dichotomous exposure variables were used to study the agenda setting power of specific ads.

The four-point ad scales incorporated measures of both exposure and attentiveness or frequency of viewing. For example, the 1974 National Election Study asked two questions: "During the recent campaign did you see any political advertisements on television about the candidates running for the U.S. Senate?" (yes or no) and "Would you say you paid close attention, some attention, or no attention to these advertisements?" These questions were combined to form the categories of (1) saw no ads, (2) saw ads but paid no attention, (3) saw ads and paid some attention, and (4) saw ads and paid close attention. Four-category measures of ad viewing were created for each of the other election years as well.[14]

It is possible that the variations in question wording from 1972 to 1992 introduce sources of error into the analysis. But as shown in Table 2-1, the frequency distributions of the values for these scales reveal that the differences are clearly related to electoral dynamics

TABLE 2-1
Frequency Distributions for Ad Exposure Scales,
Selected Elections, 1972-1992

| | Ad Exposure Scale | | | | |
| | Low | | | High | |
	1	2	3	4	*N*
1972 Presidential					
September	33%	28%	23%	17%	711
October	15	31	32	22	635
November	6	18	35	41	637
1974 Senate	32	13	43	12	1,773
1976 Presidential					
April	43	15	25	17	462
June	25	22	28	25	361
October					
Carter	14	21	33	31	769
Ford	18	20	31	32	769
1984 Presidential	11	21	32	35	1,416
1988 Presidential					
March					
Bush	71	4	16	10	438
Dukakis	80	4	8	8	789
October					
Bush	37	26	24	13	1,289
Dukakis	43	21	23	12	1,270
Early Nov.					
Bush	10	11	35	44	1,451
Dukakis	11	11	35	43	1,454
Mid-Nov.					
Bush	12	11	36	41	1,586
Dukakis	15	10	36	40	1,587
1990 Senate, R.I.					
Pell	21	25	29	25	378
Schneider	29	31	26	14	380
1990 Senate, N.C.					
Gantt	23	20	23	34	600
Helms	35	18	18	30	599
1992 Senate, Calif.					
Feinstein	20	30	20	29	577
Seymour	27	28	21	24	572
Boxer	20	25	23	32	576
Herschensohn	22	21	22	34	569

(Table continues)

TABLE 2-1
(continued)

	Ad Exposure Scale				
	Low			High	
	1	2	3	4	*N*
1992 Presidential					
March					
Clinton	43	22	17	19	520
Tsongas	42	23	18	16	519
Bush	43	22	16	18	505
Buchanan	36	22	20	22	502
September					
Bush	14	17	18	51	587
Clinton	15	17	19	50	592
October					
Bush	17	20	20	43	571
Clinton	19	20	21	41	579
Perot	13	18	18	51	583

Sources: See pp. 163-165 in Appendix for further information on each survey.

Note: Entries indicate the percentage of individuals falling within each category of the ad exposure scale.

and level of the election. Not surprisingly, attentiveness increased during the course of each campaign. For example, in 1988 the percentage seeing and paying close attention to Bush ads rose from 10 percent in March to 13 percent in October, 44 percent in early November, and 41 percent in mid-November. Meanwhile, there were few differences over time in ad viewing between 1972 and 1992. If one compares the last time point for each election, the level of ad viewing ranged from 41 percent in 1972 to 32 percent in 1976, 35 percent in 1984, 41 percent in 1988, and 41 percent for Clinton in 1992 (Bush and Perot were at 43 and 51 percent, respectively.)

Senate races, however, were considerably less visible than presidential campaigns at the top of the scale, owing to their less prominent nature. Twelve percent paid close attention in 1974, while 14 and 25 percent, respectively, were very attentive to ads for Schneider and Pell during their 1990 Rhode Island Senate race. The 1990 exposure figures for the ads of Gantt and Helms in North Carolina (34 and 30 percent, respectively) are higher than for Rhode Island because the North Carolina poll occurred later in the campaign and did not limit recall to a specific period. (Time references improve the accuracy of recall and limit the risks from poor memories.) The 1992 California Senate races between Dianne Feinstein and John Seymour for the two-year term and Barbara Boxer and Bruce Herschensohn for the six-year term also generated less ad visibility than did the presidential campaign.

The Use of Recall Measures

Despite the many advantages of public opinion surveys, one must be cautious in relying on them. Surveys are limited because they use recall data about television advertising. Recall items are dependent on respondents' memory of ad exposure. Scholars have pointed out the difficulties of these indicators in regard to the evening news and have called for the development of alternatives.[15]

However, there are conceptual reasons why exposure variables should be less problematic in ad studies than in studies of the evening news. Viewers have difficulty remembering whether they saw the evening news because of the large number of stories shown, the consistent format of the shows, and the fact that different newscasts may look alike. In contrast, ads are more easily remembered because they are novel, entertaining, and distinctive. They are made for particular elections, which also facilitates recall.

Available evidence indeed demonstrates that even when open-ended questions are asked about ad content—which is a very challenging request—a relatively high number of voters are able to describe ads accurately. Patterson and McClure argue that the novelty of campaign ads encourages citizens to remember them quite clearly.[16] When asked to engage in the very difficult task of describing a specific 1972 campaign ad, 56 percent of the TV viewers gave a remarkably complete description; only 21 percent were unable to recall anything at all about the ad. This may be even more true today, with Ad Watch commentary on television; people are as likely to see ads on the news as in a paid time slot.

A comparison of results based on recall and program logs reveals no important differences. Patterson and McClure developed an innovative perspective for measuring ad exposure based on programming logs derived from the measurement of prime-time television viewing.[17] On a program-by-program basis, they asked respondents to indicate which shows had been watched between 7 o'clock and 11 o'clock each evening: "Below is a list of nighttime television programs that are shown in this area once a week. You are to indicate your own viewing of each of these programs during the past four weeks. If you never watch the program, check the first box. If you watch the program now and then, but have not watched it in the last four weeks, check the next box. Finally, if you have actually watched the program in the last four weeks, then check the box that tells how many of the last four shows you have watched" (list of shows each night for seven nights). The analysis of ads viewed based on these detailed program logs can be compared with recall using the following four-point item from Patterson and McClure: "How often have you heard about the presidential campaign from the following source? Television advertisements: many times, several times, one or a few times, or not at any time?"

The substantive results of analyses of citizens' views derived from recall measures and program logs were similar in 1972, when both measures were available. Table A-1 presents an analysis of the effect of ad exposure on impressions of Nixon and McGovern, controlling for various political and demographic characteristics.[18] A positive number for ads indicates a direct relationship between seeing ads and believing Nixon was likely to honor commitments to other nations, while asterisks indicate the statistical significance of the relationship. It is clear that using either recall or program logs, ad exposure had a significant, positive effect on views about Nixon's honoring commitments to other nations and about his electability to the presidency. There were no significant ad effects with either measure for McGovern's top issue of withdrawing from Vietnam or for his agenda setting on foreign affairs.[19] If anything, ad recall items were a conservative test because they generally showed weaker significance values than measures derived from program logs. This suggests that critiques about the limitations of media self-reports are not very accurate in regard to campaign advertisements.

Chapter 3

The Strategic Use of Commercials

Campaign observers have long complained about the tendency of candidates to engage in simplistic and emotional advertising.[1] For example, in 1952 both parties ran controversial ads evoking World War II memories. Republicans, in an effort to support General Eisenhower and break two decades of Democratic control, reminded voters in a *New York Times* ad that "one party rule made slaves out of the German people until Hitler was conquered by Ike." Not to be outdone, Democratic print ads informed voters that "General Hindenberg, the professional soldier and national hero, [was] also ignorant of domestic and political affairs.... The net result was his appointment of Adolf Hitler as Chancellor." [2]

Nor do strategies that highlight the personal traits of candidates represent a new development in advertising. The 1964 presidential campaign between Johnson and Goldwater was one of the most negative races since the advent of television advertising. Johnson's campaign characterized Goldwater as an extremist not to be trusted with America's future. One five-minute ad, "Confession of a Republican," proclaimed, "This man scares me.... So many men with strange ideas are working for Goldwater." [3] The most notorious commercial of that year, though, was Johnson's "Daisy" ad. Although it aired only once, its dramatic image of a mushroom cloud rising behind a little girl picking daisies in a meadow helped raise doubts about Goldwater's fitness for office in the nuclear age.

Hard-hitting spots have been around since television ads were introduced, but few studies have systematically investigated the strategic use of political advertising.[4] Ads are a valuable lens on strategic behavior because candidates reveal important things about themselves through their commercials. As stated by Elizabeth

Kolbert, a news reporter for the *New York Times*, "Every advertising dollar spent represents a clue to a campaign's deepest hopes and a potential revelation about its priorities." [5] With their decisions about message and style of presentation, campaigners provide clues about their policy views and personal qualities. Through choices regarding when particular ads are aired, candidates show their sense of timing, which is important to political dynamics. Their targeting decisions reveal what constituencies are most valued by the campaign. This chapter looks at ads from 1952 to 1992 to determine what can be learned from electronic manifestations of strategic behavior.

Models of Strategic Behavior

Candidates do not choose their advertising messages lightly. Most campaigners develop commercials based on game plans that guide organizational decision making. These documents outline the desired targets of the campaign as well as the themes and issues to be addressed. [6] Candidates often test basic messages through polls and focus groups. Reagan manager Ed Rollins said in reference to the 1984 campaign against Walter Mondale: "We made some fundamental decisions at that stage to take [Mondale] on the tax issue . . . to try to drive [his] negatives back up. . . . The decision was to go with two negative commercials for every one positive commercial. . . . Let me say the commercials clearly worked, we drove [Mondale's] negatives back up again, the tax thing became the dominant issue at least in our polling, and it helped us get ready for the final week of the campaign." [7]

Different models have been developed to explain the choice of campaign strategies. The model of Anthony Downs suggests that candidates are political free agents who look for the midpoint of public opinion and direct their appeals to that place on the spectrum. [8] The reasoning is simple. Since to win an election requires the development of a broad-based coalition, it makes sense for politicians to aim for the most votes.

Increasingly, though, Downs's economic theory of democracy has been supplanted by party cleavage models, which posit the importance of party arenas to electoral appeals. As described by Benjamin Page, party cleavage models argue that candidates' positions are affected by party settings and/or the views of primary electorates.

Candidates of opposing parties often take systematically different positions.[9] According to this perspective, candidates are not ideological neuters with complete freedom to roam the political spectrum. Instead, they bring political views and strategic reasoning to bear on their campaign decisions.

As campaigns have opened up and nominating battles have become common, the strategic aspect of electoral appeals has emerged as a political determinant. Candidates face more choices than at any previous point in American history. A system of presidential selection based on popular support places a premium on these decisions. Campaigners who pursue the wrong constituencies, go on the attack prematurely, or address nonsalient issues generally end up in political oblivion.

The strategic thinking of campaign elites is significant because it sets the perimeters of voters' decision making. Citizens do not reach their electoral decisions in a vacuum. Instead, they make choices within the confines of the options presented by leaders. As Goldwater put it in his 1964 campaign slogan, nothing is more critical than candidates' decisions to offer a "choice" or an "echo."

For these reasons, it is instructive to look at ad content and style of presentation with an eye toward strategic behavior. Do ad messages vary by party? Are there differences in electronic appeals in different stages of a campaign? How have candidates' presentations changed over time? What do these patterns tell us about contemporary elections? The study of these and related questions offers valuable insights into how the media shape citizens' decisions.

The Conventional View

The classic criticism of American ads was written by Joe McGinniss following Nixon's 1968 presidential campaign. Nixon entered that race with a serious image problem. His previous loss in 1960 and public impressions of him during a long career in public service led many to believe he was a sour, nasty, and mean-spirited politician. His advisers therefore devised an advertising strategy meant to create a "new" Nixon. As described by McGinniss, who had unlimited access to the inner workings of Nixon's advertising campaign: "America still saw him as the 1960 Nixon. If he were to come at the people again, as candidate, it would have to be as something new; not this scarred, discarded figure from their past. . . . This would be Richard Nixon, the leader, returning from exile. Perhaps not beloved, but respected. Firm but not harsh; just but compassionate. With flashes of warmth spaced evenly throughout." [10]

The power of this portrait and the anecdotes McGinniss was able to gather during the course of the campaign helped create a negative impression of political ads that has endured. For example, Robert Spero describes the "duping" of the American voter in his book analyzing "dishonesty and deception in presidential television advertising." [11] Others have criticized ads for being intentionally vague and overly personalistic in their appeals.

Political commercials do not have a great reputation among contemporary viewers either. An October CBS News/*New York Times* survey during the 1988 presidential general election asked those exposed to ads how truthful they considered commercials for each candidate. The Bush ads and Dukakis ads scored the same: only 37 percent felt they were mostly truthful. The remainder believed that campaign commercials were either generally false or had some element of falsehood.

Even more interesting were overall beliefs about the impact of television ads. People felt the strongest effects of ads were to influence general feelings about the candidates and the weakest were in the communication of substantive information. Fifty percent said ads made them feel good about their candidate, while only 25 percent said ads had given them new information about the candidates during the fall campaign. Citizens furthermore believe that today's campaigns are more negative than those of the past. When asked whether the 1988 race had been more positive, more negative, or about the same as past presidential campaigns, 48 percent of the respondents said it had been more negative. Perhaps 1988 reached a high in negativity; in 1992, 36 percent felt that the presidential race was more negative than past contests. [12]

Studies of the effects of ads have rarely paid much attention to the dimensions of evaluation. Many criticisms of commercials have failed to define the elusive notion of substance or distinguish it from image-oriented considerations. One exception is a study by Leonard Shyles, who draws a distinction between image, which he defines as "character attributes of candidates," and issues, which he defines as "current topics and civic concerns linked to the national interest." [13] There can be no clear distinction between image and issues, since many ads are based on a combination of substantive matters and character attributes. In fact, a number of commercials use discussions of substantive points to create an impression of knowledge, experience, or competence; this mixture further complicates assessments of ad content.

This problem notwithstanding, there have been several efforts to investigate the content of ads. Such research generally has attempted to assess the quality of the information presented to viewers. In keeping with the interest in issue-based voting during the 1970s and recognizing the centrality of policy matters to democratic elections, much of the work on ad content focused on the treatment of issues. Surprisingly, in light of popular beliefs about the subject, most of the research has found that ads present more substantive information than viewers and journalists generally believe.

Richard Joslyn has undertaken one of the most thorough and systematic efforts in his 1980 study of 156 television spot ads aired during contested general election campaigns. He measured whether political issues were mentioned during the ad. His research revealed that 79.6 percent of presidential ads mentioned issues. Based on this work, he argues that "political spot ads may not be as poor a source of information as many observers have claimed." [14]

Others have reached similar conclusions. Richard Hofstetter and Cliff Zukin discovered in their analysis of the 1972 presidential race that about 85 percent of the candidates' ads included some reference to issues. In comparison, only 59 percent of the news coverage of McGovern and 76 percent of the news coverage of Nixon had issue content. Likewise, Patterson and McClure demonstrate, in a content analysis of the 1972 race, that issues received more frequent coverage in commercials than in network news coverage. Robinson and Margaret Sheehan report in regard to 1980 CBS news coverage that 41 percent of the lines of news transcript contained at least one issue mention. [15]

These projects have attracted considerable attention because they run contrary to much of the popular thinking and press criticism about media and politics. At the normative level, the findings are reassuring because they challenge conventional wisdom warning of the dangers of commercials. Rather than accepting the common view, which emphasizes the noneducational nature of ads, these researchers claim that commercials offer relevant information to voters.

But there has been little follow-up work on these important analyses. Few studies have extended the investigation to recent elections. Since much of this past research has focused on single elections, without considering how to generalize the results, it remains to be seen whether the results stand up over time. In addition, past research has ignored the variety of ways in which substantive messages can be delivered, beyond direct policy mentions.[16] For example, character and personal qualities are increasingly seen as vital to presidential performance. It is therefore important to assess the full range of the content of ads in order to reach more general conclusions about the rhetoric of candidates.

Typical versus Prominent Ads

The study of ad content poses several problems. Foremost is the dilemma of how to come up with a representative sample when the full universe of ads from 1952 to 1992 is not available. One approach, which was common in the past, is to use convenience samples based on ads the scholar is able to obtain. However, it is difficult to establish how representative the ads in a convenience sample are. Thus, it is impossible to generalize and account for the results.

Research is complicated because not all ads are equally important. A random sample has the unfortunate tendency to weight important, frequently aired ads the same as less important ads. The failure to distinguish prominent from less-important commercials is troubling because in each presidential year certain ads attract more viewer and media attention than others. These ads are the most central to the candidates. In addition to being aired most frequently, prominent ads are discussed and rebroadcast by the media.[17] Owing to the general noteworthiness of these ads and their heightened exposure through the free media, they are the most likely to be influential with voters. It therefore makes sense to investigate commercials generally regarded as the crucial ones in particular campaigns as well as ads typically run by the candidates.[18]

Since there is no single approach that incorporates each of these dimensions, I look at two types of ads representing different aspects of content: typical ads and prominent ads. To examine typical ads, I drew a random sample of 150 presidential thirty- and sixty-second spot ads aired from 1972 to 1992. These ads come from lengthy lists of spots collected by the Political Commercial Archive at the University of Oklahoma.[19]

I also studied prominent ads as defined by Kathleen Jamieson, the leading historian of political advertisements. For every presidential campaign since 1952, Jamieson, on an election-by-election basis, has described the presidential campaign ads that were newsworthy, entertaining, flamboyant, or effective. I used her detailed histories to compile a list of 324 prominent spot ads from 1952 to 1992.[20] This set is a complete enumeration of all the spot ads cited by Jamieson, but it is not designed to be a random sample of all ads from this period. Rather, it is a listing of all the commercials judged by one ad historian to have been among the most visible and important ones in given years. Using a single judge facilitates comparability over time; Jamieson presumably employed consistent criteria for selecting prominent commercials. Reliance on a single historian, of course, does not ensure a full list of prominent ads.[21] Every historian has to make choices, given the limits of time and space, about which commercials to include in a listing. But a perusal of *New York Times* and *Washington Post* coverage reveals that Jamieson was generally successful at identifying the commercials that attracted media attention. Most of the spots mentioned in stories are included among the prominent commercials described by her.

Appendix Table A-2 lists the party, candidate, campaign stage, and chronological breakdowns for the prominent ads. It is obvious that not all candidates who ran for president during the period are represented in this set, nor should they be. For example, there are no ads in this sample for Phil Crane, John Connally, and others who were also-rans. There is a much better representation, however, of prominent ads each year for the party nominees and major challengers. The commercials included in this analysis come from both the presidential nominating process ($N = 60$) and the presidential general election ($N = 255$), while 4 dealt with congressional races and 5 dealt with ballot measures. Overall, there were 145 Republican ads, 159 Democratic ads, and 20 independent candidate or referenda ads. The period from 1960 to 1976, when there were a number of competitive Democratic primaries, slightly overrepresents Democratic ads, while the time from 1980 to 1992 slightly overrepresents Republican spots. Intercoder reliability scores were computed for the content categories. In general, the scores were well within the range of acceptability, as about 85 percent of the content codes were consistent between reviewers.

For the typical and prominent ads, codes were compiled for each commercial based on the year of the election, type of election (presidential general election or nominating stage), sponsoring party (Republican, Democrat, or other), and content of the ad. Ad messages were classified into the areas of domestic concerns, international affairs, personal qualities of the candidates, specific policy statements, party appeals, or campaign process. Specific policy appeals involved clear declarations of past positions or expectations about future actions. General categories were subdivided into more detailed types of appeals. Domestic concerns included the economy; social welfare; social issues; crime, violence, and drugs; race and civil rights; taxes and budgets; corruption and government performance; and energy and the environment. International affairs consisted of war and peace, foreign relations, national security and defense, and trade matters. Personal qualities included leadership, trust and honesty, experience and competence, compassion, independence, and extremism. Party appeals were based on explicit partisan messages (such as the need to elect more Republicans) and references to party labels. Campaign appeals included references to strategies, personnel matters within the campaign, electoral prospects, or organizational dynamics.

The Paucity of Policy Appeals

Issue information in advertising can be assessed either as action statements or as policy mentions. The former refers to specific policy statements, that is, clear statements of past positions or expectations about future actions. For example, Reagan's 1980 ad promising a "30% federal tax cut" that would benefit every group and offer the government an actual gain in revenue was an action statement. Johnson's criticism of Goldwater for past statements proposing that Social Security become a voluntary retirement option was a specific policy mention, although Johnson never made clear whether Goldwater still supported this proposal. (One of the ads supplied the dates of Goldwater's statements.)

Few discussions of domestic or international matters reach this level of detail, however. The more common approach is the policy mention, in which general problems of the economy, foreign relations, or government performance are discussed, but no specific proposals to deal with the matter are made. For example, an Eisenhower ad about the economy in 1952 showed a woman holding a bag of groceries and complaining, "I paid twenty-four dollars for these groceries—look, for this little." Eisenhower then said, "A few years ago, those same groceries cost you ten dollars, now twenty-four, next year thirty. That's what will happen unless we have a change." [22] This commercial obviously does not suggest a plan for combating inflation, although it does portray the painfulness of price increases.

There are interesting differences between prominent and typical ads, as well as between the parties, that have consequences for the way candidates are viewed (see Table 3-1). Typical ads (27 percent) were more likely than prominent ads (22 percent) to contain the type of specific policy appeals defined as action statements. Prominent ads were more likely to emphasize personal qualities (31 percent) and domestic performance (32 percent) than were typical ads (23 percent and 27 percent, respectively).

Small differences were apparent between the parties in level of specificity. Typical ads for Republicans included more specific pledges (31 percent) than typical ads for Democrats (25 percent). The same was true for prominent ads (22 percent for Republicans and 20 percent for Democrats). However, there were bigger partisan differences in other areas. Prominent ads for Republicans were more likely to emphasize international affairs (13 percent) than prominent ads for Democrats (4 percent), whereas those for Democrats were much more likely to emphasize personal qualities (39 percent) than were those for Republicans (26 percent). Typical ads for Democrats more often referred to domestic performance (32 percent) than did typical ads for Republicans (19 percent).

The party differences reflect interests within each party and have consequences for how each party is viewed by the public. The greater attention paid by Republicans to international affairs and by Democrats to domestic areas is consistent with party coalitions. It also helps to explain why Democrats are viewed as weak on foreign policy and Republicans are seen as inattentive to domestic matters. The public and the media take cues about party priorities from the visibility of issues in political advertising.

These results offer little encouragement regarding substance in campaigns. Even if one follows the lead of other scholars and uses

TABLE 3-1
Content of Prominent and Typical Ads, 1952-1992

	Prominent Ads	Typical Ads
Personal qualities	31%	23%
Domestic performance	32	27
Specific domestic policy	18	20
Specific foreign policy	4	7
International affairs	8	11
Campaign	5	8
Party	2	3
N	(324)	(150)

Sources: Prominent ads: Kathleen Jamieson, *Packaging the Presidency*, 2d ed. (New York: Oxford University Press, 1992) for campaigns 1952-1988, and "CBS Evening News" tapes for 1992 campaign. Typical ads: Political Commercial Archive tapes, University of Oklahoma for campaigns 1972-1988, and campaign ad tapes for 1992 campaign.

Note: Entries indicate the percentage of ads devoted to each type of appeal.

the less demanding standard of policy mentions regardless of specificity, the overall level of substantive information is not impressive. Joslyn, as well as Hofstetter and Zukin, combines specific policy statements with more general discussions of domestic performance and international affairs to form a broader measure of substantive appeals. According to this more general standard, 62 percent of prominent ads contained policy mentions and 65 percent of typical commercials did. These figures are considerably lower than the 85 percent found by Hofstetter and Zukin for 1972 and the 79.6 percent uncovered by Joslyn for his sample of races.

The unwillingness of candidates to discuss policy or to propose plans of action creates obvious difficulties for models of issue-based voting. If candidates do not make statements about how they would deal with policy problems, then voters who might cast ballots based on the issues face barriers. Most commercials are not very specific, and they fail almost completely as policy blueprints.

Of course, even mentioning issues allows voters to incorporate broader notions of accountability into their choices. If candidates mention unemployment in an ad but do not say what they will do about the problem, the ad can serve an agenda-setting or a priming function. The mention may increase the importance of employment policy in voters' priorities or in campaign coverage by the media.

Scholars may turn to performance-based models, such as retrospective voting models, under which voters do not require detailed policy information to hold leaders accountable. Since the field of voting studies has evolved in recent years from issue- to performance-based models, it is important to recognize that ads may be influential even if their specific policy content is limited.

Shifts over Time

There is little reason to treat all elections the same or to assume that every contest engenders the same type of advertising appeals. Based on obvious differences in strategic goals among presidential aspirants and shifts in voters' priorities over the years, one would expect extensive fluctuations in commercials from election to election. To see exactly how advertising messages have changed, it is necessary to study ads from a series of elections.

It is commonly believed that ads have become less policy oriented and more personality based in recent years. But when one looks at changes in the making of policy appeals, it is obvious that prominent ads in the 1980s and 1990s were more substantive than those of earlier periods (Figure 3-1). Twenty-six, 45, and 41 percent of commercials, respectively, in 1984, 1988, and 1992 included specific statements about public policy.[23] These are much higher than figures from earlier periods. The only other period when specific policy messages were common was the 1960s (23 percent in 1964 and 31 percent in 1968). However, as has been found in other areas of research, the 1960s were an anomaly in terms of specific policy mentions. The more common pattern in other historical periods was a relatively low level of specificity.

Despite beliefs to the contrary, commercials in recent elections have not become more personalistic than those of the past. Although there are wide fluctuations from election to election, the trend line actually is down in this area. Ads based on personal qualities reached their high points in 1960 (69 percent of all appeals), 1976 (50 percent), and 1980 (42 percent), but dropped back to lower levels of 9, 21, and 21 percent, respectively, in 1984, 1988, and 1992. It appears that races that had the greatest emphasis on personal qualities involved challengers who were either unknown or inexperienced. For example, in 1960 many questions were raised about the qualifications and experience of

Figure 3-1 Prominent Ad Content by Election Year, 1952-1992

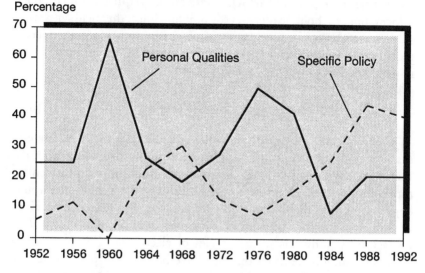

Percentage

Sources: For 1952-1988, Kathleen Jamieson, *Packaging the Presidency*, 2d ed.
(New York: Oxford University Press, 1992), and for 1992, *CBS Evening
News* tapes.

John F. Kennedy. Similarly, ads during the Ford-Carter contest in
1976, the Reagan-Carter-Anderson campaign in 1980, and the
Bush-Clinton-Perot race of 1992 devoted a great deal of attention
to personal characteristics, such as leadership, trustworthiness,
and experience. But these emphases were more a matter of
defusing or highlighting personal qualities important in a particular race than a manifestation of any general trend toward
personalistic politics.

It also is interesting to examine variations in ad categories over
time. Table 3-2 presents the breakdowns of prominent ads for the
broad categories of domestic matters (specific domestic policy appeals
combined with general domestic performance), international affairs
(both specific and general mentions), personal qualities, party
appeals, and campaign-related messages. Party appeals were stronger in the 1950s than in any period since then. Twelve percent of
prominent ads in 1956 emphasized appeals to party, the highest of
any election in this study. In fact, for many elections from 1960
through 1992, there were no prominent ads that featured direct
party pitches.

TABLE 3-2
Content of Prominent Ads, 1952-1992

	1952	1956	1960	1964	1968	1972	1976	1980	1984	1988	1992
Domestic Matters	62%	62%	24%	39%	30%	46%	38%	44%	68%	58%	68%
Economy	50	25	0	0	0	8	17	31	30	7	8
Social welfare	6	25	12	31	12	18	3	6	4	3	11
Social issue	0	0	0	0	6	0	0	2	4	0	19
Crime, violence, drugs	0	0	0	4	12	3	6	0	0	41	11
Race, Civil rights	0	0	12	0	0	0	0	0	0	0	0
Taxes, budget	0	0	0	0	0	12	6	5	26	0	17
Corruption, government performance	6	12	0	4	0	5	6	0	0	0	2
Energy, environment	0	0	0	0	0	0	0	0	4	7	0
International Affairs	6	0	6	19	37	21	3	11	17	10	6
War and peace	6	0	0	15	25	8	3	3	4	0	2
Foreign relations	0	0	6	4	12	5	0	2	4	3	2
National security, defense	0	0	0	0	0	8	0	6	9	7	0
Trade	0	0	0	0	0	0	0	0	0	0	2
Personal Qualities	24	24	69	27	18	29	50	41	8	20	21
Leadership	0	0	25	0	0	5	3	8	0	0	2
Trustworthiness, honesty	6	0	0	0	6	0	31	6	0	10	11
Experience, competence	0	12	25	4	6	8	8	18	0	3	2
Compassion	0	12	0	0	0	13	8	6	4	7	6
Independence	12	0	19	0	0	0	0	0	4	0	0
Extremism	6	0	0	23	6	3	0	3	0	0	0
Party	6	12	0	0	0	3	3	3	0	0	0
Campaign	0	0	0	16	12	3	9	0	4	10	6
N	(16)	(8)	(16)	(26)	(16)	(39)	(36)	(62)	(23)	(29)	(53)

Sources: Kathleen Jamieson, *Packaging the Presidency*, 2d ed. (New York: Oxford University Press, 1992) for 1952-1988, and "CBS Evening News" tapes for 1992 campaign.

The 1956 election may have been a high point in terms of the strength of party appeals in the post-World War II era. The classic study of voting behavior, *The American Voter,* argued that party identification was the dominant structuring principle of public opinion.[24] It may be no accident that most of the authors' data came from the 1950s. In that decade, it made sense for candidates to incorporate partisan pitches in their television advertising: partisanship allowed them to win votes from the electorate. Hence, we see Republican Eisenhower and other members of his cabinet exhorting viewers to give them a "Republican Congress." [25]

However, after the 1950s, party loyalties in the American public began to decline. In their research, reported in *The Changing American Voter,* Norman Nie, Sidney Verba, and John Petrocik show how party identification and party-based voting ebbed in strength.[26] Independents began to rise as a percentage of the overall electorate, and candidates rarely made advertising appeals based on party.

Advertising shifted toward other topics. Not surprisingly, given the nature of the times, war and peace issues rose during the Vietnam period. Fifteen percent of ads in 1964 and 25 percent in 1968 discussed war and peace topics. For example, in 1964 some of the Johnson advertising effort against Goldwater emphasized the danger of war and Johnson's record of preserving the peace. In the 1968 Democratic nominating race, print ads for Eugene McCarthy attacked Robert Kennedy for his brother's decision to send troops to Vietnam: "There is only one candidate who has no obligations to the present policies in Vietnam and who is under no pressure to defend old mistakes there." Another noted that "Kennedy was part of the original commitment. . . . He must bear part of the responsibility for our original—and fundamentally erroneous—decision to interfere in Vietnam." In the general election, both Nixon and Hubert Humphrey ran spots emphasizing Vietnam. For example, Nixon tried to tie his Democratic opponent to the unpopular war. In contrast, a voice-over in a Humphrey ad criticized Nixon's refusal to discuss Vietnam: "Mr. Nixon's silence on the issue of Vietnam has become an issue in itself. He talks of an honorable peace but says nothing about how he would attain it. He says the war must be waged more effectively but says nothing about how he would wage it." [27]

Meanwhile, domestic economy and tax/budget matters attracted considerable attention in the late 1970s and the 1980s. When the economy started to experience the twin ills of inflation and unemployment, a phenomenon that led experts to coin a new word, *stagflation,* advertising began to emphasize economic problems. In 1976, 17 percent of ads addressed economic concerns, while 31 percent in 1980 and 30 percent in 1984 touched on the economy. One has to harken back to the early 1950s to find elections with as much emphasis on the economy. Tax and budget matters were also particularly popular during this period. Republicans have repeatedly run ads challenging past Democratic performance, and Democrats have criticized Republican failures to deal with federal deficits.

There have been some interesting nonissues on the advertising front. Until 1992 advertisements on social issues, such as abortion, busing, and the Equal Rights Amendment, were not very common.[28] With the exception of a George Wallace ad against school busing in 1968 and a 1980 Carter commercial in which actress Mary Tyler Moore told viewers Carter had "been consistently in favor of any legislation that would give women equal rights," [29] political spots generally have avoided these subjects. Social issues undoubtedly are seen by candidates as very divisive, and campaigners appear reluctant to take clear stands in their ads on these matters. In fact, a 1989 decision by Virginia gubernatorial candidate Douglas Wilder to incorporate abortion rights advertising in his campaign attracted considerable attention precisely because of the novelty.

But a change of tactics in 1992 altered this situation. Along with other challengers around the country, Indiana congressional candidate Michael Bailey used graphic anti-abortion footage during his race to unseat Rep. Lee Hamilton. The goal obviously was to attract media attention and raise public awareness. Yet there is little evidence in overall results that this effort worked. Of the thirteen congressional candidates in 1992 who relied on this tactic during the nominating process, only two won their primaries and none won in the general elections.[30]

The Impact of Campaign Stage

Television ads used to be the near-exclusive purview of presidential general elections. As noted earlier, the nominating process was an elite-based activity in which party leaders exercised dominant control over delegate selection. Since voters were not central to the process, candidates made little use of television advertising. Much greater emphasis was placed on personal bargaining and negotiations with political leaders.

However, in recent years, advertising has become a prominent part of presidential nominating campaigns. Candidates spend a considerable amount of their overall campaign budget on advertising. Commercials have become a major strategic tool in the nominating process. Candidates use ads to convey major themes, make comments about the opposition, and discuss each other's personal qualities.

As pointed out previously, there are substantial differences between stages of the campaign, and one might expect to find different appeals in the nominating and general election campaigns. In nominating contests, candidates of the same party compete for their party's nomination. There are often a number of candidates on the ballot. In contrast, general elections typically are two-person battles between major party nominees. One can expect political commercials to emphasize different points in different stages.

Table 3-3 lists the distribution of prominent and typical ad appeals from 1952 to 1992 by campaign stage. Personal qualities were used more often in the nominating campaign than in the general election campaign. For example, in 1980 Carter employed so-called character ads to highlight the contrast between his own family life and that of his Democratic opponent, Sen. Edward Kennedy: "I don't think there's any way you can separate the responsibilities of a husband and father and a basic human being from that of the president. What I do in the White House is to maintain a good family life, which I consider to be crucial to being a good president." Personal qualities also played a major role in Carter's 1976 nominating campaign effort. Taking advantage of public mistrust and skepticism following Watergate disclosures, Carter pledged he would never lie to the public: "If I ever do any of those things, don't support me." [31]

Structural and strategic differences between the nominating and general election stages of the campaign help to explain the use of personal appeals in the primary season. The nominating stage often generates more personal appeals because, by the nature of intraparty battles, personality and background more often than substantive matters divide candidates. With Democrats competing against Democrats and Republicans against Republicans, there are at this time usually as many agreements as disagreements on policy issues and general political philosophies. Politicians therefore use personal

TABLE 3-3
Ad Content by Campaign Stage, 1952-1992

| | Prominent Ads | | Typical Ads | |
	General Election	Nominating	General Election	Nominating
Personal qualities	31%	38%	22%	30%
Domestic performance	34	22	28	25
Specific domestic policy	14	23	21	10
Specific foreign policy	3	8	8	5
International affairs	8	7	9	25
Campaign	6	2	9	7
Party	2	0	3	0
N	(255)	(60)	(130)	(20)

Sources: Prominent ads: Kathleen Jamieson, *Packaging the Presidency,* 2d ed. (New York: Oxford University Press, 1992) for campaigns 1952-1988, and "CBS Evening News" tapes for 1992 campaign. Typical ads: Political Commercial Archive tapes, University of Oklahoma for campaigns 1972-1988, and campaign ad tapes for 1992 campaign.

Note: Entries indicate the percentage of ads devoted to each type of appeal.

qualities to distinguish themselves from the field and point out the limitations of their fellow candidates.

Domestic performance appeals in prominent ads were less common in the nominating process than in the general election campaign. One standard appeal concerned credit claiming on economic matters. A 1976 Ford ad showed a woman with bags of groceries meeting a friend who was working for the Ford campaign. The Ford supporter asked the shopper whether she knew that President Ford had cut inflation in half. "In half?" responded the shopper. "Wow!" In an 1980 ad, Democratic contender Kennedy had the actor Carroll O'Connor say that Carter may "give us a Depression which may make Hoover's look like prosperity." [32]

The attention devoted to domestic matters is important, and several articles have addressed issue-based voting by primary voters.[33] But few of these projects address the role of candidates in providing substantive cues. For there to be extensive issue-based voting, candidates must emphasize substantive matters and provide issue-based cues. Although a fair amount of attention is paid to domestic affairs in the nominating process, for prominent ads these types of appeals occupy a smaller percentage in the spring than in the fall.

International relations are emphasized on prominent ads at about the same levels in the nominating contests and general election but were mentioned much more often in the nominating process among typical ads. Trying to capitalize on a United Nations vote seen as harming Israel, Kennedy in 1980 ran an ad saying Carter "betrayed Israel at the U.N., his latest foreign policy blunder." Meanwhile, on the Republican side in 1980, a Reagan ad noted, "Our foreign policy has been based on the fear of not being liked. Well, it's nice to be liked. But it's more important to be respected." A 1976 Ford ad aimed at Reagan said, "Last Wednesday, Ronald Reagan said he would send American troops to Rhodesia. On Thursday he clarified that. He said they would be observers or advisers. What does he think happened in Vietnam?" The ad then concluded with the tagline, "Governor Reagan couldn't start a war. President Reagan could." [34]

The Rise of Negative Advertising

Critics have widely condemned the advertising style in recent elections for being among the dirtiest and most negative in the nation's history. One leading commentator, Larry Sabato, described the 1988 elections as "a dreary, highly negative, and trivial general election campaign." [35] The tone of the campaign was so appalling that in an unprecedented action, one candidate actually broadcast an ad complaining about the tenor of the race and attempting to blame his opponent for that situation. The ad by Dukakis, "Counterpunch," proclaimed, "I'm fed up with it ... [I] never have seen anything like this in twenty-five years of public life.... George Bush's negative TV ads [are] distorting my record." [36] The 1992 campaign also featured sharp attacks through campaign commercials. One reporter, Eric Engberg of CBS, described the primary contest as a "political food fight." [37]

Despite the widespread consternation regarding these attacks, few have defined what they mean by negativity. Observers often define negativity as anything they do not like about campaigns. Defined in this way, the term is so all-encompassing as to become almost completely meaningless. The broadness of the definition brings to mind former justice Potter Stewart's famous line about pornographic material. When asked how he identified pornography, Stewart conceded that he could not define it. But, the justice asserted, "I know it when I see it." [38]

William Riker undertook an imaginative study of negative campaigning during the constitutional ratification effort of 1787-1788.[39] Unlike others, who lump together a variety of topics, he distinguished direct criticism; charges of threats to civil liberties, governmental structure, and state power; and other types of appeals. Relying upon contemporaneous documents employed by each side in the ratification campaign, he was able to define negativity more clearly and to show that the modern period has no monopoly on negative campaigning.

Following his lead, I examined the 324 prominent ads for the period from 1952 through 1992 and the 150 typical ads from 1972 through 1992 to determine the tone and object of attack. For example, if a candidate challenged an opposing campaigner in terms of policy positions or personal qualities, the ad was described as negative. If unflattering or pejorative comments were made about the opponent's domestic performance, the ad was labeled negative. Overall, negative comments were classified into the categories of personal qualities, domestic performance, specific policy statements, international affairs, the campaign, and political party. Fifty-three percent of prominent ads during this period were critical, with ads in the general election stage being slightly less negative (52 percent) than those in the nominating stage (55 percent). Republicans (60 percent) were more negative in their prominent ads than Democrats (47 percent). Forty-three percent of typical ads were negative, with Republicans (48 percent) being more negative than Democrats (43 percent).[40]

Campaigns through 1960 were not particularly negative in their advertising (Figure 3-2). Twenty-five percent of prominent ads in 1952 were negative, and 38 percent were negative in 1956. The low point occurred in 1960, when only 12 percent of the prominent ads featured critical statements. However, starting in the Johnson-Goldwater race of 1964, advertising turned more negative. Fifty percent of the prominent ads in 1964 and 69 percent of the prominent ads in 1968 were negative. The 1964 campaign produced a successful effort on Johnson's part to portray his opponent as a political extremist and threat to world peace. This race, as mentioned previously, featured the "Daisy" ad and others that damaged Goldwater's political prospects. One of the most visible ads of that campaign claimed that Goldwater would try to saw off the eastern seaboard of the United States. An ad that never aired linked

Figure 3-2 Negative Ads as a Percentage of Total, 1952-1992

Percent Negative

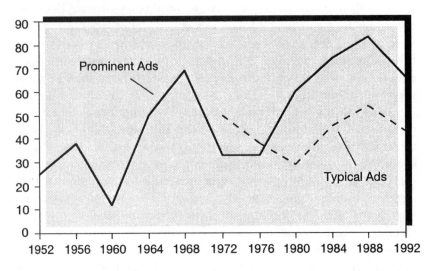

Sources: Typical ads for 1972-1988, Pol. Commercial Archive tapes, University of Oklahoma, and for 1992, Campaign Ad tapes. Prominent ads for 1952-1988, Kathleen Jamieson, *Packaging the Presidency,* 2d ed. (New York: Oxford University Press, 1992), and for 1992, *CBS Evening News* tapes.

Goldwater to the Ku Klux Klan. Although the ad was produced and given the go-ahead for regional airing, it was pulled at the last minute, according to one Johnson aide, because it "strained the available evidence, it was going too far." [41]

The effectiveness of Johnson's television ad campaign undoubtedly encouraged candidates in 1968 to use negative advertising. The race that year, between Nixon, Humphrey, and Wallace, was quite negative. The presence of Wallace in the race threatened both Nixon and Humphrey, and each responded with ads attacking the Alabama governor. Humphrey ran an ad showing a large picture of Wallace while actor E. G. Marshall explained: "When I see this man, I think of feelings of my own which I don't like but I have anyway. They're called prejudices. . . . Wallace is devoted now to his single strongest prejudice. He would take that prejudice and make it into national law." [42] Democrats also sought to take advantage of popular displeasure over the vice presidential qualifications of Spiro Agnew. One of their ads opened with a poster of "Spiro Agnew for Vice President," while in the background a man looking at the picture gradually collapsed in laughter.⁴³

Republicans sought to capitalize on the bloody riots that occurred during the 1968 Democratic convention in Chicago by running an ad linking the street disorder with Humphrey. In one of the campaign's most controversial ads, Nixon contrasted footage of the bloody riots with pictures of a smiling Humphrey accepting the nomination. With music from the song "Hot Time in the Old Town Tonight" playing in the background, the ad ended with the tagline, "This time vote like your whole world depended on it." ⁴⁴

The elections of 1972 and 1976 were not nearly as negative in tone. In both races only about one-third of prominent ads and about one-half of typical ads were negative. Campaigners may have become more reluctant to air negative commercials because of the backlash that followed the highly emotional ads of the 1964 and 1968 races. McGinniss's exposé of the electronic merchandising of Nixon in the 1968 campaign created a climate of skepticism among reporters that increased the risks of negative campaigning. Moral outrage against attack ads dominated the 1976 elections, which followed the "dirty tricks" associated with Watergate.

These sentiments, though, dissipated with time. As the memory of Watergate receded, the outrage associated with it also began to decline. Voters no longer associated attacks on the opposition with unfair dirty tricks. The result was that presidential contests in the 1980s reached negativity levels even higher than those of the 1960s. In 1980, 60 percent of prominent ads were negative; 74 percent were negative in 1984; and 83 percent were negative in 1988. Sixty percent of typical ads in 1988 were negative. For example, the 1980 campaign featured efforts, albeit unsuccessful, to portray Reagan as a dangerous extremist, in the mold of Goldwater. Carter employed "person-in-the-street" ads in an effort to portray Reagan as danger-ous: "I just don't think he's well enough informed. . . . We really have to keep our heads cool and I don't think that Reagan is cool. . . . That scares me about Ronald Reagan." ⁴⁵ Another ad sought to characterize the Californian as trigger happy by listing cases in which Reagan had backed military force, including the time he said a destroyer should be sent to Equador to resolve a fishing con-troversy.

Mondale used a similar strategy in 1984 when he ran an anti-Reagan ad showing missiles shooting out of underground silos, while

David Crosby, Stephen Stills, Graham Nash, and Neil Young sang lyrics from their song, "Teach Your Children." [46] The Minnesotan also sought to play on concerns about Gary Hart's leadership ability in the nominating process by running an ad featuring a ringing red phone to raise doubts about Hart's readiness to assume the duties of commander-in-chief.

The 1988 campaign attracted great attention because of numerous negative ads like the "Revolving Door." This Bush commercial sought to portray Dukakis as soft on crime by saying the Massachusetts governor had vetoed the death penalty and given weekend furloughs to first-degree murderers not eligible for parole. Although Willie Horton was never mentioned in this ad, the not-so-veiled reference to him generated considerable coverage from the news media, with numerous stories reviewing the details of Horton's crime of kidnapping and rape while on furlough from a Massachusetts prison. The Bush team, headed by Roger Ailes, also hammered Dukakis for his failure to clean up Boston Harbor. Dukakis meanwhile ran ads that reminded viewers of concern about Bush's most important personnel decision, the choice of J. Danforth Quayle as the Republican vice presidential nominee. Widespread doubts about Quayle's ability gave Dukakis a perfect opportunity to run an ad criticizing this selection. The ad closed with the line, "Hopefully, we will never know how great a lapse of judgment that really was." [47]

The 1992 race featured sharp attacks from Clinton and Perot on Bush's economic performance and from Bush on Clinton's past record and trustworthiness, but a lower level of negativity than in 1988. Overall, 66 percent of prominent ads and 44 percent of typical ads were negative. One memorable spot for Clinton tabulated the number of people who had lost jobs during Bush's administration. Bush meanwhile portrayed Clinton as just another "tax and spend" liberal who had a weak record as governor of Arkansas and who was shifty in his political stances. Perot ran a generally positive campaign, with commercials and infomercials that addressed the national debt, job creation, and the need for change. However, in the closing days of the campaign, Perot ran the infomercial entitled, "Deep Voodoo, Chicken Feathers, and the American Dream," which attacked both Bush and Clinton. One of the most memorable segments of this program featured a map of Arkansas with a big chicken in the middle to convey the message that job growth during

Clinton's governorship had occurred mainly through low-paying jobs in the chicken industry.

The Objects of Negativity

Attack ads are viewed by many as the electronic equivalent of the plague. Few aspects of contemporary politics have been as widely despised. Many observers have complained that negative campaign spots are among the least constructive developments of recent years. Furthermore, they are thought to contribute little to the political education of voters.

But in reviewing the objects of attack ads, it is somewhat surprising to discover that the most substantive appeals actually came in negative spots. For example, the most critical prominent commercials during the period from 1952 to 1992 appeared on foreign policy (86 percent of which were negative) and domestic policy (67 percent), followed by international affairs (56 percent), domestic performance (52 percent), personal qualities (45 percent), campaign appeals (35 percent), and party mentions (17 percent).[48]

There were some differences in the objects of negativity based on campaign stage. Negative prominent ads were more likely to appear on international affairs during the nominating stage (75 percent) than during the general election campaign (52 percent). Personal qualities attracted more negativity during the general election campaign (46 percent) than during the nominating stage (39 percent), as did domestic performance (53 percent in the general election campaign and 46 percent in the nominating stage).

If one charts the percentage of negative ads from 1952 to 1992 by type of message contained in the commercials, it is apparent that in recent years domestic performance and specific policy statements more than personal qualities have been the object of the negative prominent ads. In 1980, 95 percent of ads dealing with domestic matters were negative, as were 73 percent of those in 1984 and 83 percent in 1988. Similarly, 100 percent of the ads dealing with specific policy appeals in 1984 and 1988 were negative. In contrast, fewer of the prominent negative ads in 1984 and 1988 dealt with personal qualities (50 and 67 percent, respectively). The same trends are seen in typical ads. This pattern reinforces the point that attack ads are more likely to occur on substantive issues than on personality aspects of presidential campaigns.

Candidates often employed attack commercials to challenge the performance of the government or to question the handling of particular policy problems. Despite the obvious emotional qualities of the commercial, Bush's infamous "Revolving Door" ad was quite specific in attacking Dukakis's record: "As governor, Michael Dukakis vetoed mandatory sentences for drug dealers. He vetoed the death penalty. His revolving-door prison policy gave weekend furloughs to first-degree murderers not eligible for parole." [49]

Negative commercials are more likely to have policy-oriented content because campaigners need a clear reason to attack the opponent. Specificity helps focus viewer's attention on the message being delivered. Issue-oriented ads often attract public attention and are likely to be remembered.

Political strategists need to be clear about the facts in case of challenges from the media. Reporters often dissect negative ads and demand evidence to support specific claims. [50] In addition, campaigners are reluctant to criticize candidates personally for fear that it would make themselves look mean-spirited. Carter in 1980 ran ads challenging Reagan's experience and qualifications, and he was roundly criticized for being nasty. Research by Karen Johnson-Cartee and Gary Copeland demonstrates that voters are more likely to tolerate negative commercials that focus on policy than on personality. Voters' reactions help to reinforce the patterns noted above. [51]

Critics often condemn attack ads for disrupting democratic elections. While fears for democracy are certainly warranted, my research suggests a quandary for political observers. Negative commercials provide a considerable amount of policy-oriented information. Negative ads are not always specific. But candidates' desire to target their messages, combined with their need for a plausible defense against attacks on them, creates incentives to attack via the issues.

From the standpoint of substantive content, therefore, negative ads contribute to public education when they are accurate. Of course, other problems can arise from attack ads. Negative commercials are often inaccurate or deceptive, and they may involve emotionally charged subjects. In addition, their effects can fall disproportionately on inattentive viewers. But observers interested in increasing the amount of substantive information in commercials should know that negative ads are more informative than is commonly believed.

Chapter 4

Media Coverage of Ads

The influential role of the media is a vital new element of the
American electoral system. Reporters clearly have become
major power brokers in contemporary elections.[1] Together, print and
electronic journalists provide much of the information we receive
about both campaigns and candidates. These journalists teach us
about candidates' backgrounds, personalities, strategies, and goals.
When a campaign starts to accelerate, the press becomes almost
insatiable in its curiosity about the personal and political lives and
objectives of these individuals.

With the increasing influence of the media, criticism has
surfaced concerning how reporters perform their jobs. The media
have been challenged for their well-documented emphasis on horse
race and personality considerations rather than policy issues.[2]
There often is a faddish quality to media reporting that can propel
candidates into the type of momentum Bush once described as "Big
Mo." [3] Surprise winners can become the beneficiary of extensive
coverage, which then allows them to raise additional money,
broadcast more ads, and often win greater public support. Conversely, those who fail to beat the expectations game see their free
coverage vanish, ad budgets disappear, and campaigns forced into
premature bankruptcy.[4]

The way in which reporting about political advertising has
changed over the past few decades has not received much attention.
Political commercials generate much greater attention from the
news media today than they generated in the past. At the same
time, there have been important developments in the format of
ad coverage. Media coverage of ads therefore deserves serious
attention.

From Old- to New-Style Journalism

Reporters used to be governed by the norms of old-style journalism, the "who, what, where, when, and how" approach to newsgathering. Candidates' statements were reported more or less at face value; behind-the-scenes machinations fell outside the news; and, by implicit agreement, the private behavior of political leaders was ignored. If a leader's personal life included excesses in the areas of drinking, philandering, or gambling, as was true with John F. Kennedy, it was kept quiet on the assumption that these activities would not affect performance in office. Leaders—such as Sen. Edmund Muskie (Maine) a Democratic candidate in 1972—who were subject to temper tantrums and uncontrollable emotional outbursts in private were not questioned publicly regarding whether they would be able to withstand the pressures of high office.

However, Johnson's deception in the Vietnam War and Nixon's lying in the face of the deepening Watergate scandal led reporters to take more interpretive and investigative approaches to newsgathering.[5] Rather than sticking to hard news, journalists today see a responsibility to put "the facts" in broader context. Reporters want to enable readers and viewers to see the real picture of political events, not just the version public officials place before them.[6] Why do leaders act the way they do? What hidden motives govern leadership behavior? How can outsiders make sense of the ups and downs of daily political events?

This new-style journalism also led reporters to a different approach to campaign coverage. Once content to cover candidate speeches and travel, reporters began to emphasize behind-the-scenes activities.[7] What strategies were candidates pursuing? What blocs of voters were seen as most critical to electoral success? What clues did campaigns provide about underlying beliefs and preferences? Following the lead of Theodore White, who revolutionized coverage of presidential campaigns, reporters began to devote greater attention to analysis.[8]

Changes in the nature of presidential selection following the 1968 election created new opportunities for reporters.[9] The decline in the power of party leaders, rise in the number of primaries, and extension of races over a number of months made it dramatically easier for reporters to explore behind-the-scenes maneuvering. In fact, the entry into open nominating contests of little-known candidates made it mandatory that reporters cover the backgrounds and goals of candidates. Who were these new candidates and why were they running for president? Journalists rightly saw their mission as informing the public about these people as well as describing how they were running their campaigns.

The open electoral process also made it easier to investigate campaign events. This system brought candidates out of the back rooms into public view. Disclosure requirements associated with campaign finance reforms brought an avalanche of background material out into the open. Reporters gained access to information that allowed them to probe further than ever before.

But according to many observers, the media have not fulfilled their responsibility. There have been a number of critical analyses of how the media cover campaigns. The most common approach has been to distinguish coverage based on policy content from reports regarding the campaign and the personal qualities of the candidates. The assumption is that policy reporting is the type of coverage most relevant to voters. This assumption ignores the fact that knowledge about personal qualities of candidates is equally important to those interested in how well particular individuals will cope with the office or deliver on promised commitments.

Nevertheless, research generally has found that the media devote little space to policy matters. A thorough study by Henry Brady and Richard Johnston of every United Press International story on the Democratic candidates from January 1 through July 31, 1984, revealed that press coverage devoted only 16 percent of lines to policy positions. The more common topic included discussions of the campaign (50 percent overall, which included 21 percent devoted to prospects of election, 20 percent devoted to campaign appearances, and 9 percent devoted to sources of support), personal qualities of the candidates (23 percent), and comments about the opposition (11 percent). These figures are comparable to what Doris Graber found in her study of *Chicago Tribune* coverage of the 1983 mayoral election. In that race, 42 percent of the lines dealt with the campaign, 20 percent were devoted to policy matters, 19 percent dealt with personal qualities, and 20 percent involved other matters, such as ethics or party affairs.[10]

These findings have been disappointing to those who believe the media should play a central role in educating the electorate. In past eras, a variety of institutions assumed the role of civic educator.

Political parties helped to define voters' choices, while voluntary associations and interest groups tried to instruct their members in the issues of the day. Today, however, parties engender little respect and group leaders have difficulty representing their followers. This situation has created an information vacuum, which reporters are attempting to fill.

But rather than devoting space to matters that would facilitate public education, the press focuses most often on who is ahead and who is behind. Robinson and Sheehan show in their study of the 1980 presidential campaign that once the nominating season gets under way, "horse race" coverage far outpaces coverage of issues and candidates. They found that in March 76 percent of the campaign coverage time on CBS was devoted to the horse race, compared with 18 percent to the issues and 6 percent to candidate characteristics. Similarly, in September 62 percent of the news time emphasized the horse race, while 25 percent dealt with policy matters and 12 percent involved personal qualities.[11] Just at the point when voters start to pay attention to politics, reporters devote relatively little coverage to the candidates' stances on issues and substantial attention to the contest.

This pattern of reporting has affected voters. In their pathbreaking survey research on the 1948 presidential campaign, Berelson, Lazarsfeld, and William McPhee discovered that 67 percent of voters' conversations with one another dealt with the policy positions and personal qualifications of candidates, whereas about 25 percent involved questions of winnability.[12] But by 1976, these numbers had reversed in public opinion surveys. According to Patterson, the "game was the major topic of conversation in 1976." [13] In June of that year, near the end of the nominating cycle, 69 percent of conversations involved the game and only 18 percent dealt with substantive matters.

The horse race has become a popular object of press attention because it often involves drama and suspense. Nothing attracts the attention of the media more than a surprise showing that surpasses their expectations. Candidates who have come out of nowhere and do well in early caucuses and primaries attract a disproportionate share of media coverage.[14] Carter was the classic case: his campaign's momentum was fueled by media coverage. In the months before the 1976 Iowa caucuses, Governor Carter of Georgia was a virtual unknown. Public opinion polls a year before the election had put him on the list of "asterisk" candidates, those individuals who fell in the "others" category because their public preference ratings fell under 5 percent. When Carter did better than expected in Iowa, he received an extraordinary amount of news coverage, much of which dealt with his success in the horse race. He then skyrocketed in the polls, was able to raise much more money, and eventually became the nominee of the Democratic party.

The Increasing Coverage of Ads

Although there has been great interest in media coverage of presidential campaigns, limited attention has been paid to how journalists cover television ads. As noted earlier, candidates devote considerable effort to the messages presented in their ads. They also use strategy in choosing where and when to show their ads.

To see how advertising is covered, I made a tabulation of the number of *New York Times* articles from 1952 to 1992, *Washington Post* articles from 1972 to 1992, and "CBS Evening News" stories from 1972 to 1992 that covered political advertising.[15] As a reflection of differences in time periods and scope of coverage, there were 368 articles about political commercials in the *New York Times,* 296 articles in the *Washington Post,* and 174 stories on the "CBS Evening News."[16] For the *New York Times,* 183 articles (50 percent) dealt with the nominating stage, while 185 involved the general election. In the case of the *Washington Post,* 170 (57 percent) involved nominations and 126 dealt with the general election. For CBS, 107 (61 percent) of the stories covered the nominating stage and 67 involved the general election. However, if only articles from 1972 to 1992 are included for the *New York Times* for comparability with the other outlets, 160 (56 percent) of the stories dealt with the nominating phase and 127 (44 percent) covered the general election.

There were some differences between the news outlets, but the general trend has been a substantial increase in coverage of advertisements in the 1980s and 1990s.[17] For both nominating and general election contests, the 1970s did not generate many television stories about political spot ads (see Figures 4-1 and 4-2, respectively, for the stages). For example, in 1972 only seven CBS stories about ads appeared during the nominating process and four during the general election campaign. In 1976, there were fourteen stories on

Figure 4-1   Media Coverage of Nomination Campaign Ads, 1952-1992

Number of Stories

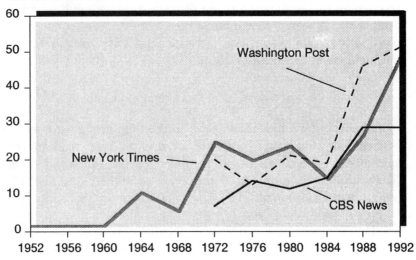

Sources: *New York Times, 1952-1992; CBS Evening News, 1972-1992; Washington Post, 1972-1992.*

CBS in the spring and five in the fall. However, the numbers started to rise in 1980 and reached their zenith in recent elections. The 1988 race produced five times the number of ad stories (twenty-nine in the nominating process campaign and twenty-one in the general election campaign) than had the elections of the 1970s. Meanwhile, the 1992 contest generated twenty-nine nomination and twenty-four general election campaign stories.

This increase in television attention to advertising has had major consequences for candidates and voters. People today are about as likely to see ads through the news as they are to see them directly. This means ads are seen along with comments provided by the media. Thus, journalists have gained great influence in shaping public interpretations of the objectives and impact of ads.

In regard to the *New York Times,* the critical turning point in ad coverage for the nominating process occurred in 1972. Before then, there were few stories about political advertising. In 1952, 1956, and 1960, there were two *New York Times* articles about ads each year in the presidential nominating period from January to June. A March 26, 1960, article, for example, described Stuart Symington's

Figure 4-2 Media Coverage of General Election Campaign Ads, 1952-1992

Number of Stories

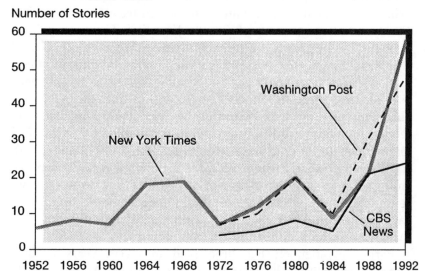

Sources: *New York Times,* 1952-1992; *CBS Evening News,* 1972-1992; *Washington Post,* 1972-1992.

decision not to launch a preconvention television drive against Nixon. In 1968, for the same period, six stories appeared. An article on May 8 recounted Robert Kennedy's decision to spend heavily on television in Indiana because of Gov. Roger Branigan's control of the party organization. Most of the other articles dealt with the content of or strategies behind ads.

However, after Democratic reforms and the rise in the number of primaries, the number of stories on ads during the nominating process rose dramatically. The 1972 campaign was the first election conducted under the new nomination reforms, which had been designed to open up the process and give citizens a more direct voice in delegate selection. Not surprisingly, press coverage of ads during the nominating period increased considerably. Twenty stories appeared in the *Washington Post* in 1972, compared to thirteen in 1976, twenty-one in 1980, nineteen in 1984, forty-six in 1988, and fifty-one in 1992. Twenty-five articles about campaign commercials appeared in the *New York Times* between January and June of 1972, twenty in 1976, twenty-four in 1980, fifteen in 1984, twenty-seven in 1988, and forty-nine in 1992. A May 22, 1976, *New York*

Times story reported Frank Church's (Idaho) accusations that Gov. Edmund Brown, Jr. (Calif.) was trying to "buy" votes in the Oregon primary by spending large sums of money on television advertising. Earlier that spring, on March 28, the *New York Times* had printed a long article by Joseph Lelyveld on Carter's media adviser, Gerald Rafshoon, and his use of television ads in crucial primary states.

Newspaper coverage of general election advertising has changed as well. In general, the number of stories has fluctuated considerably, depending on the closeness of the race. Campaigns that were seen as competitive (1968, 1976, 1980, 1988, and 1992) generated many more stories than those seen as runaways (1972 and 1984). This was particularly true in 1992, as the three-way battle between Bush, Clinton, and Perot prompted a dramatic increase in news stories. In close elections, the media devote more coverage to campaign phenomena, such as television advertising, that are thought to make a difference in voters' choices.[18]

Particular attention has been paid in recent years to how television advertising shapes the dynamics of a race. An October 10, 1988, *New York Times* story described how both Bush and Dukakis ran commercials that attacked the opposition, with little positive reference to platforms or promises. Dukakis's inability to produce timely, effective ads was cited in an October 19 article as an indicator of larger failings within his campaign organization.

In 1992 news coverage emphasized the backlash against Bush's attack ads and the big audiences Perot was attracting to his thirty-minute infomercials. Special attention was paid to new media formats that emerged that year: the morning shows, "Larry King Live," the "Arsenio Hall Show," and the new style of debates in the fall. Reporters discussed the major changes that were taking place in the industry and the way in which the new outlets were taking attention away from the traditional media.

Horse Race Coverage of Ads

The increase in the coverage of ads highlights the blurring of free and paid media, but the raw figures do not reveal what reporters actually said. There has been widespread criticism about media attention to horse race considerations and the limited time spent on policy matters. Since television is the major news source for most Americans, I examined in detail all the stories about campaign

TABLE 4-1
Content and Tone of CBS News Coverage, 1972-1992

	Descriptions of Ads	News Stories about Ads
Personal qualities	22%	8%
Domestic performance	31	9
Specific policy statements	33	16
International affairs	7	1
Campaign	6	66
Party	1	0
N	(174)	(174)
Negativity Level	66%	46%

Sources: Vanderbilt Television News Index and Abstracts for campaigns 1972-1988, and "CBS Evening News" tapes for 1992 campaign.

Note: Entries indicate the percentage of "CBS Evening News" stories devoted to each type of appeal.

advertising that appeared on the "CBS Evening News" from 1972 through 1992. Two features were analyzed: (1) the content of the ad reference and (2) the general topic of the news story in which the ad was discussed. Several categories were developed to assess the quality of coverage and to facilitate comparison with the results for ads themselves, as discussed in Chapter 3.

There were interesting differences between the descriptions of ads in news stories and the content of the news stories. As shown in Table 4-1, the major contrast concerned the tendency of reporters fascinated with the horse race to convert substantive ad messages into news stories about campaign prospects or strategies. Ads that were reported on in the news were more specific (33 percent) than either the news stories themselves (16 percent) or the prominent ads analyzed in the preceding chapter (22 percent). They also were more specific than those documented by Brady and Johnson (16 percent) for the 1984 nominating process. CBS often rebroadcast ad segments that were particularly pointed in their charges about opponents' policy positions. For example, a Nixon ad featured in the "Evening News" on October 30, 1972, lambasted McGovern's defense posture and noted which specific weapons programs the Democrat would oppose. In the same vein, CBS showed a Jack Kemp ad on January

19, 1988, which attacked Bush and Robert Dole for being willing to reduce Social Security benefits. Spring campaign coverage tended to be more specific about policy (36 percent) than coverage of the general election campaign (21 percent).

In contrast, most of the news stories about ads dealt with the campaign (66 percent), a figure similar to the 76 percent reported by Robinson and Sheehan for general coverage in 1980.[19] Many of these stories included discussions of how particular ads fit strategic goals of the campaign (35 percent), affected the electoral prospects of the candidate (18 percent), or had been produced and financed within the campaign organization (12 percent). For example, CBS broadcast a story on January 29, 1980, describing an Edward Kennedy ad that addressed the Chappaquidick incident. The ad itself dealt with personal qualities, such as Kennedy's trustworthiness and honesty, but the news story emphasized the change in the candidate's strategy, which had been designed to reassure voters about the senator's past conduct. Another example appeared February 12, 1988, when a Dukakis ad on the economy was analyzed in terms of its contribution to the candidate's campaign strategy.

The news media were more likely to report specific ad claims for Republicans (44 percent) than for Democrats (21 percent). They also were more likely to cover ads based on international affairs for Republicans (14 percent) than for Democrats (5 percent). In contrast, Democrats earned more news coverage for ads on domestic performance (33 percent) than Republicans (26 percent) and on personal qualities (28 percent) than Republicans (14 percent). There were few partisan differences in other areas of coverage.

News reports generally placed much less emphasis on personal qualities, domestic performance, or specific policy statements than did the ads themselves. Reporters often blame candidates for not discussing the issues, but it appears that fascination with the horse race leads journalists to turn substantive messages into campaign stories.

In addition, ads broadcast as part of news stories tended to be more negative than the news stories were. Sixty-six percent of ads described in the news were negative in orientation, compared with 46 percent of the news stories themselves. As noted in Chapter 3, negative ads have become more common. Negative commercials tend to be more controversial, which produces greater coverage than otherwise would be the case, especially in Ad Watches. But the media devote considerable time to rebroadcasting negative ads, which reinforces the widespread public view about the negativity of television ads. In fact, it is well known in political circles that one of the easiest ways to attract press coverage is to run negative commercials. Media adviser Ailes explained it this way: "There are three things that the media are interested in: pictures, mistakes, and attacks.... If you need coverage, you attack, and you will get coverage." [20]

Shifts over Time in Ad Coverage

An intensive study of *New York Times* ad coverage since 1952 shows exactly how press coverage of commercials has shifted over the last four decades. In the 1950s, consistent with the old-style journalism practiced at that time, considerable attention was devoted to the use of celebrity endorsements in the presidential campaign. For example, Eleanor Roosevelt filmed an endorsement of Adlai Stevenson that generated press attention simply because of her celebrity status. In 1960 an April 20 story discussed a New York telethon plan to raise money for fall advertising time, while a March 26 article recounted Symington's decision not to spend $400,000 in a preconvention television drive against Nixon.

Both of the 1960 articles are noteworthy because of their emphasis on factual events. Each clearly illustrates the "who, what, where" approach to newsgathering. Hard facts were emphasized and announcements from campaign officials taken at face value. There was little discussion of how the decision fit broader strategic goals. There was no analysis of campaign maneuvering or how candidates actually reached particular decisions. Furthermore, there was no attention paid to the motivations of campaign decision makers. Reporters did not examine the true motives or goals of Symington or the telethon planners to determine what they "really" were trying to accomplish or who was winning organizational battles.

A similar example of hard news coverage occurred in 1968. On May 27 the *New York Times* reported that Humphrey had hired the firm Doyle Dane Bernbach as his advertising agency. This seemingly bland news item is noteworthy because of what it did not say. The article more or less stayed on the surface. It did not delve into strategic considerations. It furthermore did not address the consequences of the decision for the power balance within the Humphrey organization. There was no speculation about who won and who lost in this decision or what it revealed about the type of campaign Humphrey might run.

However, the *New York Times* began to cover political advertising in a different sort of way during the 1970s and 1980s. A January 14, 1972, article describing Senator Muskie's use of television in his bid for the Democratic nomination illustrates the new tendency to put the campaign in context and tell the story behind the event. The article noted that television would be the dominant element in Muskie's campaign. Muskie's strategy was described as contrasting himself to Nixon's weak credibility. Muskie also planned to stress his own position on sensitive issues and avoid staged scenes characteristic of most political commercials. The newspaper's approach was clearly a departure. The story emphasized strategic considerations—how advertising furthered vote getting. This story also illustrated the effort to report the behind-the-scenes story. Why was Muskie employing particular ads? What was he really trying to accomplish? The attention to the candidate's motivations and goals reflects the new direction in the coverage of political ads.

Later years saw further development of this style of coverage. For example, a March 28, 1976, article discusses the crucial importance of television ads to presidential candidates. It describes the dramatic impact Rafshoon had in Carter's primary victories. The article describes how Rafshoon put together ads and how polls by Pat Caddell helped Carter officials decide where to place their television commercials. The story analyzed the implications of this approach for Carter's success.

This is not to imply that strategic considerations were the reporters' only focus. Journalists also devoted attention to the substance of television ads. A March 21, 1984, article covering Democratic party ads focused on the "ethical and moral" violations of the Reagan administration. Rep. Tony Coelho (Calif.) was quoted as criticizing President Reagan's willingness to blast welfare cheats but not those who violate the public trust.

There were stories in 1988 that discussed Rep. Richard Gephardt's trade ads in Iowa. The Democratic representative from Missouri used highly effective commercials blasting Far East trading partners for closing their markets to American products while flooding the United States with cheaper imports. These ads noted the threat to American jobs and described Gephardt's legislative plans to force Japan and other countries to open their markets to U.S. goods. A September 1, 1988, story described how Dukakis planned to run commercials that featured the slogan "Bringing Prosperity Home." According to the article, the point of this slogan was to appeal to the economic anxiety of the middle class and help Dukakis regain his lead over Bush.

But even this type of coverage often incorporated considerations of candidates' strategic thinking. A number of stories describing the content of ads showed how particular messages were designed to appeal to particular constituencies. For example, the Coelho articles noted that these commercials were meant to call attention to the nomination of Edwin Meese III as attorney general. Democratic officials hoped that the sleaze factor associated with Meese's questionable private dealings would damage Republican prospects in 1984 and win Democrats the support of voters cynical about American politics. Likewise, the Gephardt ads were described in substantive terms but were used to illustrate the strategic goals of his campaign. His protectionism ads were designed to win labor support and votes from workers worried about losing their jobs. These ads furthermore helped to make Gephardt distinctive from his Democratic rivals, some of whom played down their protectionist sentiments. Therefore, this form of press coverage used substantive messages presented in ads to describe strategic plans within campaign organizations.

Media Coverage of Negative Ads: Daisy and the Revolving Door

Nothing illustrates the change in media orientation better than the subject of attack commercials. Although there were many stories condemning the rise of negative ads in 1988, journalists have become over the years quite tolerant of these ads. A simple comparison of reactions to two of the most notorious negative ads—"Daisy" in 1964 and the "Revolving Door" ad in 1988—illustrates the change. Both commercials dealt with emotional subjects and generated criticisms about playing on citizens' fears—of nuclear war in 1964 and of crime in 1988.

The "Daisy" commercial was probably the most infamous ad in television history. This ad opens with a young girl standing in a meadow plucking petals from a daisy. After she counts "1, 2, 3, 4, 5, 6, 7, 8, 9," a solemn voice begins its own countdown: "10, 9, 8, 7, 6, 5, 4, 3, 2, 1, 0." At zero, the picture of the child dissolves and a mushroom cloud fills the screen. Johnson closes the ad by warning, "These are the stakes. To make a world in which all of God's children can live, or to go into the dark. We must either love each other or we must die." [21]

This ad aired only once, during NBC's "Monday Night at the Movies" showing of "David and Bathsheeba" on September 7, 1964. But condemnation came almost immediately. As recalled by Bill Moyers, then Johnson's press secretary, "The president called me and said 'Holy shit. I'm getting calls from all over the country.' Most of them said that it was an effective ad. Others said they didn't like it." Press reaction was swift. According to Lloyd Wright, an advertising strategist for Johnson, "The first night it aired, it created such a media flap that the next night it was used in its entirety on the newscasts on all three networks." Johnson pulled from the ad. [22]

Bush's "Revolving Door" ad received quite a different reception. CBS covered this commercial in its broadcast on October 7, 1988. (News stories about Horton had been broadcast September 22.) The story described the commercial as a crime ad that would highlight the prison furlough policy of Governor Dukakis. Clifford Barnes and Donna Cuomo, joint victims of an assault by a convict who had been released on a weekend furlough, were reported to be participating in a speaking tour with a pro-Bush group. Bush meanwhile was shown campaigning with police officers. This was followed on October 20 with another story, this time showing in great detail Horton's crime record and supplying background on the Bush ad. Bush was shown campaigning in New York City at a police union rally. It was not until October 24 and 25—almost three weeks after the commercial appeared—that opponents appeared on the news to claim that the "Revolving Door" ad had racist undertones. But in keeping with the horse race mentality of the media, a second story on October 25 also quoted media consultant Tony Schwartz as saying that Bush's ads were successful and that the "Revolving Door" was particularly effective.

The contrast with the coverage of the "Daisy" ad could not have been more stark. Whereas the 1964 ad was immediately condemned and removed from the airwaves, reporters in 1988 treated the furlough ad as a typical news story. Its airing was reported. It was described as being quite effective. Criticisms came late and were never solidly addressed; the spot was not pulled off the air.

This subdued and delayed reaction was in keeping with the general rumor of news coverage about attack ads in 1988. A number of CBS stories and *New York Times* articles during the general election campaign emphasized the overall effectiveness of negative political commercials. A September 18 *New York Times* article, for example, discussed the role of advertising in contemporary campaigns. Former governor Brown was quoted, saying that media and professional campaign advisers think negative commercials work better. A number of politicians and consultants were cited as saying that Bush and Dukakis would be foolish to delve deeply into policy issues. This was followed on October 10 with an article that cited campaign officials who believed that the electorate had become accustomed to sharp-elbow tactics.

In addition, political professionals quoted on October 19 sharply derided Dukakis's advertising effort. Several experts complained about the ever-shifting focus of his ad campaign and the fact that his commercials were not well timed. An October 13 story noted that 1988 was the first time candidates used more ads to criticize opponents than to promote themselves. A number of analysts even attributed Bush's lead in the polls to the success of his negative commercials and the lack of an appropriate response by Dukakis.

This tolerance of negativity, combined with the grudging respect reporters had for the effectiveness of the GOP ads, created a pattern of coverage that benefited Bush. Rather than condemning the ad, as reporters had in 1964 with the "Daisy" ad, the reporters of 1988 did not complain when the "Revolving Door" commercial stayed on the air. They even rebroadcast the ad repeatedly throughout the last month of the campaign.[23] This behavior effectively erased the traditional difference between the free and paid media. It gave Bush more air time and therefore lent him more credibility than any campaign organization alone could have managed. This style of news coverage helped make Bush's 1988 advertising campaign one of the most effective of the past twenty years.

Ad Watches

The style of coverage in the 1988 campaign was profoundly disturbing to voters, political professionals, academic experts, and even reporters themselves. Countless seminars, conferences, and white papers urged journalists to alter their approach, particularly as it related to campaign commercials. The feeling was that by not having challenged Bush more effectively, reporters let the candidate set the campaign agenda, to the detriment of democratic discussion. The inevitable conclusion was that fundamental changes in media coverage would have to be made.

One way in which the news media have altered their response has been through Ad Watch features. Ad Watch stories review the content of prominent commercials and discuss their accuracy and effectiveness. Designed to provide media oversight of candidates' claims, they have become regular features in leading newspaper and television outlets around the country. As described by Jamieson, one of the originators of the concept, Ad Watches were created to provide a "grammar of evaluation." [24]

According to Jamieson, though, focus groups revealed in 1988 that the few Ad Watches that appeared that year did not achieve their purposes. Viewers often remembered the ad, but not the media corrections. For example, negative ads that year, such as Bush's "Revolving Door," had such powerful visuals that replaying the ad, even with criticism and commentary, only served to boost Bush's campaign message. Jamieson found the same thing in focus groups when she showed a story by Richard Threlkeld of CBS debunking Bush's "Tank" ad. This spot revealed a helmeted Dukakis riding around in a military tank while the graphics claimed the Massachusetts governor opposed major weapons programs. Threlkeld ran a lengthy critique of this ad showing that Dukakis actually supported a number of weapons systems, but because he rebroadcast the ad full screen, viewers who saw this story were more likely to believe Bush's charges against Dukakis than the news story's rebuttal.

Based on these reflections, according to Jamieson, it was decided to change Ad Watches in fundamental ways. In the reviews, accuracy/fairness issues were separated from notions of strategic effectiveness. In many newspapers, a box labeled "Ad Watch" was created, with distinctive sections providing the complete script of the ad (along with a photo of the most important visual), an assessment of the accuracy of the ad, and a discussion of its effectiveness. It was hoped that viewers would realize there were different standards of evaluation and that it was important to judge ads on several levels.

In 1992 the media devoted considerable space to Ad Watches. The *Boston Globe* offered some of the most comprehensive coverage in the country. It printed Ad Watches on forty-eight of the fifty-three commercials broadcast during the New Hampshire primary campaign alone (as well as many thereafter). Overall, the *New York Times* ran fifteen separate reviews throughout the nominating process, while the *Washington Post* ran twenty-one. The television networks also incorporated ad segments in a number of stories. The general election campaign featured twenty-nine Ad Watches in the *New York Times* and twenty-four in the *Washington Post.*

According to reporters, Ad Watches have become effective oversight tools. Howard Kurtz of the *Washington Post* says they are "a great step forward for democracy because they keep candidates honest." The same sentiment was expressed by Mara Liasson of National Public Radio, who said that "candidates are more careful because they know they will be scrutinized." Renee Loth of the *Boston Globe* felt that Ad Watches "inoculate viewers against the potion of ads." [25]

Ad Watches have had a big impact on candidates. Recent elections have seen the rise of what can be called ads with footnotes. Reporters' scrutiny has forced candidates to document their claims more carefully. Some aspirants in 1992 even included citations of factual information directly on the screen. For example, Clinton ads routinely listed the source and date of publication of a quote or fact for viewers to see. This was an obvious effort to boost the credibility of partisan ads by citing nonpartisan sources, such as newspaper articles and government reports. Clinton media adviser Frank Greer said his campaign's research "consistently found that viewers believed Bush's negative ads—such as one suggesting that Clinton would raise taxes on middle-class workers—lacked documentation. . . . They [the Bush advisers] never figured out that you needed to offer people substantiation and details. Ross Perot figured that out." [26]

Because of the attention devoted by the media, it is not surprising that Ad Watches are noticed by the viewing public. A Boston metropolitan survey taken March 2-9 revealed that 57 percent of the area's residents said they had seen Ad Watches, 28 percent said they had not, and 15 percent did not remember. Viewers were generally likely to see Ad Watches as helpful. A survey in May 1992 taken in Los Angeles asked residents how helpful news stories analyzing ads had been.[27] Of those expressing an opinion, 21 percent indicated the stories had been very helpful and 47 percent said they had been somewhat helpful. Only 32 percent felt the Ad Watch analysis had been not very helpful.

When it comes to reporting on the most controversial commercials, however, there remains a big difference between media outlets. The clearest example of this came in the 1992 primaries following Buchanan's airing of his controversial Georgia spot, "Freedom Abused," criticizing Bush for supporting public subsidies of homoerotic art. The video footage for this commercial was taken from a Public Broadcasting Service documentary, *Tongues Untied,* which had been subsidized by the National Endowment for the Arts. The ad blasted Bush for spending tax dollars on pornographic art that glorified homosexuality. Clearly designed to appeal to traditional voters in the South, the spot generated widespread press attention and prompted direct comparisons with Bush's 1988 "Revolving Door" commercial.

In general, newspaper reporters were quite critical of this ad. On February 27, almost immediately after the commercial started running, the *Washington Post* printed an article by E. J. Dionne, Jr. reporting the ad's airing and reactions from the Bush campaign calling the ad a "blatant distortion of truth." [28] Buchanan's response was that the ad "has nothing to do with anti-gay prejudice. It has to do with not spending people's tax dollars on values that insult them." Ad Watches followed on February 28 by Kurtz in the *Washington Post* and by Loth in the *Boston Globe.*[29] The *New York Times* did not run an Ad Watch feature, but had detailed stories by Robin Toner and Kolbert on that day with critical comments from campaign strategists and by Alessandra Stanley on March 8 giving the reactions of gay groups.[30]

The *Washington Post* Ad Watch noted that Bush was not personally responsible for the decision to subsidize the film. The film-maker, Marlon Riggs, had been given $5,000 by the Rocky Mountain Film Institute, which received the money from the American Film Institute, which got it from the National Endowment for the Arts.[31] Loth, in her *Boston Globe* Ad Watch, was even more critical. She pointed out the limited political control of the White House over the National Endowment for the Arts and wrote, "For sheer appeal to intolerance and shock value, this ad pushes all the right buttons. It features a slow-motion film clip from "Tongues

Untied," a frank documentary on black gay life. While the ad may galvanize the religious right in Georgia, it also reveals what many could see as an unattractive side of Buchanan." [32]

Others were not nearly as critical. Almost completely unfazed by this commercial was Eric Engberg in a February 28 "CBS Evening News" report dealing with negative ads (specifically, Bush's "General Kelley" ad questioning Buchanan's position on the Persian Gulf War and Buchanan's quota and antipornography ads). Engberg's closing remarks in the story gave a remarkably upbeat interpretation of the anti-NEA ad and stressed its general effectiveness: "By staking a claim to the racially sensitive quotas issue and by coming on as a strong supporter of traditional values, Buchanan is cutting into Mr. Bush's base, something of a surprise for a president who was able to make effective use of Willie Horton just four years ago." No mention was made of the antihomosexual overtones of the ad or the difficulties noted by Kurtz and Loth in attributing responsibility to Bush for NEA funding decisions. This story, of course, was not a formal Ad Watch, and its tone reflected the general tendency of reporters to focus on strategy.

A second feature by Engberg that discussed Buchanan's ad appeared March 2 on the "CBS Evening News." There again was no critique of the commercial, although Engberg was more circumspect in describing the candidate's political fortunes. In his story, Engberg said that Buchanan's advertisements were "turning Georgia into a political mud-wrestling contest that will determine whether Pat Buchanan has political legs or is just a one-time wonder."

Lisa Myers of NBC was much more critical in a February 28 story. After she aired a Buchanan segment promising no discrimination and then discussed the new television ad, she raised questions about whether Buchanan was guilty of racism. Buchanan's past statements regarding Martin Luther King, Jr., and women serving in the Persian Gulf War were outlined, as were previous comments on David Duke and the State of Israel. Chris Bury of ABC was not personally critical of Buchanan in a February 28 story, but statements from White House spokesman Marlin Fitzwater and Vice President Quayle attacking Buchanan were used.

While the CBS stories obviously failed to point out major shortcomings of "Freedom Abused," it may be that television itself has greater problems than print outlets in evaluating ads. Television is a powerful medium because of its combination of audio and visual communications. This makes it quite difficult to shield voters from the candidate's message when rebroadcasting advertisements.[33] The most controversial ads almost always use emotionally charged visuals. For example, the backdrop of "Freedom Abused" included apparently gay men in chains dancing around a stage. Similar difficulties arose in the case of the "Revolving Door" ad, which featured slow-motion frames of prisoners streaming through a revolving door, while an armed guard watched over them.

But there are ways of overcoming barriers to effective television Ad Watches. In 1992 Brooks Jackson of the Cable News Network made an innovative effort on the show "Inside Politics" to review ads without hyping the candidate. The trick, according to Jackson, was to use what Jamieson calls a "truth box" to rebroadcast the commercial in a smaller square on one side of the screen.[34] This shrinking of the video in the Ad Watch is an important advance because it undercuts the visual impact of the advertisement. Rather than forcing news analysts to compete with powerful visual images, the CNN approach allows reporters to superimpose their own graphics—such as "misleading," "false," or "unfair"—over the ad. This puts them on a fairer footing and gives them a chance to overshadow the campaign commercial.

The "CBS Evening News" in the fall made a valiant effort to oversee candidates' claims. In a periodic feature called Reality Check, reporters subjected political speeches, debate claims, and advertising messages to close scrutiny. A feature by Engberg on October 19, for example, examined some of the scathing radio ads being used in the campaign. In Florida, for example, Clinton ran commercials accusing Bush of wanting to cut Medicare, despite Bush's claims to the contrary. Bush meanwhile tried to tie Clinton in New Jersey to unpopular tax hikes by Gov. Jim Florio.[35]

It remains to be seen how effective these features are. Focus groups during the 1992 primaries worried that Ad Watches would give too much power to the media. For example, one participant from Boston claimed after seeing a television Ad Watch that: "ad watch just . . . shows you what . . . the media wants to show you." Another person from the same group found them confusing: "It's so editorial, and it's just bits and pieces put together to confuse you." [36]

In spite of these sentiments, it appears that Ad Watches have had an important impact. These ad critiques have had some effect in terms of nationalizing campaign coverage. It is more difficult for candidates to target specific ads on local audiences when there is media oversight. For example, Buchanan's effort in his "Freedom Abused" spot to deliver a message about lifestyle values to conservative Republican voters in Georgia backfired when newspapers and television stations from around the country ran stories about it. Ad Watches make it riskier to broadcast commercials in different parts of the country to cater to local interests.

At the same time, the disparity in how news outlets cover advertisements suggests a need for further refinement of the Ad Watch concept. Liasson of National Public Radio notes that "the media is an organism without a head. There are no standard rules on coverage and there is no punishment if [the coverage] is not good." [37] Some local television stations have repeated mistakes made in 1988—for example, rebroadcasting ads full screen. Many local television reporters have been much less critical of candidates' ads than newspaper and CNN reporters have. Local television has taken on a much more limited oversight function in regard to ads.

Chapter 5

Learning About the Candidates

One preoccupation of advertising research has been to assess the impact of campaign commercials on citizens. Early efforts to ascertain the effects of ads looked at voters' perceptions of candidates' positions on the issues and personal qualities. Although they do not all agree, these analyses generally have shown that ads do not alter views about candidate qualities. Contrary to the fears of the public and hopes of the candidates, campaigners were unable to change impressions of their personal characteristics.[1] Citizens were, however, able to learn about candidates' issue positions from ads. Far from being a detrimental force, as is popularly believed, commercials actually informed the electorate about the policy views of presidential aspirants.[2]

The undeniable trend found in these studies notwithstanding, researchers persist in their efforts to examine the effects of advertising. Great changes have been made in the structure and nature of political campaigns since the earlier research was completed; new arenas do not have the stabilizing features of past settings. Furthermore, recent campaign experiences run contrary to interpretations that emphasize the educational virtues of commercials. Television is thought to have played a crucial, and not very positive, role in a number of races, a state of affairs that has renewed concern about the power of ads to alter citizens' beliefs.[3]

This chapter looks at television advertising in several electoral settings: general election campaigns, presidential nomination campaigns, and Senate races. I examine a broad range of ad effects, from informing voters about issues and personal characteristics to new types of effects that have arisen with changes in the election process. Each type of effect has its own consequences for campaigning as well as implications concerning the role of advertising. By studying a wide range of advertising effects, the research reported here demonstrates how political commercials influence citizens' perceptions of candidates.

From Cognition to Effect

Most research on the power of the media has depended on cognitive models derived from work in social psychology.[4] Cognitive models address ideas and beliefs held about an object. Do the media provide information that increases voters' knowledge and awareness of the candidate? Since a major question about television ads has concerned their impact on voters' perceptions of the candidates' positions on issues and their personal characteristics, a number of studies have explored the "issue/image" controversy. Put simply, this literature discusses whether ads help viewers learn about the policy positions and personal qualities of the candidates.

Many observers assume that, because so much money is spent on ads, commercials must be effective in shaping viewers' perceptions. Most critiques of political advertising—as well as recent legislative restrictions on the advertising of certain products, such as liquor and cigarettes—are based on the assumption that television ads are influential in a variety of ways. If this were not the case, advertisers would be spending large sums of money without much payoff.

But the scholarly literature reveals that the impact of campaign commercials is segmented. The most widely cited body of evidence on issues and images is Patterson and McClure's landmark study concerning the effects of advertising on voters' perceptions of candidates' issue positions and personal characteristics.[5] Their pathbreaking analysis has been extensively quoted and even reproduced in prominent textbooks. In brief, their argument has shown that ads do not alter voters' perceptions of candidates' personal qualities. Citizens can, however, use ads to learn about candidates' issue positions. Voters who watched ads—as opposed to network news—were remarkably better informed about the policy views of presidential aspirants.

Other researchers have studied the impact of advertising on perceptions of issues and images; they have supported the conclusions of Patterson and McClure. Gina Garramone found that experimental subjects were more confident about what they knew about issues information than about personalities. Ronald Mulder's study of the 1975 Chicago mayoral race between Richard Daley and William Singer also shows that voters' evaluations of candidates were more difficult to change than their positions on issues. Experimental work by Charles Atkin and Gary Heald, and by Atkin, Lawrence Bowen, Oguz Nayman, and Kenneth Sheinkopf reiterates the claim of Patterson and McClure about the educational virtues of commercials.[6]

The findings were surprising to those who worry that ads allow candidates to develop new images. Because they affirmed the educational value of political ads, Patterson and McClure allowed other scholars to proclaim the wrongheadedness of conventional critiques. Many people found the new portrait of ads reassuring.

However, recent studies have found that voters do not cast ballots based on the issues very often, and that their evaluations of candidates and views about the prospects are often decisive.[7] Citizens form many impressions during the course of election campaigns, from views about candidates' issue positions and personal characteristics to feelings about the electoral prospects of specific candidates. As ads have become more gripping emotionally, affective models—which describe feelings—have been seen as crucial to evaluating candidates' fortunes.[8]

Favorability is an example of an affective dimension that is important to vote choice. There is a well-documented relationship between voters' likes and their candidate preferences. Citizens often support the candidates they like and oppose those they dislike. If all are disliked, they vote for the one favored the most. Anything that raises a candidate's favorability also increases his or her likelihood of being selected.[9] Candidates devote great attention to presenting themselves in ways that make them appear more likable. For example, it is a common strategy in political campaigns to appeal to basic community and family values. Values that are widely shared, such as patriotism and pride in national accomplishments, help candidates increase their favorability ratings among voters. Conversely, hard-hitting ads are used to pinpoint flaws of the opposition, although such efforts can backfire.

The opening up of the electoral process has brought new factors such as electability and familiarity to the forefront. *Electability* refers to citizens' perceptions of a candidate's prospects for winning the November election. Since many citizens do not want to waste their vote on a hopeless choice, impressions of electability can increase voters' support of a candidate; people like to support the winner. Familiarity is important as a threshold requirement. Candidates must become known in order to do well at election time. In earlier epochs most campaigners were nationally known; but today's candidates may not be well known, and they may have to use ads to raise their name recognition and catapult themselves out of the pack. The development of a campaign structure that encourages less widely known candidates to run makes citizens' assessments of a candidate's prospects potentially a very important area of inquiry.

Advertising in the Electoral Context

Past work on television advertising has focused on a particular kind of electoral setting—presidential general elections. For example, Patterson and McClure's findings were based on the campaign that ended in Nixon's 1972 landslide victory over McGovern. The apparent absence of effects of ads on voters' assessments of the personal qualities of candidates in the two-and-one-half-month span of that campaign may not be surprising in light of the lopsided race and the fact that by the time of the initial survey in September, public perceptions of the two candidates had largely been determined. In that situation, it may have been appropriate for Patterson and McClure to conclude that people "know too much" to be influenced by ads.[10]

However, as Patterson and McClure themselves have pointed out, other electoral settings display greater opportunities for advertising to have measurable effects. Nominating affairs and Senate races show extensive shifts in voters' assessments of the candidates. Presidential nominations often have unfamiliar contenders vying for the votes of citizens who hold few prior beliefs about the candidates. As described in earlier chapters, changes in the nominating process in recent years have increased concern about advertising.[11] In the nomination race, television commercials can play a major role in providing crucial information about unknown candidates.[12]

Advertising is particularly important when news media time is scarce. Ken Bode, then a reporter for NBC, recounts a letter written to him by Senator Dole following the 1980 nominating campaign: "Dear Ken, I would appreciate knowing how much coverage my campaign received by NBC from the date of my announcement to my final withdrawal. I've been told my total coverage by NBC amounted to fourteen seconds." [13]

Senate races have become heavily media oriented. Candidates spend a lot of money on television advertising, and Senate contests have taken on the roller-coaster qualities of nominating affairs. Many Senate elections feature volatile races involving unknown challengers. Some observers have speculated about the effects of advertising in producing shifts in the nature of campaigns. It is therefore important to study advertising in nominating and Senate campaigns to determine whether the impact of advertising varies with the electoral setting.

Citizens' Knowledge and Evaluations of Candidates

Elections in recent decades represent an interesting opportunity to study the impact of political commercials. Structural changes have allowed individuals who are not very well known nationally (such as McGovern in 1972, Carter in 1976, Gary Hart in 1984, Dukakis in 1988, and Clinton and Perot in 1992) to run for president and do surprisingly well. Other changes include a growing independence of voters, rising skepticism about the Washington establishment, and increasing prominence of the media in campaign affairs. Again we face questions about the role of ads in changing citizens' impressions of candidates.

Opinion surveys provide one way of determining how the public felt about the candidates. Information is available on a number of different contests at various levels from 1972 through 1992: Senate contests for 1974, 1990, and 1992; presidential nominating races for 1976, 1988, and 1992; and presidential general elections for 1972, 1976, 1984, 1988, and 1992. These surveys give a sense of the public's recognition of the candidates, overall views about favorability, and impressions of each candidate's electability. By comparing elections over a period of years and at several levels, one can see how the effects of ads change in different contexts.

Table 5-1 presents baseline information on a number of major Senate and presidential candidates during this period. The results illustrate the wide variation in citizens' assessments. There were clear differences in recognition levels depending on electoral setting. Presidential general election candidates were the best well-known, with a range of recognition levels from a low for Clinton and Perot in 1992 to

TABLE 5-1
Evaluations of the Candidates, 1972-1992

	Recognition	Likability	Electability
U.S. Senate			
1974	52%	—	—
Democrats	—	34%	—
Republicans	—	24	—
1990 R.I.			
Democrats	84	75	65%
Republicans	78	66	17
1990 N.C.			
Democrats	92	—	—
Republicans	92	—	—
1992 Calif. (2 yr.)			
Democrats	62	37	60
Republicans	60	17	20
1992 Calif. (6 yr.)			
Democrats	66	34	49
Republicans	67	23	26
General Election			
1972			
Democrats	—	—	1
Republicans	—	—	50
1976			
Democrats	92	35	37
Republicans	95	32	29
1984			
Democrats	82	38	—
Republicans	90	66	—
1988			
Democrats	74	42	15
Republicans	75	55	85
September 1992			
Democrats	73	39	62
Republicans	80	35	37
Independent	67	12	1
October 1992			
Democrats	83	53	71
Republicans	84	23	18
Independent	67	26	3

TABLE 5-1
(Continued)

	Recognition	Likability	Electability
Nominating Campaigns			
1976			
Carter	77	42	52
Udall	37	25	1
Ford	93	34	49
Reagan	89	27	14
1988			
Dukakis	40	44	39
Gore	38	34	12
Bush	67	49	62
Dole	56	44	30
1992			
Clinton	70	27	45
Tsongas	80	64	45
Bush	90	32	92
Buchanan	77	19	8

Sources: See pp. 163-165 in Appendix for further information on each survey.

Note: Entries represent the percentage of respondents recognizing the candidate, evaluating him or her favorably, and seeing him or her as electable in November. The North Carolina recognition number is based on familiarity with the race.

— No data available.

a high for Ford in 1976. The average recognition level across general elections was 80 percent, significantly higher than the 68 percent for nominating candidates and 52 percent for Senate contenders in 1974. The 1990 Senate races in Rhode Island between Pell and Schneider and in North Carolina between Gantt and Helms were exceptions to this pattern because, with the exception of Gantt, the candidates started with high recognition levels. The average recognition level in the 1992 California Senate races was 64 percent.

There have been extensive variations in citizens' perceptions of candidates' likability and electability. Of recent nominees, Reagan has been the best liked and Bush became the least liked by October 1992. The average rating for general election nominees was 38 percent, higher than the 36 percent for candidates in the nominating process, 29 percent for Senate candidates in 1974, and 28 percent for California Senate candidates in 1992.[14] In regard to electability

TABLE 5-2

Top Issue and Trait for Parties and Candidates, 1972-1992

	Top Issue	Top Trait
U.S. Senate		
1974		
Democrats	Equal rights	—
Republicans	Urban unrest	—
1990 R.I.		
Democrats	Education	Caring
Republicans	Environment	Caring
1990 N.C.		
Democrats	Oil drilling	—
Republicans	Death penalty	—
General Election		
1972		
Democrats	Immediate Vietnam withdrawal	Govt. experience
Republicans	Commitment to other nations	Govt. experience
1976		
Democrats	Welfare spending	Ability
Republicans	Defense spending	Trustworthiness
1984		
Democrats	—	—
Republicans	Budget deficit	Caring
1988		
Democrats	Helping blacks	Attacking
Republicans	Economy	Attacking
September 1992		
Democrats	Improving economy	Feeling hopeful
Republicans	Improving economy	Leadership
Independent	—	—
October 1992		
Democrats	Improving economy	Leadership
Republicans	Improving world standing	Feeling disgusted
Independent	Improving world standing	Feeling excited
Nominating Campaigns		
1976		
Carter	Tax cuts	Leadership
Udall	Guaranteed jobs	Personality
Ford	Defense spending	Trustworthiness
Reagan	Defense spending	Trustworthiness

TABLE 5-2
(Continued)

	Top Issue	Top Trait
Nominating Campaigns con't		
1988		
Dukakis	Military	Saying what believes
Gore	Japanese competition	Caring
Bush	Deficit reduction	Leadership
Dole	Military	Leadership
1992		
Clinton	Improving economy	Caring
Tsongas	Japanese competition	Honesty
Bush	Improving economy	Caring
Buchanan	Improving economy	Honesty

Sources: See pp. 163-165 in Appendix for further information on each survey.

Note: This list consists of those issues and traits having the strongest association with each candidate's appeals. No data were available for the 1992 California Senate campaigns.

during the fall, McGovern in 1972 was the candidate who was seen as least electable, while Bush in 1988 was seen as the most electable. There were variations in impressions of electability during the nominating process as well, with the strongest nominee being Bush in 1988 and 1992.

Voters furthermore have a sense of the main policy issues and personal traits associated with each candidate. Table 5-2 lists the issues and traits identified by voters which were most closely connected to campaign appeals. Many issues and traits were correlated with ad exposure for each candidate, and the issue and trait most closely tied to the candidate's ad pitches were selected.

There were interesting contrasts over time in the types of matters mentioned by survey respondents. Foreign policy considerations were prominent in 1972 for McGovern and Nixon because of the Vietnam War, while domestic matters dominated thereafter. There were also interesting shifts in the types of personal traits identified with candidates. This period began with candidates' experience being the most cited and ended with leadership being the most cited.

Of course, it remains to be seen how political commercials influenced perceptions of recognition, likability, and electability. Since several qualities are subject to influence by ads, a screening

TABLE 5-3

Difference in Candidate Evaluations with Low or High Ad Exposure, Selected Elections 1972-1992

	Recognition	Likability	Electability	Top Issue	Top Trait
U.S. Senate					
1974	39 [3]	—	—	—	—
Democrats	—	29 [3]	—	13 [2]	—
Republicans	—	25 [3]	—	4	—
1990 R.I.					
Democrats	19 [3]	19 [3]	−2	3	−12
Republicans	10 [2]	21 [3]	7	11 [1]	22 [3]
1990 N.C.					
Democrats	18 [3]	—	—	2	—
Republicans	22 [3]	—	—	8 [1]	—
1992 Calif. (2 yr.)					
Democrats	27 [3]	10	−3	—	—
Republicans	38 [3]	2	0	—	—
1992 Calif. (6 yr.)					
Democrats	32 [3]	14	6	—	—
Republicans	40 [3]	2	9	—	—
General Election					
1972					
Democrats	—	—	0	21 [3]	8 [2]
Republicans	—	—	6 [1]	19 [3]	6 [1]
1976					
Democrats	12 [3]	16 [2]	8 [1]	5	18 [3]
Republicans	11 [3]	0	1	9 [2]	12
1984					
Democrats	7 [2]	−2	—	—	—
Republicans	13 [3]	6	—	7	7
1988					
Democrats	16 [3]	1	3 [1]	20 [3]	12 [1]
Republicans	20 [3]	−1	−3	14 [3]	7
September 1992					
Democrats	4	12	15 [2]	13 [1]	15 [1]
Republicans	4	−1	−5	−6 [1]	−11
October 1992					
Democrats	6	13 [1]	−2	16 [1]	23 [3]
Republicans	4	6	0	10	3 [1]
Independent	10	15 [2]	2 [1]	21 [2]	24 [3]

TABLE 5-3
(Continued)

	Recognition	Likability	Electability	Top Issue	Top Trait
Nominating Campaigns					
1976					
Carter	21 [3]	6	21 [1]	9	26 [1]
Udail	48 [3]	−14	−2	4	4
Ford	11 [3]	−1	10	4	11
Reagan	15 [3]	−6	2	9	2
1988					
Dukakis	18 [1]	8	21 [3]	19 [1]	15 [1]
Gore	21 [3]	17 [3]	6	22 [3]	19 [3]
Bush	19 [1]	28 [3]	11 [1]	17 [1]	16 [1]
Dole	11	3	1	5	3 [2]
1992					
Clinton	0	2	2	16 [2]	11 [1]
Tsongas	−5	−16 [1]	4	19 [2]	−11 [1]
Bush	−2	−1	−11 [2]	−14 [2]	−17 [1]
Buchanan	6	12 [1]	11 [2]	20 [2]	10 [1]

Sources: See pp. 163-165 in Appendix for further information on each survey.

Note: Entries indicate percentage-point difference in citizen knowledge and candidate evaluations between low and high ad exposure. The superscripts show the statistical significance of those differences.

— No data available.

[1] $p < .05$ [2] $p < .01$ [3] $p < .001$

tool is needed to identify areas of possible impact. The characteristics that are significantly associated with commercials then can be evaluated through more sophisticated statistical techniques to make sure the ad effects are not spurious.

Table 5-3 presents the results of tests showing the statistical significance of percentage differences in citizens' knowledge and evaluation of candidates between the low and high ends of four-point ad exposure scales. These measures can be used as screening devices to compare those with high and low ad exposure on their impressions of the candidates. Ads cannot be proved to be the cause of the association, but at least we can identify relationships that warrant additional analysis. For example, if 70 percent of the least attentive television watchers recognized Clinton, while 75 percent of the most attentive did, the recognition difference reported in Table 5-3 would be +5 percentage points. Superscripts indicate the statistical probability that such differences hold for the population at large. The relationships that were strongest are marked with superscripts, while those that were not significant have no superscripts.

In general, Senate races showed the strongest advertising effects, with exposure to campaign ads associated with high recognition of political contenders. The average difference in recognition between respondents who scored high on ad viewing and those who scored low was 27 percentage points.[15] Senate campaigners typically are not as well known as presidential contenders, which means that political commercials can be more influential in raising the visibility levels of those who run for senator.

Presidential elections showed a lower, albeit still significant, association for recognition based on advertising exposure. From 1976 through 1992, there was a difference of 10 percentage points in the general election campaign and 14 percentage points in the nominating process. The largest general election difference in recognition came during the 1988 Bush-Dukakis race. These men were among the least known of the recent party nominees. Dukakis was not known nationally; and, despite having been vice president for eight years, Bush was not very visible in that office.

In the nominating process, the magnitude of the difference varied according to how well known the individuals were. Candidates who were not well known used advertising to advance their name recognition. For example, in April 1976, polls from the Pennsylvania primary revealed that Carter had a difference of 21 points and Udall a difference of 48 points between the high and low ends of their ad exposure scales. Dukakis and Sen. Al Gore, Jr. (Tenn.), also showed substantial differences in 1988. In 1992 Buchanan had the greatest rating differential for visibility.

Ads also had effects on citizens' perceptions of favorability; the strongest were for Senate and nominating races.[16] In both the 1974 and the 1990 Senate campaigns, ad viewing produced favorability gains for Democratic and Republican candidates. The effects were not as consistent in the nominating process, but there were strong differences for Gore and Bush in 1988. Both ran aggressive advertising campaigns, and their strategies appear to have paid off. Gore, for example, emphasized a populist image designed to win the support of white southerners. Bush ran a hard-hitting campaign designed to persuade voters that he was the logical heir to the Reagan legacy. Interestingly, Dukakis's ads were not associated with changes in favorability ratings. The Massachusetts governor later would have difficulties during the fall in overcoming public impressions that he was cool and aloof.

In 1992 Buchanan displayed the highest improvement in favorability between the low and high ends of his ad exposure scale. He ran the spring's most prominent ad, "Read Our Lips." This commercial painted a negative picture of Bush and questioned the president's character for breaking his promise of no new taxes. The ad featured a catchy narrative related to betrayal of the common person. Eventually, according to Bush adviser Teeter, the president was able to beat back the Buchanan challenge through attack ads that told voters "[Our] guy's the goddam president and the other guy's a goddam typewriter pusher, and the toughest thing he's had to do in his whole life is change the ribbon on his goddam Olivetti." [17]

Sen. Paul Tsongas (Mass.) suffered the ignominy of a negative relationship, as frequent viewers of his ads were *less* favorable by 16 percentage points toward him than those people who did not see his commercials, a difference that was statistically significant. Tsongas clearly had difficulty using the paid media to his advantage after his surprise New Hampshire victory. Clinton showed a difference score of +13 percentage points in the October 1992 phase of the general election campaign, while Perot had a difference of +15 points.

In terms of electability, ads were associated with significant effects for Nixon in fall 1972, Carter in spring and fall 1976, Dukakis and Bush in spring 1988, and Buchanan and Clinton in spring and fall, 1992, respectively.[18] Seeing ads for these candidates was related to believing that the candidate was politically strong. Dukakis's ads created the impression of electoral strength. Despite the fact that his commercials did not make voters feel any more favorable toward him, they helped generate a sense of inevitability about his campaign. Carter in 1976 also received a boost, as did Bush in 1988 and Buchanan and Clinton in 1992. Of the candidates examined in this study, Bush in 1992 was the only one whose ad exposure actually hurt the perception of electability. Frequent ad viewers were 11 percentage points less likely to see him as electable than infrequent viewers were. The difference was statistically significant.

One of the most persistent criticisms of campaign advertising has been that advertising can manipulate citizens' views about candidates. If one looks at the most prominent issues and personal traits, 1972 stands out. For 1972 the results of the presidential race conform to the findings of Patterson and McClure that the effects of advertising on citizens' perceptions of issues were substantially larger than the influence on assessments of personal traits.[19] Recall that 1972 was the election they studied. However, other races show different patterns. For example, in 1976 Carter ran an image-based campaign that produced stronger advertising effects for evaluations of personal traits than of issue positions.[20] In the 1988 nominating process, Dukakis, Gore, and Bush had ads with strong effects on both assessments of issues and traits.[21]

Clinton was able to use his 1992 nominating campaign commercials to help viewers see him as caring and capable of handling the economy. He used ads (such as his commercial, "Ron") to tell the story of a family and their problems in affording quality health care. Visuals in these commercials allowed him to convey his positive, caring side. His fall ads helped project an image of hopefulness and being able to improve the economy that was important to voters discouraged by the dismal economy. His campaign slogan emphasized that the contest was a "race of hope against fear," and ads were run noting Clinton's origins in a town called Hope, Arkansas.[22] Buchanan also used ads to connect salient issues with personal character. In the process, he was able to boost citizens' impressions of his honesty and knowledge of economics.

Interestingly, Bush was the only major candidate in 1992 who was unable to boost impressions of himself either on his positions on issues or on his character.[23] This was true for both the nominating and the general election campaigns. Part of the problem obviously was structural in nature. When domestic problems prove intractable, it is nearly impossible for incumbents to improve their political image through advertising. But Bush also had serious problems developing ads that could resonate with voters and attract favorable media coverage. For these reasons, he was unable to repeat his successful 1988 experience in 1992.

The Mediating Effects of Prior Beliefs

The analysis to this point has suggested a tie between advertising and voters' assessments of candidates. It is likely, of course, that other factors influence this relationship in meaningful ways. As pointed out previously, advertisements are merely one part of the cacophony of information heard by voters during election campaigns. Various sources of citizens' impressions must be examined to determine whether ads have any independent effect. For example, partisanship and ideology are often important to how people respond to ads. Citizens bring different values and beliefs to the political arena, and they are likely to see the same event in very different ways. Selective exposure may influence the results based on the differential impact of educational attainment, race, age, and sex. Finally, interest in politics and exposure to the media in general may make a difference since impressions can be altered in ways that are independent of campaign ads.

Regression models are widely used in the social sciences to determine the impact of particular factors on citizens' impressions, controlling for other influences. Using regression, which produces estimates of the magnitude and direction of relationships, one can evaluate the independent effect of commercials on voters' assessments. Regression furthermore has the virtue of incorporating a significance test, which ensures that the particular results obtained do not arise purely by chance.

Table 5-4 presents the results of a series of regression analyses for evaluations that showed significant effects for ads. Controls for party identification, education, age, race, sex, ideology, political interest, and media exposure were included in each regression to ensure against spuriousness.[24] Only effects that stayed significant after the introduction of these factors are reported here. A positive coefficient indicates a direct relationship between seeing ads and the quality under consideration.

Even after the controls were incorporated, ad viewing still had a major impact on citizens' knowledge. Those who saw Nixon ads in 1972 were more likely to see him as wishing to uphold commitments made to other nations. The same phenomenon emerged in the 1988 nominating process. During that year, exposure to ads influenced people's perceptions of the issue positions of Dukakis (on the military), Gore (on unfair competition from Japan), and Bush (on deficit reduction). The 1992 race helped viewers understand Buchanan on the economy, Clinton on the economy, and Tsongas on competition from Japan. Each candidate ran ads that made these subjects a central part of his campaign. Buchanan's ads from New Hampshire criticized Bush for insensitivity on the economy, Clinton

TABLE 5-4

Ad Effect on Citizens' Perceptions of Candidates, 1972-1992

	Ad Coefficient	(SE)	N
Likability			
Senate Democrat 1974[b]	.17	(.05) [4]	693
Senate Republican 1974[b]	.18	(.05) [4]	666
Gore (1988 nom.)	.09	(.03) [3]	426
Bush (1988 nom.)	.11	(.04) [4]	369
Pell (1990 Senate)	.05	(.03) [2]	311
Schneider (1990 Senate)	.10	(.04) [3]	286
Buchanan (1992 nom.)	.06	(.04) [2]	393
Tsongas (1992 nom.)	−.07	(.04) [2]	417
Perot (1992 Oct. gen. elect.)	.08	(.04) [2]	438
Electability			
Nixon (1972 gen. elect.)	.13	(.06) [2]	343
Carter (1976 nom.)	.16	(.09) [2]	333
Dukakis (1988 nom.)[b]	.17	(.04) [4]	560
Buchanan (1992 nom.)[b]	1.19	(.48) [3]	415
Bush (1992 nom.)[b]	−1.16	(.49) [3]	418
Clinton (1992 Sept. gen. elect.) [b]	.44	(.30)[1]	457
Top Issue			
Nixon (1972)	.10	(.05) [2]	342
Dukakis (1988 gen. elect.)	.07	(.02) [4]	1,082
Bush (1988 gen. elect.)	.07	(.01) [4]	1,167
Dukakis (1988 nom.)	.06	(.03) [2]	597
Gore (1988 nom.)	.09	(.02) [4]	515
Bush (1988 nom.)	.04	(.02) [2]	374
Helms (1990 Senate)	.03	(.01) [2]	471
Buchanan (1992 nom.)	.11	(.06) [2]	315
Clinton (1992 nom.)	.12	(.06) [2]	363
Tsongas (1992 nom.)	.08	(.04) [3]	280
Top Trait			
Carter (1976 gen. elect.)	.14	(.06) [2]	524
Gore (1988 nom.)	.06	(.01) [4]	546
Bush (1988 nom.)	.05	(.02) [2]	348
Clinton (1992 nom.)[b]	.18	(.08) [2]	356
Tsongas (1992 nom.)	−.09	(.03) [3]	371

Sources: See pp. 163-165 in Appendix for further information on each survey.

Note: Entries are unstandardized regression coefficients with standard errors in parentheses. Coefficients marked with superscripts were statistically significant. Effects of control variables (party identification, education, age, sex, race, ideology, political interest, and media exposure) are not shown. Names followed by [b] are based on logistic regression estimates because the dependent variables were dichotomous.

[1] $p < .10$ [2] $p < .05$ [3] $p < .01$ [4] $p < .001$

emphasized the need for a middle-class tax cut, and Tsongas called for reinvigorated efforts against Japan's trade practices.

Clinton's nominating strategy was marked by a tendency to run ads filled with lists of matters of concern to him. His sixty-second ad "The Plan" illustrates this approach (see Appendix). According to Kolbert of the *New York Times,* as soon as this ad started airing in New Hampshire, Clinton strategists found their candidate jumped 13 percentage points in tracking polls. The commercial was "designed to counter the Tsongas plan. It provided a sense of specificity for Clinton," said Kolbert.[25] It furthermore had the long-term effect of staking out claims to particular issues, in order to prevent Republicans from trespassing on traditionally Democratic issues, as Bush had done in 1988 when he campaigned on promises to become the environmental and education president. But his strategy also created problems for Clinton. One of the criticisms directed against him in spring focus groups was that he was difficult to pin down: "If you asked his favorite color he'd say 'Plaid,' " stated one focus group participant.[26]

However, the effects of ads were not simply that citizens learned about policy matters. If that were the case, critics would have much less ammunition against political commercials. Instead, ads also had an impact on assessments of candidates' images, likability, and electability that was at least as strong as the effect on assessments of issue positions. In terms of perceptions of likability, seeing commercials had a significant impact in many elections. For Gore and Bush, ad exposure was related to favorability ratings during the 1988 nominating process, and the same was true for Buchanan and Perot in 1992 and for Senate candidates in 1974 and 1990.

Political commercials furthermore had an impact on perceptions of electability. The strongest impact came with Dukakis in the 1988 nominating process, but effects were present for Nixon in 1972, Carter in 1976, and Buchanan and Clinton in 1992. Conversely, people who saw Bush's ads in 1992 had a negative sense of the president's electability.

In addition, campaigners were able to mold public perceptions of personal traits. Those who watched Carter ads saw him as an able leader, while those who saw Gore ads felt he was likely to care about people. Clinton was able to use his spring 1992 commercials to persuade people that he was a caring individual. The ads helped create a positive view of his character, which counterbalanced the negative coverage received after Gennifer Flowers came forward to say he had an affair with her.

Tsongas was hurt in spring 1992 because his advertisements did not help him create a more positive image. Several members of a focus group study conducted on the nominating contest mentioned Tsongas's low-key personality and unkempt appearance. One described him as having "the charisma of a bull dog." Another said, "He looks like an unmade bed. He looks like he got out of bed in the morning, threw on the first thing that he picked up off the floor, like my son does sometimes, and combed his hair with a piece of toast." [27]

The Media Connection

There are several ways to understand the relationships just described. One interpretation is to attribute the results to the content of commercials, on the grounds that if voters see ads extolling particular virtues, they will be more likely to view candidates in those terms. In fact, a review of 1988 and 1992 campaign histories as well as videotapes of the ads reveals that viewers' assessments of images and issues generally corresponded to portraits presented in paid advertisements. For example, Gore's ads in 1988 trumpeted his ability to represent the little person. Not surprisingly, in light of this message, viewers who saw his ads were likely to see him as a caring individual. Clinton also was successful in using commercials that emphasized his concern about the economy in 1992.

This linkage mechanism, though, is not very persuasive for arguments about electability. An analysis of advertising histories reveals that few candidates ran ads directly proclaiming that they could win. Neither Jamieson nor Pat Devlin reports in discussions of prominent ads that anyone made the ability to win the general election a central part of his paid advertisements. [28] Ads by Kerrey, Clinton, and Perot in 1992 were noteworthy precisely because they did discuss the candidates' ability to win elections. [29]

One instead must look toward the media coverage of candidates' ads to understand electability. An analysis of television coverage shows how coverage of the nominating process created particular clusters of meaning among voters. [30] The tendency of reporters to convert substantive ad messages into news stories about campaign strategy or election prospects was more pronounced during the primaries than in the fall. Whereas 64 percent of the fall news stories about ads emphasized strategy or prospects, 71 percent of spring stories did. Both of these figures were much higher than the rate of campaign messages presented in ads themselves. Thus, it should not be surprising that there were gains in assessments of electability for particular candidates during the primaries. By the manner in which they covered commercials, reporters converted ad appeals into horse race messages.

The power of the media can be seen in Table 5-5 through full models of impressions about the electability of Nixon in 1972, Carter in 1976, Dukakis in 1988, and Buchanan, Bush, and Clinton in 1992. These were the candidates who in earlier results displayed significant ad effects for electability—ad exposure was linked to beliefs about their electability. But general media exposure and political interest were also important to views about campaign prospects.[31] This suggests that both seeing ads and watching television news are associated with viewing candidates as electable.

Change During the Campaign

Ad effects do not simply materialize at the end of a campaign. They develop over the course of the race, depending on strategic moves by the contenders and on the dynamics of the contest.[32] Panel surveys, which are designed to study the dynamics of attitude change, are an ideal way to look at ad effects. They are based on reinterviews with the same people at various points during the race. Both in 1972 and in 1976, panel studies were conducted to investigate the impact of ads on changes in voters' assessments of candidates.

There were few changes in people's views of issues and traits in 1972 and in 1976. No change took place between September and October in people's view of Nixon's likelihood of maintaining commitments to other nations. There was a slight gain, 5 percentage points, between October and November. Similarly, there were few changes in views of Carter's position on welfare spending in 1976 or perceptions of personal traits in 1972 or 1976.

However, there were substantial alterations in assessments of Carter's electability during the 1976 nominating process. It is an indication of the momentum that developed for the Georgia governor that 8 percent saw him as electable in February, 52 percent in April, and 74 percent in June. That means there were improvements of 44 percentage points between February and April and another 22

TABLE 5-5
Models of Electability, Selected Candidates

	Nixon 1972 b	(SE)	Carter 1976 b	(SE)	Dukakis 1988 b	(SE)	Buchanan 1992 b	(SE)	Bush 1992 b	(SE)	Clinton 1992 b	(SE)
Ads	.13	(.06)[2]	.16	(.09)[2]	.17	(.04)[4]	1.19	(.48)[3]	1.16	(.49)[3]	.44	(.30)[1]
Party	.16	(.03)[4]	.04	(.06)	−.00	(.04)	1.38	(.89)[1]	−1.67	(.90)[2]	1.39	(.34)[4]
Education	−.01	(.01)	−.08	(.07)	.09	(.04)[2]	−3.55	(.95)[4]	3.54	(.92)[4]	−.14	(.39)
Age	.00	(.00)	.08	(.12)	−.05	(.05)	−.93	(.51)[2]	.78	(.48)[1]	−.19	(.30)
Sex	.14	(.12)	−.12	(.22)	.03	(.09)	.35	(.71)	−.10	(.70)	−.20	(.42)
Ideology	.06	(.03)[2]	.01	(.09)	.03	(.06)	−.62	(.60)	.47	(.59)	−.02	(.42)
Race	1.75	(.33)[4]	−.64	(.78)	.10	(.11)	.59	(.94)	−.35	(.95)	1.28	(.60)[2]
Political interest	.04	(.05)	.11	(.12)	.15	(.10)[1]	.20	(.57)	−.32	(.57)	.75	(.34)[2]
Media exposure	.03	(.03)	.15	(.10)[1]	—	—	−.64	(.49)	.72	(.50)[1]	−.08	(.31)
Constant	−.75	(.59)	3.37	(1.19)	5.45	(.36)	5.87	(.84)	4.23	(.82)	5.31	(.38)
N	343		333		560		415		418		457	

Sources: See pp. 163-165 in Appendix for further information on each survey.

Note: Entries are unstandardized regression coefficients with standard errors in parentheses for Nixon and Carter and logistic regression estimates with standard errors in parentheses for Dukakis, Buchanan, Bush, and Clinton. Coefficients marked with superscripts were statistically significant.

— No data available.   [1] $p < .10$ [2] $p < .05$ [3] $p < .01$ [4] $p < .001$

points between April and June. As befits the stability of the 1972 general election, Nixon saw no significant change in electability between October and November.

When one examines the extent to which panelists' impressions were influenced by campaign ads, it becomes apparent that ad exposure is important at various stages in the process. In the early stage of the nominating campaign, ad exposure was critical to those who switched from not believing to believing that Carter was electable. This situation, though, contrasts with developments later in the nominating process. Between April and June, after Carter's actual electability was established, ad exposure displayed a strong reinforcement effect rather than a conversion effect: seeing ads made people more likely to retain their view of Carter's electability than to change their view.

The Electoral Consequences of Electability

Advertising is important for voters' assessments of electability, but it has not yet been shown to have electoral consequences. The 1988 Democratic and 1992 Republican nominating campaigns offer interesting opportunities to investigate the vote as well as strategic interactions among the candidates. The Democratic nominating process was a wide-open, seven-candidate affair with no well-known front runner until Dukakis began to forge ahead at the time of the March Super Tuesday primaries. The 1992 Republican process, in contrast, featured a two-person race between President Bush and challenger Buchanan. (The third candidate, David Duke, was not a serious factor.)

At the time of the 1988 Super Tuesday contests, a number of candidates were running hard-hitting ads challenging the substantive positions and personal qualifications of their opponents. For example, Gephardt's ads in Iowa and South Dakota criticized Dukakis for claiming naively that farmers could reverse their financial problems by planting Belgian endive. Dukakis's ads later accused Gephardt of flip-flops on policy matters.[33] Gore and Jesse Jackson also ran strong campaigns in key southern states.

The victories by Dukakis on Super Tuesday were vital to the sense of inevitability that began to surround his candidacy. Prior to this time, Dukakis had put together a strong organization and had been very successful in terms of fund raising. But it was the voter and delegate support expressed at the time of Super Tuesday that began to propel him toward the nomination. As summarized by Jack Germond and Jules Witcover right after Super Tuesday, "Dukakis was now clearly the front-runner, in terms of both the number of delegates he had captured and the strength demonstrated in winning not only in the Northeast but also in the Far West and South." [34]

But how did this sense of momentum develop? To answer that we need a technique that allows us to examine the complex relations between ads, electability, and the vote in greater detail. Path analysis is designed to look at these types of interrelationships. As described by Asher, it is a way of estimating "the magnitude of the linkages between variables and using these estimates to provide information about the underlying causal processes." [35] It has the advantage of distinguishing direct from indirect effects, and therefore can be used to examine advertisements in more depth than previously available.

The path models reported here use a two-stage least squares estimator to examine the possibility of nonrecursive relations. Because relevant factors are purged of contaminating associations before being modeled, it is possible through this process to be more explicit about causal linkages. Ideally, one wants to find instruments external to the relationships being studied. This allows for independent estimates of each direction of the causal linkage to be made. But, in practice, it is difficult to find pure measures.

Behr and Iyengar (and later Iyengar and Kinder) pioneered a technique that offers some promise in their study of news agenda setting on inflation, unemployment, and energy. [36] Since the link between public concern for a particular issue and news coverage can be reciprocal in nature, they used a two-stage estimator in which concern for one other issue (inflation) was measured through concern for other issues (unemployment and energy) as well as presidential speeches. Following this example, I measured the electability of Dukakis in 1988 through views about the electability of his competitors for the Democratic nomination. Similarly, the Dukakis nomination vote was modeled through support for opposing candidates. The same process was followed in 1992.

A two-stage path model of the Dukakis vote during the critical period of the 1988 Super Tuesday primaries can be used to deal with the possibility of reciprocal relations between voters' preferences in candidates and views regarding electability. [37] Even after these variables were purged of joint effects, electability clearly was quite decisive for the Dukakis vote. The more he was seen as being electable, the more likely voters were to support him. But other factors—race, sex, and party identification—were also directly linked to support for Dukakis. Race was important, owing to the presence of Jackson in the contest. There was a clear polarization of voters, with Jackson receiving the vast majority of the black vote and Dukakis and Gore dividing the white vote. Sex and party identifications had a strong effect on support for Dukakis, with women and strong Democrats being most likely to vote for him.[38]

Dukakis's advertising had indirect consequences for the vote through views regarding electability. The strongest predictor of electability in this model was exposure to spot commercials. Ads shown prior to Super Tuesday, more than race, sex, or partisanship, influenced voters to see the Massachusetts governor as the most electable Democrat.[39]

These results hold up when strategic considerations are incorporated into the model. Voters do not make decisions about candidates in isolation. They see ads for all the major contestants and form impressions based on the campaigns' strategic interactions. The major competition for Dukakis among white voters on Super Tuesday was Gore. As a senator from Tennessee, Gore had a home-region advantage in southern states. Other than Jackson, whose base clearly was black voters, Gore was the major obstacle to Dukakis's nomination drive at the time of Super Tuesday.

When the ads of competing candidates are included in the path model, the results correspond to those just reported. Seeing ads for the Massachusetts governor was positively correlated with feeling Dukakis was the most electable Democrat. Electability also had a clear impact on the vote.[40] Spot commercials thus were important even when strategic interactions were factored into the model.

In the 1992 Republican primaries, advertising played a different role. At the start of the race, President Bush was on the defensive over his handling of the economy and his inattention to domestic politics in general. Buchanan ran a series of ads castigating Bush for breaking his famous "no new taxes" pledge. In part because of saturation coverage of the New Hampshire and Massachusetts markets, these commercials achieved a remarkably high level of visibility. Tom Rosenstiel, a news reporter for the *Los Angeles Times* who covered the media, noted that "little kids all over New

Hampshire were running around schoolyards chanting, 'Read our lips, No new taxes'." [41]

A March survey of the Boston metropolitan area asked viewers which ad run by a Republican presidential candidate had made the biggest impression. Of the 590 people interviewed, 92 (about 16 percent of the entire sample) were able to name a specific ad. The most frequently named commercial by far was Buchanan's "Read Our Lips" spot, which was cited by 64 people, followed by Buchanan's "Freedom Abused" spot against the NEA, which was named by 11 people. Overall, 85 viewers cited specific ads for Buchanan, compared with 6 for Bush and 1 for Duke.

The situation for Democrats was different: 86 people (14 percent) named specific ads, but the ads mentioned were spread among the candidates: Kerrey ($N = 29$), Tsongas ($N = 25$), Tom Harkin ($N = 23$), Clinton ($N = 6$), and Brown ($N = 2$). The most frequently cited ads were Kerrey's hockey rink ad ($N = 20$), Tsongas's swimming ad ($N = 17$), and Harkin's empty mill ad ($N = 10$).

Not only were Bush's commercials unmemorable, they also had a negative impact on views about the president. Rosenstiel said the president's ads about the need for change "weren't connected to reality. People smelled that. They knew he wasn't the candidate of drastic change." In contrast, Buchanan's advertisements "weren't bull. They were real. Bush had broken campaign promises." When people were exposed to ads from both candidates in a path model, they were less likely to see the president as electable and also less likely to vote for Bush.[42] These results are surprising not only because they are negative but because they contrast so clearly with Bush's 1988 ad performance. In that election, Bush's commercials dominated those of Dukakis.

Part of the problem was that Bush's 1992 spots simply were not as catchy as Buchanan's. The challenger's ads, according to Rosenstiel, had a "crude simplicity that suggested someone who was not slick, someone who was an outsider type of candidate." Rosenstiel felt that Bush's commercials started out effectively but lost their punch close to the New Hampshire primary, just when people started paying attention to the race.

Bush's advertising did not successfully use visual symbols and narrative to develop his connection with salient issues. In one ad, for example, he referred to the Persian Gulf war and also attacked Congress to show how strong he was. But the main issue of concern to voters—getting the economy going again and helping the unemployed with new jobs—did not relate to this appeal. According to Robin Roberts, Bush's ad tracker, this spot was the most frequently run in the nominating process.[43]

The president suffered because media coverage of his 1992 nominating campaign was quite negative. Reporters in New Hampshire questioned Bush's campaigning ability, concern about human suffering, and disjointed speaking style (which also was caricatured by "Saturday Night Live" comedian Dana Carvey). This pattern of coverage undermined the president's message and made it difficult for him to impress people who saw his ads. Although he ultimately was able to win his party's nomination, Bush's spring commercials did not lay a strong foundation for the fall campaign.

Chapter 6

Agenda Setting

Few subjects are more central to the political system than agenda formation. It is well established that issues come and go, and that at any given time only a few matters receive serious consideration by government officials.[1] *Agenda setting* refers to the process by which issues evolve from specific grievances into prominent causes worthy of government consideration. In a political system where citizens pay only limited attention to civic affairs, it is a mechanism through which the public can influence official deliberations by conveying its sense of which problems are important. Agenda setting is also a means of maintaining popular control in democratic societies because the process provides a link between citizens' concerns and the actions of leadership.

One avenue of agenda setting that has attracted considerable attention is the mass media.[2] There has been extensive discussion of how television shapes priorities and influences public perceptions about the nation's most serious problems. Television is thought to play a crucial role in presidential strategies of going public. Iyengar and Kinder's experimental work also strongly supports a model of media agenda setting. Their respondents regarded any problem covered by the media as "more important for the country, cared more about it, believed that government should do more about it, reported stronger feelings about it, and were more likely to identify it as one of the country's most important problems."[3]

However, there has been little extension of this work to political advertising. No one has used an agenda-setting model to determine whether ads influence citizens' policy priorities. In a campaign, agenda setting is potentially very important. Candidates often use election contests to dramatize issues that previously were not high on the public agenda or to show their awareness of issues that are. They also try to deemphasize matters that may be problematic for themselves. Bush's strategy in 1988 clearly involved a redefinition of the agenda away from certain aspects of Reagan's record and toward furloughs and flag factories (Dukakis's vulnerable areas) in an effort to move the campaign debate onto terms more advantageous for Republicans. Candidates' advertising therefore should be assessed to gauge its ability to change citizens' perceptions of what is important and how the campaigns are run.

The Media's Role in Agenda Setting

Studies of agenda setting have emphasized how issues move from societal matters to top priorities of governmental decision makers. At its most general level, this subject entails studying the wide range of actors who turn personal concerns into matters deserving political action. There are a large number of societal problems that warrant government attention. Some are domestic in nature, involving fundamental questions of poverty, justice, and social welfare. Others include the broad contours of macroeconomic performance. War and peace are recurring concerns, as are more general issues of foreign affairs.

But not all matters of social concern get defined as political problems that deserve government attention. In the United States, many problems are considered to be outside the sphere of government. According to Stanley Feldman, it is common in the individualistic political culture of the United States for subjects to be defined as private matters related to the personal characteristics of individuals. Whereas other societies attribute responsibility for difficulties more generally, a belief in economic individualism weakens attributions of collective responsibility in the United States.[4]

Some are seen as problematic but not as a priority for institutional deliberations. Only a few questions occupy the attention of government decision makers at any point. Paul Light demonstrates convincingly in his study of presidential agenda setting how important it is for leaders to conserve their political capital and focus their attention on a limited number of issues.[5] The chief executives who are the most successful develop specific priorities and are able to communicate their preferences clearly to voters.

From the standpoint of researchers, the most interesting question is how topics move from private concerns to top priorities and what role the media play in this process. Roger Cobb and Charles Elder argue that agenda setting is a way for citizens to convey preferences to leaders in a system characterized by limited participation. They demonstrate how the characteristics of particular policy areas (such as concreteness, social significance, long-term relevance, complexity, and novelty) influence the scope and intensity of political conflicts. These authors suggest that the media—because of its crucial role in defining the nature of conflict—can "play a very important role in elevating issues to the systemic agenda and increasing their chances of receiving formal agenda consideration." [6] Their conclusions are in line with a number of public opinion studies which have found that media exposure is a major factor in how people rank policy concerns.[7] Issues that receive a lot of attention from the press generally are seen as important problems facing the country. Saturation coverage by the media, as occurred during the Watergate scandal, can have a decisive effect on the public agenda.[8] Likewise, it also is true that journalists pay a lot of attention to issues of general public concern.

Other scholars have been more sanguine about media influence. John Kingdon studies agenda formation using lengthy interviews with leaders as well as detailed studies of congressional hearings, presidential speeches, polling data, and media coverage. Interestingly, his interviews reveal that few leaders attributed much of an agenda-setting effect to the mass media. Policy entrepreneurs were seen as very significant, and there also was emphasis placed on interest groups (named as important by 84 percent) and researchers (named by 66 percent). In contrast, only 26 percent of the leaders he interviewed said the media were important.[9]

Kingdon does suggest ways in which the media can elevate particular issues. Reporters often influence agenda formation by acting as a conduit of information for policy makers. Kingdon cites the case of federal officials who were unable to gain access to the White House. One day a report about their concern was published in the *Washington Post,* and the president immediately called up the secretary of the relevant department to resolve the problem.[10] Because policy makers are swamped with the daily demands of governing, it is not uncommon for them to use media coverage to determine which problems deserve immediate attention.

The press also can act as a triggering mechanism for agenda setting by using particular styles of coverage. Through crisis reports or investigative journalism, the media can magnify particular events and turn them into catalysts for official action. Even when there is widespread agreement regarding the importance of a particular policy problem, it still takes a specific incident to galvanize public attention and move the concern onto the formal agenda of government.

The exact magnitude of the media's impact appears to depend considerably on institutional setting. For example, Light's analysis of agenda setting in the presidency attributes more influence to the media than much of the work conducted on Congress. Light finds, like Kingdon, that the media often act as an indirect channel to the White House. While they rarely serve as an incubator of new ideas, they are a "source of pressure." One of Carter's aides is quoted as saying, "We all read the papers and we notice if an event is causing a reaction. We watch the evening broadcasts and recognize the lead stories. If an item makes a stir and we haven't noticed it, we are in trouble." [11]

Preliminary investigations have documented the impact of television ads on the public agenda during campaigns. For example, Atkin and Heald studied advertising in a 1974 open seat election to the House of Representatives.[12] Through a survey of 323 voters in the closing weeks of the campaign, they found that ad exposure altered voters' impressions of the most important policy issues in the race. Thomas Bowers meanwhile examined a number of Senate and governor's races in 1970 and demonstrated that exposure to newspaper ads corresponded with survey results about most important issues.[13]

Policy and Campaign Components of the Public Agenda

Agenda-setting studies commonly have investigated people's perceptions of the policy agenda, the substantive problems deemed worthy of government attention. In the campaign world, though, the agenda also includes a number of other matters. In recent years, the campaign agenda has been dominated by matters such as who is doing well and who has made major progress or blunders. The media devote most of their attention to nonpolicy matters. Such topics often have consequences for candidates' fortunes. For example, the so-called character issue effectively derailed the fortunes of candidates Hart and Joseph Biden in the 1988 presidential campaign and came close to doing the same thing to Clinton in spring 1992.[14]

The policy agenda and the campaign agenda have different characteristics. The policy agenda is generally rooted in the real conditions of people's everyday lives. If unemployment rises, there will be a parallel increase in concern about jobs. When oil tankers spill their cargo, worry arises regarding the environment. In contrast, campaign issues are more ephemeral and less rooted in objective realities. Questions related to momentum and mistakes often arise quickly, based on electoral developments and media coverage.[15] The mass media are quick to jump on unexpected events. They provide saturation coverage of things that are politically surprising, and this can influence the dynamics of the electoral contest.

Opinion polls from 1972 through 1992 have included a series of open-ended questions examining citizens' views about the most pressing policy concerns for the country and about the most important campaign events.[16] From the 1970s through the 1990s there was a fundamental shift in priorities (see Table 6-1). In 1972, foreign affairs and economic matters dominated the fall general election campaign between Nixon and McGovern. By the 1974 Senate races, inflation was starting to rise nationally; at the same time, the Watergate scandal that forced the resignation of President Nixon in August of that year was renewing public concern about honesty in government. Economic issues returned to the forefront in 1976, when both unemployment and inflation were cited as the most important problems. In the 1980s, foreign affairs returned as the most important problem after a period off the list of most pressing needs. Tax and spending issues also emerged for the first time during this period as the most important problem. Both Reagan and Bush devoted great attention in their advertising and political speeches to keeping down the size of government. Bush's most famous line in the 1988 campaign occurred during his convention speech, when he said, "Just read my lips—no new taxes." [17] But in 1992, prosperity disappeared and the economy and concern over unemployment again emerged as the top issues.

Surveys also asked about the most notable campaign events from 1976 through 1992. In 1976, that Carter and Reagan did well and

TABLE 6-1

Problems and Campaign Events Most Often Named as Most Important, 1972-1992

Elections	Most Important Problems		Most Notable Campaign Events	
1972 Presidential	Foreign affairs	36%	—	
	Economy	33		
1974 National Senate	Inflation	40	—	
	Honesty in govt.	33		
1976 Presidential	Unemployment	40	Presidential debates	42%
	Inflation	17	Carter doing well	23
			Reagan doing well	16
1984 Presidential	Soviet relations/		Reagan mistakes	
	Arms control	24	in debate	60
	Tax/spending	18	Restore U.S. pride	7
1988 Presidential	Tax/spending	39	Bush attacking Dukakis	54
	Social welfare	14	Dukakis bad campaign	23
			Dukakis not responding	14
			Bush campaign	11
1990 R.I. Senate	Economy/budget	19	Pell's age/memory	10
	Foreign affairs/			
	defense	15		
1992 Presidential (March)	Economy	50	Buchanan doing well	15
	Unemployment/			
	jobs	13	Clinton scandals	11
1992 Presidential (September)	Economy	42	Perot candidacy	19
	Unemployment/			
	jobs	14		
1992 Presidential (October)	Economy	56	Debates	28
	Unemployment/			
	jobs	14	Perot candidacy	22

Sources: See pp. 163-165 in Appendix for further information on each survey.

Note: Entries are the percentages on open-ended questions citing the particular problem or campaign event as most important that year.

— No data available.

won key primaries were the top developments
the presidential debates were the most notable ε
1984 CBS News/*New York Times* survey bι
important campaign events for individual candi
cited Reagan's mistakes in the debates. In 198
Bush's attacks on Dukakis as the most importa
fall campaign. The 1992 primary race saw voters naming
an's unexpected showing in New Hampshire and Clinton's scandals
as the most important developments of the nominating campaign,
and Perot's candidacy and the debates as the most important aspects
of the general election campaign.

Ads and Agenda Setting

Candidates seek to influence citizens' priorities and to base their
strategies on issues that are already on the public's mind. But it is
not obvious how ad exposure corresponds to the agenda. A preliminary analysis in Table 6-2 breaks down the impact of ad viewing on
mentions of policy priorities and campaign events. Percentage
measures were used to compare citizens' knowledge of issues and
evaluations of candidates between the low and high ends of four-
point ad exposure scales. If 15 percent of the least attentive and 25
percent of the most attentive viewers cited honesty in government as
the most important problem, the difference would be +10 percentage points. Superscripts indicate the statistical significance of the
differences.

In 1972, 1976, and 1984, ads were not associated with particular
policy views. Many of the differences were either not very large or
not in the expected direction. For example, the top issue cited in
1972 was foreign affairs, and there were no significant differences
based on ad exposure. Concern over the economy actually was
stronger among those who were not ad viewers than among those
who were. There also were weak effects in 1976 on unemployment
and inflation and in 1984 on peace and arms control as well as on
tax and spending matters.

However, there were exceptions in the 1974 and 1990 Senate
races, Bush's 1988 general election campaign, and Clinton's fall
1992 campaign. Honesty in government was significantly linked to
advertising in the 1974 Senate races.[18] Thirty-four percent of people
who reported not seeing ads cited honesty in government as the most

TABLE 6-2

*Difference in Most Important Mentions with Low and High
Ad Exposure, 1972-1992*

Year	Most Important Problems	Ad Impact	*N*	Most Important Events	Ad Impact	*N*
1972	Foreign affairs	2	613	—		
	Economy	−14	613	—		
1974	Inflation	1	1,663			
	Honesty in government	8 [2]	1,617			
1976	Unemployment	−2	756	Carter doing well	9 [1]	318
	Inflation	0	756	Reagan doing well	9 [1]	318
				Presidential debate	2	560
1984	Soviet relations/ Arms control	2	1,302	Reagan mistake in debate	26 [3]	658
	Tax/spending	3	1,302	Restore U.S. pride	10	648
1988	Tax/spending	25 [3]	1,373	Bush attacking Dukakis	−3	951
	Social welfare	−1	1,373	Bush campaign	6 [2]	640
				Dukakis bad campaign	−3	992
				Dukakis not responding	11 [3]	992
1990	Economy/budget	17 [2]	335	Pell's age/memory	−1	292
	Foreign affairs/ defense	−1	335			
March 1992	Economy	−9	520	Buchanan doing well	−2	502
	Unemployment/ jobs	21 [3]	520	Clinton scandals	2	520
Sept. 1992	Economy	9 [1]	592	Perot candidacy	3	592
	Unemployment/ jobs	4	592			
Oct. 1992	Economy	2	579	Debates	10 [1]	579
	Unemployment/ jobs	6	579	Perot candidacy	−11	579

Sources: See pp. 163-165 in Appendix for further information on each survey.

Note: Entries indicate percentage-point difference in most important mentions between low and high ad exposure. The superscripts show the statistical significance of those differences.

[1] $p < .05$ [2] $p < .01$ [3] $p < .001$

— No data available.

important problem, compared with 42 percent of those who had paid close attention to ads, a statistically significant difference of 8 percentage points. In 1990, those who saw ads were more likely than others to cite the economy and budget matters as the most important problem. Bush's 1988 ads on tax and spending matters paid off in a big way, as did Clinton's 1992 ads. Among those who did not watch ads, 21 percent cited tax and spending matters as most important in 1988, while 46 percent of those who had paid attention to Bush's ads cited tax and spending issues, a whopping difference of 25 percentage points.

Differences also occurred on citizens' assessments of campaign events. In 1976, 27 percent of those who did not watch ads cited Carter's doing well as the most important development in the campaign, compared with 36 percent of those who had paid attention to ads, a difference of 9 percentage points. In June of that year, Reagan also achieved a 9 point difference among ad viewers, with attentive viewers more likely to report that his doing well was the most notable aspect of the campaign. The Californian experienced a substantial effect of 26 percentage points based on ad viewing for those who cited his debate performance as the most important thing he did in the campaign.

There were also advertising effects in 1988 regarding which campaign events were most important. Eight percent of those who had not seen ads cited Bush's campaign as his top accomplishment, compared with 14 percent of those who had paid attention to Bush's ads. There were significant differences based on ad exposure in criticism of Dukakis for not responding to Bush. Among those with low attentiveness, 6 percent named this problem, whereas among those with high attentiveness, 17 percent mentioned it.

It is less clear whether ads have an independent effect once other factors are incorporated in the analysis. Party identification, education, age, race, sex, ideology, political interest, and media exposure are thought to structure people's reactions to policy problems and political matters.[19] It is important to examine the impact of ad exposure controlling for these determinants.

Table 6-3 presents the findings of a series of regression analyses for mentions of most important problems and most notable campaign events. Only factors that were significant previously were included in this analysis. The results conform to those just reported. Four policy problems (honesty in government in 1974, tax and spending matters

TABLE 6-3

Ad Effect on Mentions of Most Important Problem and Most Notable Campaign Event

	Ad Coefficient	(SE)	N
Most Important Problem			
Honesty in government (1974) [b]	.19	(.07) [2]	1,176
Tax/spending (1988)	.15	(.03) [3]	1,344
Economy/budget (1990 Senate)	.05	(.02) [2]	328
Unemployment/jobs (1990 nom.)	.20	(.07) [3]	431
Most Notable Campaign Event			
Carter doing well (April 1976)	.10	(.06) [1]	287
Reagan doing well (June 1976)	.05	(.08)	262
Reagan mistake in debate (1984)	.09	(.04) [1]	641
Restored U.S. pride (1984)	.27	(.10) [3]	634
Bush campaign (1988)	.17	(.09) [1]	536
Dukakis not responding (1988)	.17	(.06) [3]	869
Debates (October 1992)	.50	(.28) [1]	467

Sources: See pp. 163-165 in Appendix for further information on each survey.

Note: Entries are logistic regression estimates with standard errors in parentheses. Coefficients marked with superscripts were statistically significant. Effects of control variables (party identification, education, age, sex, race, ideology, political interest, and media exposure) are not shown. Items marked with [b] are ordinary least squares estimates.

[1] $p < .05$ [2] $p < .01$ [3] $p < .001$

in 1988, the economy and budget in 1990, and unemployment in 1992) showed significant advertising effects. Even after controls were introduced, exposure to advertising was associated with naming the problem the most important problem facing the country. In 1974, seeing and paying attention to ads were linked to citing honesty in government as the most important problem. Similarly, in 1992, ad exposure was related to naming unemployment as the country's most important problem.

There were significant advertising effects related to a number of notable campaign events. Ad watching was linked to mentions that Carter was doing well, that Reagan had performed poorly in television debates, that Reagan had restored pride in the United States, that Dukakis had erred in not responding to Bush during the 1988 campaign, and that the debates were the most important campaign event in 1992. Characteristics of the phenomenon under scrutiny appear to affect the ability of the media to influence people. As shown in Chapter 5 in regard to electability, ephemeral qualities are amenable to ad effects. Just as it is possible to shape people's impressions of how well candidates are doing, television ads can influence and reflect views of the campaign agenda.

The Influence of Individual Ads

General exposure to campaign ads are associated with citizens' assessments of the public agenda. But what about individual ads? Most past work has examined ad exposure in aggregated form with no distinction being made between ads. To explore the impact of individual ads, I analyzed the most frequently named ads in the 1984, 1988, and 1992 presidential general elections. In 1984 the CBS News/*New York Times* survey asked: "Both presidential candidates had a lot of television commercials during this campaign. Was there any one commercial that made a strong impression on you? (If so) Which commercial?" The top Mondale ad named in the postelection survey was the "Future" commercial, while Reagan's top ad was the "Bear in the Woods" ad (see Appendix). In 1988, the CBS News/*New York Times* poll again asked which ads made the biggest impression: "Tell me about the commercial for [Bush/Dukakis] that made the biggest impression on you." Viewers picked the "Revolving Door" as Bush's top ad and the Family/Education ad for Dukakis.

In 1992 an October 26-31 survey asked, "Which television ad run by a presidential candidate this Fall has made the biggest impression on you?" One hundred forty-five people (24 percent of the sample) were able to name a specific ad. Perot received by far the most mentions: 109 people cited his ads, 27 cited Clinton's, and 9 cited Bush's. Perot's most memorable ads were his infomercials, mentioned by 38 people, followed by his spot discussing job creation ($N = 19$), his sixty-second spot discussing the legacy of national debt being left to our children ($N = 18$), and the commercial in which he discusses having received a purple heart in the mail from a supporter ($N = 10$). Clinton's top commercials were "How're You Doing?" ($N = 7$) and "Read My Lips" ($N = 5$). Bush's top ad accused Clinton of raising taxes ($N = 3$). (See Appendix for descriptions.)

The ads remembered by viewers received plenty of attention from the news media. In the case of Reagan, Mondale, Bush, Clinton, and

Perot, the evening news rebroadcast the top ads and featured them in news stories about the campaign. The only exception was Dukakis's ad, which in keeping with the low respect professionals had for his ad campaign, did not receive free air time. Today this spot is not considered very memorable and is not widely associated with the Dukakis campaign.

The conventional wisdom is that commercials for Reagan, Bush in 1988, and Clinton were effective, while those for Mondale, Dukakis, and Bush in 1992 were not. But these judgments are based on the views of political professionals, not the assessments of the American public. To see what effects these ads had on citizens' views about the policy agenda, I conducted an analysis of ad exposure on those matters seen as the country's most pressing policy problems, controlling for party identification, education, age, race, sex, ideology, political interest, and media exposure.[20]

Table 6-4 presents the findings, and they are quite striking. In the case of Bush, Dukakis, Clinton, and Perot, the findings conform to conventional wisdom. However, with regard to Reagan and Mondale, the common view is not supported. Mondale's "Future" ad on defense matters was very effective, at least from the standpoint of having the strongest tie to people's priorities. Among those who had not seen the ad, 20 percent cited peace and arms control as the most important problem, whereas 38 percent of those who had seen it did, a difference of 18 percentage points. Mondale's ads also influenced beliefs that restoring pride in the United States had been the most important aspect of the 1984 campaign.

Interestingly, for all the attention devoted to Reagan's "Bear in the Woods" ad, this commercial had no significant effect on either of the concerns noted: peace and arms control or restoring pride in the United States. Part of the problem may have been the abstractness of the ad. Although the Reagan campaign was apparently confident of the public's ability to understand this ad, the spot contained abstract allusions both to dovishness—the bear may not be dangerous—and hawkishness—we need to be strong. The complexity of this ad may have limited its effect on the agenda.

In 1988, Bush's "Revolving Door" ad was linked to mentions of crime and law and order as the most important problems facing the United States.[21] Among those who had not seen the ad only 5 percent cited these problems, while 12 percent of those who had seen the ad named this area. This fits with longitudinal evidence cited by

TABLE 6-4

Effects of Individual Ads on Mentions of Most Important Problem

	Ad Coefficient	(SE)	N
1984			
Soviet Relations/Arms Control			
Mondale "Future"	.32	(.14) [2]	452
Reagan "Bear"	.08	(.13)	452
Restoring U.S. Pride			
Mondale "Future"	.68	(.25) [3]	261
Reagan "Bear"	−.08	(.24)	261
1988			
Crime/Law and Order			
Dukakis Family/Education	−.50	(.35)	301
Bush "Revolving Door"	.40	(.23) [1]	357
1992			
Economy			
Bush "Clinton Economics"	.11	(.29)	476
Perot Infomercials	.25	(.09) [2]	476
Unemployment			
Clinton "How're You Doing?"	.18	(.11) [1]	476

Sources: November 8-14, 1984, CBS News/*New York Times* Survey; October 21-24, 1988, CBS News/*New York Times* Survey; October 26-31, 1992, Los Angeles Survey.

Note: Entries are logistic regression estimates with standard errors in parentheses. Coefficients marked with superscripts were statistically significant. Effects of control variables (party identification, education, age, sex, race, ideology, political interest, and media exposure) are not shown.

[1] $p < .05$ [2] $p < .01$ [3] $p < .001$

Marjorie Hershey, who found that "the proportion of respondents saying that George Bush was 'tough enough' on crime and criminals rose from 23 percent in July to a full 61 percent in late October, while the proportion saying Dukakis was not tough enough rose from 36 to 49 percent." [22] Interestingly, the Dukakis ad did not produce significant effects on any domestic policy dimension. [23]

In 1992, Perot's infomercials were quite effective at focusing attention on the economy, as was Clinton's "How're You Doing?" ad on unemployment. Perot's ads had a simplicity and directness that in an antipolitician year appealed to viewers. Clinton's spot was able to raise public awareness of jobs as an important problem.

Focus group tests within the Clinton campaign showed that his commercial "zoomed off the charts" when played for voters.[24]

The Special Case of Women and the Revolving Door Ad

No commercial since the "Daisy" ad, has generated more discussion than Bush's "Revolving Door." This spot was aired frequently during the evening news and extensively discussed by news commentators. In looking at the effects of this ad on agenda setting, fascinating differences arise based on the personal circumstances of viewers.

Table 6-5 breaks down group reactions to ads by Mondale, Reagan, Bush, and Dukakis in regard to agenda setting. Among the people most likely to cite crime as the top problem after seeing Bush's "Revolving Door" commercial were midwesterners and young people. Reagan's "Bear in the Woods" ad meanwhile had its greatest effect on peace concerns among men and those aged thirty to forty-four. Mondale's ad about the future was quite influential among women, young people, and those who lived in the Northeast and West. Dukakis's family/education ad had its strongest agenda-setting effect on women.

But most interesting were the differences between men and women in regard to Bush's 1988 ads. One of Bush's strongest agenda-setting effects from his "Revolving Door" ad, for example, was among women on the crime issue.[25] After seeing this commercial, as well as the widely publicized Horton ad produced by an independent political action committee, women became much more likely than men to cite crime as the most important issue.

It is no accident that this appeal was so influential among women. The fact that the ads mentioned rape, a crime of particular significance to women, clearly accentuated their impact. According to Dukakis's campaign manager, Susan Estrich, herself a rape survivor, "The symbolism was very powerful . . . you can't find a stronger metaphor, intended or not, for racial hatred in this country than a black man raping a white woman. . . . I talked to people afterward. . . . Women said they couldn't help it, but it scared the living daylights out of them." [26]

The "Revolving Door" case demonstrates how the strategies of campaign elites and the overall cultural context are important factors in mediating the significance of advertisements. The way in which

TABLE 6-5

Difference in Effect of Individual Ads on Peace and Crime Concerns for Selected Groups with Low or High Ad Exposure

	Concern after Seeing Mondale's "Future Ad"	Concern after Seeing Reagan's "Bear in the Woods"	Crime Concern after Seeing Bush's "Revolving Door"	Social Welfare Concern after Seeing Dukakis's Family/ Education Ad
Sex				
Male	9	11 [1]	−6	−2
Female	26 [3]	−4	21 [3]	14 [2]
Age				
18-29	34 [3]	−2	17 [3]	9
30-44	8	12 [1]	10 [1]	12 [1]
45-64	1	1	−5	10 [1]
65+	30	−26	2	−13
Region				
Northeast	28 [2]	−11	2	−1
Midwest	13	6	31 [3]	10
South	−6	12	−9	9
West	26 [2]	9	9	6

Sources: November 8-14, 1984 CBS News/*New York Times* Survey. October 21-24, 1988 CBS News/*New York Times* Survey.

Note: Entries indicate the percentage-point difference in peace and crime mentions for selected groups between low and high ad exposure. Superscripts indicate the statistical significance of the difference.

[1] $p < .05$ [2] $p < .01$ [3] $p < .001$

this commercial was put together—in terms of both subject area and timing—was a major contributor to its impact on viewers. If Horton had stolen a car from a fifty-year-old black man while on furlough from a state prison, it is not likely that the "Revolving Door" ad would have affected voters' policy priorities as it did.

Change Within Campaigns

So far, this chapter has investigated ads and agenda setting from a longitudinal perspective. Ad exposure from 1972 through 1992 has been explored to determine whether seeing ads influenced citizens' views about what problems were most important and what aspects of the campaign were most notable. To examine change within particular campaigns, researchers have panel data from the 1972 and 1976 presidential elections. Using these data, researchers can see how agendas have varied within particular campaigns and whether ad exposure influences changes over time (September, October, and November in 1972 and April, June, and October in 1976).

There was remarkable stability in the policy arena in 1972 and 1976. Foreign affairs and economic matters headed the policy agenda in 1972, while unemployment and inflation were the most frequently cited issues in 1976. Unemployment rose in importance: 28 percent mentioned the problem in June 1976 and 40 percent cited it in October. Most other issues were quite stable in terms of being listed as the most important. Carter's doing well was the most notable campaign development in April and June 1976, while the presidential debates were the top event in October.

The stability of these figures suggests that change was quite limited in these campaigns and that the power of ads to influence citizens' views of problems and campaign events was limited. However, aggregate figures can conceal considerable variation, so it is important also to examine levels of change at the individual level.[27] A four-point scale was created for each time period, indicating whether the person had mentioned a particular problem in both periods, had not mentioned it in the first wave but had in the second, had mentioned it in the first but not in the second wave, or had not cited it in either time period.

There was no significant advertising effect on policy priorities. Change between panels ranged from a low of 15 percent on inflation between April and June to 29 percent on economic matters between September and October. An average of about one-quarter of each sample changed their answer about the most important policy problem between time points of the panel study, but there was no significant advertising effect on the changes.

But there was a significant advertising effect on people's views about Carter's election prospects. Seeing ads was associated with a shift toward believing that Carter was doing well. Almost one-third of the sample changed their assessment between April and June. This was when Carter developed momentum in the nominating process and gained enough delegates to earn the Democratic nomination.

TABLE 6-6

*Effect of Ads on Change in Belief that Carter Was Doing Well,
April-June 1976*

	Ad Coefficient	(SE)
Ads	.15	(.08) [1]
Party identification	.01	(.05)
Education	−.10	(.06) [1]
Age	−.06	(.09)
Sex	−.28	(.18)
Race	.28	(.30)
Ideology	.12	(.06) [1]
Political interest	.01	(.09)
Media exposure	−.02	(.08)
Intercept	4.09	(.82) [3]
N	141	

Source: April and June, 1976 Patterson Panel Survey.

Note: Entries are unstandardized regression estimates with standard errors in parentheses. They show the relationship between each factor and the change in the belief that Carter was doing well from April to June. Coefficients marked with superscripts were statistically significant.

[1] $p < .05$ [2] $p < .01$ [3] $p < .001$

The result held up even after multivariate controls were added. Table 6-6 presents the results of an analysis of change in Carter momentum based on exposure to ads, controlling for party identification, education, age, sex, race, ideology, political interest, and free media exposure. Seeing ads was linked to change in the direction of believing that Carter was doing well. The same was true for those who were well educated and liberal in their political outlook. Hence, at the level of individual change, advertising contributed to the sense of momentum developed by Carter in 1976.

The Strategic Dimensions of Agenda Control

Agenda setting is an interactive process in political campaigns. It was not just Bush's use of attack ads in 1988 that was important to the outcome of the election. Instead, it was the combination of Bush's attack strategy with the high road taken by Dukakis. One must go beyond ads aired by particular candidates to examine the strategic interactions of electoral competition.[28]

Strategic interactions revolve around two key campaign decisions—what subjects to cover in advertisements and whether to attack the opposition. Topics often are chosen with an eye toward public saliency. Matters that have attracted citizens' concern, such as rising unemployment, oil spills, or ethics in government, are the natural subjects of television advertising.

The decision to "go negative" is another important part of strategic decision making. In the past decade, it has become widely accepted that negative ads work. Most recent contests have produced a high proportion of commercials devoted to attacking the opposition. Yet how negative ads influence viewers is not well understood. Attack commercials may help candidates control the agenda, thereby enabling them to set the tone of the campaign. An axiom in politics is that the person "who sets the agenda, wins the election." The rationale is simple. Setting the agenda allows candidates to define the terms of debate and to dictate the dynamics of the campaign.

No case provides a better illustration of campaign strategy than the Bush-Dukakis race in 1988. Bush seized the initiative at the very beginning of the fall campaign. Recognizing that Dukakis was one of the least-known nominees in recent years, Bush advisers developed a plan designed to define the terms of the campaign. When it became obvious that Dukakis was the likely Democratic nominee, Atwater gave his staff instructions for what euphemistically is called opposition research, that is, gathering material on the opponent's background. Speaking to Jim Pinkerton, the research head, Atwater said, " 'I want you to get the nerd patrol. . . . We need five or six issues, and we need them by the middle of May'. . . . I gave him a three-by-five card and I said, 'You come back with this three-by-five card, but you can use both sides, and bring me the issues that we need in this campaign.' " [29]

The Bush campaign also picked up attack clues from Dukakis's Democratic opponents in the nominating process, for example, Al Gore. This included the case of Horton and Dukakis's veto of legislation that would have mandated the recitation of the Pledge of Allegiance in schools.[30] After testing these themes in a series of focus groups, the Bush campaign consciously pursued agenda control through an attack strategy. As stated by Bush's media adviser Ailes, "We felt as long as the argument was on issues that were good for

us—crime, national defense, and what have you—that if we controlled the agenda and stayed on our issues, by the end we would do
all right." [31]

Dukakis, on the other hand, chose a very different route. He
had earned the nomination by generating a sense of inevitability
about his campaign. Through early fund raising, the development
of a strong organization, and cultivation of the view that he
was the most electable Democrat, Dukakis was able to play the role
of the long-distance runner in the race. Because his advertising
generally was positive (with the exception of his timely attack
on Gephardt's flip-flops), he did not offend his opponents' voters.
Dukakis thereby was able to gain opposition support when
voters' preferred candidates bowed out due to lack of money. The
lesson he learned from the nominating contest, then, was that
if he was patient and took the high road, victory would come
eventually.

According to his campaign manager, Estrich, Dukakis decided
that his fall race would, among other things, center on character and
integrity. She said, "An important element of our fall strategy . . .
would emphasize competence . . . [and] the value of integrity. You
saw this at the convention and throughout the campaign—that Mike
Dukakis stood for high standards. That's the kind of campaign he
would run, the kind of governor he had been, the kind of President
he would be." [32] Along with the nomination experience, which had
rewarded a positive campaign, this decision inevitably led to the
choice of a high-road strategy, one that would not respond to Bush's
fierce attacks.

However appropriate this approach may have been in the
nominating context, with its sequential primaries and Democratic
supporters of other candidates to be wooed as their top choices
dropped out, it was disastrous in the two-candidate context of the
general election. Dukakis's decision allowed Bush to set the tone of
the campaign and to define the terms of debate. It was Bush's
issues—flags, patriotism, "tax and spend" liberalism, and crime—
that became the agenda of the campaign. Little was heard about
homelessness, rising poverty, and the unmet social needs of the
Reagan years.

The consequences of these campaign choices are reflected in a
two-stage path analysis of a paired ads design. This technique was
developed specifically to look at strategic interactions. People were

questioned regarding whether they had seen each candidate's top ads: Bush's "Revolving Door" and Dukakis's family education ad. The answers were jointly evaluated through path analysis techniques to determine whether responses had any agenda-setting and voting implications.

The results illustrate how strategic behavior helped set the tone of the campaign when ads of both candidates were seen. Bush was able through his "Revolving Door" commercial to widen the perception of crime as the most important problem facing the country. In contrast, exposure to Dukakis's ad decreased the saliency of crime. Viewers who thought crime was the most pressing policy problem also were more likely to say they would cast ballots for Bush over Dukakis.[33]

Bush's attacks took a toll on the Massachusetts governor. Not only did they allow the vice president to dictate the terms of debate in the campaign, they created the perception that Dukakis was not a fighter. As stated by Estrich, "the governor was hurt by the attacks on him—the mental health rumors, the attacks on patriotism, the harbor and furlough issues—and perhaps most of all by the perception that he had failed to fight back, which went to his character. . . . We did fight back on occasion. The problem is we didn't fight back effectively, and we didn't sustain it. We created a perception that we weren't fighting back, and I think that hurt us much more." [34]

Dukakis's decision was even more harmful in light of the very favorable media coverage reaped by Bush. Kiku Adatto undertook an intensive analysis of network news coverage in 1988. She found that newscasts ran segments from the "Revolving Door" ad ten times in October and November, making it the most frequently aired commercial of the campaign. Overall, twenty-two segments about Bush's crime ads were rebroadcast during the news, compared with four for Dukakis's ads. Only once was the deceptive information from Bush's crime ads challenged by reporters.[35]

These news reports unwittingly reinforced Bush's basic message. A number of stories appeared during the general election campaign citing political professionals who believed that Bush's tactics were working and that Dukakis's strategy was a complete failure. Because these assessments appeared in the context of news programs, with their high credibility, they were more believable than had they emanated from paid ads.

Redefinition of the Agenda in 1992

The agenda in 1992 differed significantly from that of 1988. The 1988 race took place in a setting characterized by a fluid agenda. Since the economy was still growing, no single concern dominated the agenda. Instead, a variety of concerns, such as taxes, government spending, social welfare, and crime, were on people's minds. In 1992, everyone's favorite line about the agenda was that the top three issues were jobs, jobs, and jobs. Clinton campaign adviser James Carville kept a sign posted in the Little Rock headquarters reminding workers, "THE ECONOMY, STUPID." About two-thirds of Americans identified the economy and unemployment as the crucial problems facing the country. These numbers did not drop during the campaign.

The presence of a fixed agenda altered the strategic terrain of the presidential campaign. Rather than attempting to redirect people's priorities, as had been the case in 1988 when peripheral concerns such as crime were made central to voters, candidates geared their appeals to jobs and economic development. In the case of Clinton and Perot, the message was simple. Economic performance was dismal under Bush and a new plan was needed to reinvigorate the economy. President Bush also discussed the economy, although he wavered between claiming that things were not as bad as his opponents charged and admitting that the economic picture was terrible but blaming congressional Democrats. Because Clinton led in the preelection polls throughout the summer and fall, he had the strategic luxury of targeting his economic message to eighteen states. Bush, on the other hand, ran many of his ads on the national networks in order to raise support across the country.

The one effort at agenda redefinition attempted by Bush—raising questions about Clinton's character in order to deflect attention from Bush's own record—was not very successful. After being urged privately by Ailes to "go for the red meat [and] get on the bleeping offensive," the president challenged Clinton on numerous personal dimensions in speeches, interviews, the debates, and spot commercials.[36] In one of his most hard-hitting ads, Bush used a series of ordinary men and women to criticize Clinton's integrity: "If you're going to be President you have to be honest." "Bill Clinton hasn't been telling anything honestly to the American people." "The man just tells people what they want to hear." "About dodging the draft." "I think he's full of hot air." "I wouldn't trust him at all to be Commander in Chief." "I think that there's a pattern, and I just don't trust Bill Clinton." "I don't think he's honorable. I don't think he's trustworthy." "You can't have a President who says one thing and does another." "Scares me. He worries me. You know, and he'll just go one way or another." [37] Interestingly, the campaign deleted a criticism about Clinton's trip to Russia because a backlash developed against Bush on this charge. In a play on Carville's sign, the Bush people also posted a message in their headquarters: "TRUST AND TAXES, STUPID."

But national opinion surveys demonstrated little increase in concern about Clinton's character during the fall campaign. For example, in a CBS News/*New York Times* survey taken September 9-13 42 percent of the respondents thought Clinton responded truthfully to the charge that he had avoided the draft and 25 percent did not. Seventy-nine percent felt the allegation would have no effect on their vote.[38] In an October 12-13 poll by CBS News/*New York Times* 79 percent claimed that their votes were unaffected by Bush's attacks on Clinton's antiwar activities at Oxford University.[39] Clinton's focus groups revealed little damage: "Many people indicated that they thought he [Clinton] had been evasive or had even lied, but they said that wouldn't affect their vote." [40]

Bush's efforts to redefine the agenda were unsuccessful because of unfavorable media coverage and the strategic response by Clinton and Gore. Although the media devoted considerable time and space to Bush's allegations, the spin on the story generally was negative to Bush and his chief adviser, Baker. Headlines repeatedly emphasized Bush's "assaults" on Clinton and "smears" on Clinton's character. Spokespeople for the Arkansas governor meanwhile labled the tactics McCarthyite. News of State Department searches of the passport records of Clinton, as well as of his mother, brought this stinging rebuke from Gore: "The American people can say we don't accept this kind of abuse of power. We've had the Joe McCarthy technique and the smear campaign; now we have the police state tactics of rummaging through personal files to try to come up with damaging information." [41] Combined with sympathetic news coverage, this response undermined the legitimacy of Bush's attack strategy.

In addition, Bush's advertising attacks suffered because they were unfocused. After the election, Bush's advisors said their efforts were hampered because "we never knew if we were focusing on Arkansas or Clinton's character or big spending. I don't think it ever clicked. I don't think the character assault was framed very well." [42] Bush's focus groups furthermore revealed a boomerang effect from voters on the trust issue: "They didn't trust Clinton's word or Bush's performance." For a while, Bush's advisers had the candidate substitute truth for trust. But new wording did not change the final outcome. [43]

Chapter 7

Priming, Defusing, and the Blame Game

Citizens rarely incorporate all available information into their political decisions.[1] Politics is but one of many activities for American voters. Most people are involved in several social, religious, and educational communities, and therefore face multiple demands on their time. Some pay extensive attention to election campaigns, while others devote only sporadic attention to them. The traditional notion that individuals review every option before making choices has been supplanted by models that incorporate information grazing, or sporadic searches for material.

Priming is a new theoretical model that builds on this way of thinking about political information. Developed in regard to the evening news, the priming model proposes that people use readily available material to evaluate candidates and that in the media age one of the most accessible sources is television. By its patterns of coverage, television can influence voters' choice between candidates by elevating particular standards of evaluation. For example, television shows that devote extensive coverage to defense matters can increase the importance of defense policy in citizens' assessments. Likewise, news accounts that dwell on environmental concerns can raise the salience of those matters in voting choices.[2]

Priming has attracted growing attention in relation to television news, but there has been little attention paid to its conceptual counterpart, defusing. This term refers to efforts on the part of candidates to decrease the importance of particular standards of evaluation. Candidates often have problematic features, such as being seen as weak on defense or lacking a clear vision for the future. It obviously is in their interest to defuse their shortcomings. They can do this either by lowering the overall salience of the topic to the public or by shortening the distance between the candidates to the point where the subject no longer affects the vote.

The concepts of priming and defusing are particularly applicable to the study of campaign advertising. Impressionistic evidence is available regarding the ability of television commercials to prime (or defuse) the electorate by shifting the standards of evaluation. This chapter examines priming and defusing through campaign ads and demonstrates that commercials can alter the importance of various factors in voters' decision making. Bush in 1988 was a masterful candidate whose political ads helped him defuse some standards that could have been problematic.[3]

Informational Shortcuts

To understand priming we need to understand the notion of information costs. This idea has been popularized by game theorists and incorporated into theories of social psychology. The assumption is that acquiring information costs people time and effort. Particularly during election campaigns, it is not easy for ordinary citizens to compile a full record of candidates' backgrounds, policy views, and personal attributes. Citizens lack the inclination to search for all relevant material.

Given the high costs of acquiring information, it is not surprising that people look for informational shortcuts, or what Daniel Kahneman, Paul Slovic, and Amos Tversky call heuristics.[4] Rather than conducting a complete search that incorporates every nugget of material about candidates, voters use readily available information. In the media era, television provides some of the most accessible material. By its patterns of coverage and emphasis on particular information, the electronic medium plays a significant role in influencing the standards of evaluation used in voters' selection of candidates.

For most elections, voters can call on many standards to evaluate candidates: views about their prospects for election, assessments of their positions on issues, and feelings about their personal attributes. Candidates attempt to prime the electorate by promoting standards that benefit themselves. If their strength lies in foreign policy as opposed to domestic policy, as was true for Bush in 1992, they seek to elevate foreign policy considerations in voters' decision making. Alternatively, if their strength is being seen as the most caring or trustworthy candidate, they will try to persuade voters to make personal qualities the basis of their choice.

Conversely, candidates attempt to defuse matters that may be problematic for them. They try to lower the salience of problem areas. Bush, for example, was seen as wimpish and uncaring at the start of the 1988 presidential campaign. He obviously was not able to remake his personality, but Bush did alter the terms of the campaign in a way that defused those perceptions and focused voters' attention on other matters.[5]

Considerable evidence has surfaced about the ability of television to prime viewers, although little attention has been devoted to defusing. Iyengar and Kinder as well as Jon Krosnick and Kinder have undertaken pathbreaking work on priming; they have shown that television can shape standards of evaluation in regard to presidents and political candidates.[6] Iyengar and Kinder analyze a range of filtering mechanisms that allow voters to deal with complex political phenomena without being paralyzed or overloaded with information. Briefly, their research documents the power of priming through the evening news: "By calling attention to some matters while ignoring others, television news influences the standards by which governments, presidents, policies, and candidates for public office are judged."[7]

Krosnick and Kinder demonstrate the importance of priming with regard to a real-world issue, the Iran-contra affair, which was demonstrably salient to voters in late 1986. Using data from surveys taken before and after the revelation of the scandal, this study showed that intervention in Central America "loomed larger" in popular evaluations of President Reagan after saturation coverage by the media than before the event was publicized. Priming was also more likely to occur among political novices than experts.[8]

Neither project, though, has addressed the role of television commercials in altering voters' standards. Candidates have obvious incentives to attempt to change the importance of matters in ways that benefit themselves.[9] In fact, based on recent campaigns, political commercials appear to be particularly influential as a means of altering voters' assessments of candidates. Ads are designed to be persuasive, and campaigners frequently seek to shift voters' standards of evaluation. The power to mold the judgments of voters through commercials, if demonstrated, would represent a major strategic resource for the contesting of elections.

Determining the Standards of Evaluation

The study of priming during election campaigns is complicated by
uncertainties concerning the nature of voters' evaluations and the kind
of standards actually used to evaluate candidates.[10] Past work has
devoted little attention to the mechanism by which a voter's heightened
interest in a subject leads to the incorporation of that factor into the
voter's assessments of candidates. For example, Krosnick and Kinder
assume in their study of the Iran-contra affair that the increased
coverage of the scandal led to the decline in support for Reagan.
However, Richard Brody and Catherine Shapiro argue that the
criticism of Reagan by elites of both parties was the crucial factor in
the decline, not simply the news of the arms-for-hostages deal.[11]

Both studies, though, ignore a third possibility: the strategic
behavior of the participants. In the campaign arena, voters' assessments depend on media coverage, the views of political elites, and the
strategic actions of the candidates. In fact, the candidates' activities
may be the crucial mechanism because they generate coverage by
news organizations and reaction by political elites.

Electoral strategies generally involve efforts to alter voters' concerns about domestic and foreign policy, views about the personal
traits of candidates (such as leadership, trustworthiness, and appearance of caring), and impressions of the electability of particular
candidates. The large number of determinants distinguishes electoral
from nonelectoral priming. Government scandals, such as the Iran-
contra affair, typically provoke a change in policy standards. But in
the electoral arena, other types of standards are also important to
voters' assessments.[12]

Experimental studies have solved the problem of how to determine which standards are most salient to voters by assumption.
Iyengar and Kinder conducted a series of experiments in which
viewers were shown newscasts emphasizing defense. They found
that if the evening news emphasized defense matters, that subject
became important in evaluations of the president. Conversely, factors
that did not appear on the nightly news showed no effect on voters'
decision making.[13] But outside of the experimental setting, there is no
way of knowing whether citizens actually would incorporate defense
as a factor in their vote choices. This research technique simply
cannot guarantee that voters in the field will act the way they did in
the lab.

Other studies, such as that of Krosnick and Kinder, ensure salience by using an issue, in this case the Iran-contra scandal, which had obvious relevance for citizens.[14] Iran-contra received saturation coverage from the mass media over a period of several months. There were banner headlines and numerous stories on the latest disclosure. That kind of reporting all but guaranteed salience for voters.

However, neither making assumptions nor choosing obviously salient issues solves the relevancy problem. Voters use many standards to evaluate candidates, and these dimensions are neither obvious nor stable over time. Studies of priming and defusing in electoral settings must recognize the diversity of possibilities and develop a research approach that deals with the complexity.

One way to address the saliency matter is to ask citizens which factors were most crucial in their voting choices. After determining overall relevance based on self-reports, one can measure whether exposure to television ads altered the importance of the factors cited. There are clear limitations to relying on self-reports, especially given evidence that voters are not aware of the standards they employ. But this technique can be a starting point in the analysis of voters' standards of evaluation.

In 1984 and 1988, CBS News/*New York Times* surveys inquired about which general factors were most important to voters. In 1984 the survey asked in its pre- and post-election waves: "When you vote/voted for president on Tuesday, what will be/was more important in deciding how you vote/voted—the economy of this country, or the U.S. military and foreign policy, or mainly the way you feel/felt about Reagan and Mondale?" In 1988 the item was: "Some people choose among Presidential candidates by picking the one closest to them on important issues. Some other people choose the one who has the personal characteristics—like integrity or leadership—they most want in a President. Which is most important when you choose—issues or personal characteristics?"

One of these questions emphasizes the agenda while the other focuses on vote choice. But the results show that voters differ in what is considered important to them. The top factor cited by voters in 1984 was the economy (49 percent), followed by the candidates (37 percent), and foreign policy (14 percent). Issues were named in 1988 as the most important factor by 76 percent of the sample, while 24 percent cited personal characteristics as more important.

Figure 7-1 Priming Presidential Voting (Self-Reports), 1984-1988

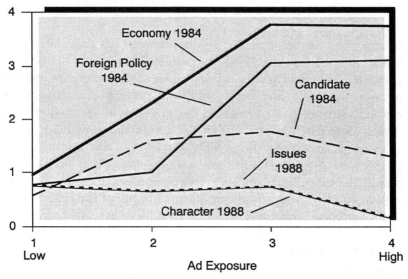

Impact of Each Factor on Vote
(T values)

Ad Exposure

Sources: November 8-14, 1984 *CBS News/New York Times* survey; October 21-24, 1988 *CBS News/New York Times* survey.

The crucial question for this research is, What impact does television advertising have on these assessments? As people saw and paid more attention to ads, did their standards of evaluation change? A voting model that reflects how the importance of particular standards changed with different levels of ad exposure can be used to investigate the interpretations of priming, defusing, and no effect. A priming effect is present when the impact of the factor on the vote rises with level of ad exposure. In contrast, defusing is evidenced by a reduction in the importance of the factor, and no effect is demonstrated by a flat line for importance of the factor based on ad exposure or a zig-zag line revealing random fluctuations.

Figure 7-1 presents the results of a regression analysis of the effect of each of the factors on the 1984 and 1988 vote, respectively. Four levels of ad exposure, from low to high, were incorporated, as were controls for intervening factors (party identification, education, age, sex, race, ideology, political interest, and [for 1988] media exposure). Vote choice was a dichotomous measure of candidate preference for Reagan or Mondale in 1984 and Bush or Dukakis in 1988. Since T coefficients are used to indicate the statistical significance of each relationship, I use them to show the importance of each factor for the vote.

In 1988, there was little evidence of priming or defusing for people who felt that issues or personal characteristics were important. The lines zig-zagged, indicating that among those with low or high ad exposure, there was no systematic difference in the weighting of issues or personal characteristics as factors in vote choice.

However, in 1984, there was significant evidence of priming. Foreign policy moved from unimportant to important as a determinant of the vote as level of exposure to television ads increased. Those who watched ads were much more likely than those who did not to cite foreign policy matters as influencing their vote for Reagan. There was also a significant priming effect for economic matters. The more ads people saw, the more likely they were to cite economic matters as an influence on their vote. The sharp change in the slope of these lines indicates that campaign ads raised the importance of foreign and economic policy matters as factors in vote choice.

Interestingly, although a number of media stories proclaimed the power of Reagan's personal traits, there was no evidence of ad priming in regard to personal candidate qualities in 1984. Politicians were unable to shift standards in this area despite journalists' reporting on Reagan's "Great Communicator" status. According to voters, ads actually had more influence on substantive than on personal dimensions of evaluation.

Beyond Self-Reporting

Ads can influence general standards of evaluation, but it remains to be seen whether political commercials can prime or defuse specific factors in vote choice. Self-reporting methods are limited by their dependence on the subjective impressions of voters. Citizens may feel that particular factors are important to their vote choice when in reality other things matter more.

Elections since 1972 present an interesting opportunity to examine ad priming and defusing in greater detail. Individual elections need to be investigated to determine exactly how ad exposure influences the factors generally considered to have been important standards of evaluation. The years 1972 through 1992 cover a range of general election and nomination settings. They encompass election campaigns that exhibited a variety of political features: both victories and losses of incumbents, differing levels of political visibility, and so on. Each of these races has received extensive analysis, which aids our reconstruction of the factors that were important in the contest.

Nixon and the Politics of Inevitability

The 1972 presidential general election is an interesting setting for an examination of priming. Nixon's general strategy in this race was to characterize himself as a trusted, capable, and responsible leader, in sharp contrast to what he portrayed as an irresponsible and not very trustworthy McGovern. Nixon also sought to portray the McGovern candidacy as hopeless, in a clear effort to elevate electability as a standard of evaluation.[15]

The question in this case is whether the president's ads shifted the standards of evaluation to magnify the significance of personal traits and electability. Respondents were asked to rate the salience of various personal qualities: "Now would you tell us how you personally feel about the unimportance or importance of some of the personal qualities needed by a President?" (Rating on a 1 to 7 scale). Trustworthiness was the most commonly cited important trait (61 percent). This item indicates directly what quality was significant to respondents, thereby resolving the salience problem. In addition, the survey asked about the most important policy problems facing the country. Foreign affairs (36 percent) and the economy (33 percent) were ranked as the most important problems. Assessments of Nixon's electability also were used to determine how likely respondents thought he was to win the November election.

Figure 7-2 lists how important each of these qualities was for the general election vote (a dichotomous measure of support for Nixon versus McGovern) by level of ad exposure, controlling for demographic, political, and media exposure factors. There were weak priming effects in regard to the policy problems of foreign affairs and the economy. Neither played a strong role in voters' decision making, and there appears to have been little significant variation based on exposure to campaign ads.

However, there were stronger priming effects for personal traits and electability. The more ads viewers saw, the more likely they

Figure 7-2 Priming the Nixon Vote, 1972

Impact of Each Factor on Vote
(T Values)

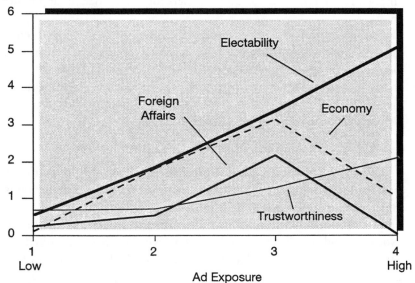

Source: September and October 1972 Patterson and McClure surveys.

became to elevate trustworthiness in their voting decisions. Trustworthiness went from being an unimportant consideration in the vote among those who were not exposed to ads to a statistically significant factor among those who watched many ads.

Electability also displayed strong evidence of priming. Its role in voters' decision making became much more important as viewers were exposed to ads. Among those who had seen ads, electability was a statistically insignificant contributor to vote choice. But among attentive viewers, electability had a substantial impact on the vote.

These effects were consistent with the general strategy employed by Nixon against McGovern. Based on his media advertising, the president appears to have shifted the standards of evaluation in a way that elevated personal traits and electability.[16] Voters who saw his ads were more likely to incorporate these factors in their decisions and to use standards favorable to the president.

There also were interesting shifts in the importance of these qualities during the course of the campaign. Between September and

November, 28 percent of the sample shifted from not seeing to seeing trustworthiness as the most important trait. Seven percent shifted in the opposite direction, 33 percent cited trustworthiness as most important in both waves, and 32 percent mentioned it at neither point.

Campaign advertising appears to have had some influence. Among those who consistently rated trustworthiness as important, 31 percent of those who did not see ads and 37 percent of those who saw many ads thought trustworthiness was important, a statistically significant difference of 6 percentage points. Political ads therefore demonstrated a priming effect over time.

Defusing Potential Problems: Bush in 1988

George Bush started his fall presidential campaign in a difficult position. Dukakis held a substantial lead in the early-summer polls. Bush was reeling from bad publicity surrounding the Reagan administration's negotiations with Panamanian dictator Manuel Noriega and disclosures that Nancy Reagan had consulted an astrologer during her husband's presidency. Bush himself was seen as weak and ineffective.[17]

However, according to the theory of priming and defusing, careful advertising can help a candidate by shifting the standards of evaluation. This is exactly what Bush set out to do in 1988. Through priming, Bush sought to elevate factors advantageous to himself. Meanwhile, matters that hurt him would be defused through television ads and favorable coverage from the news media. If he could not remove his own negatives, he could at least shift the standards to his advantage.

Figure 7-3 presents an analysis of the influence of various factors on the Bush vote.[18] On certain issues, there was little evidence of priming or defusing. For example, there was little shift in the importance of the death penalty. The impact this matter had on the vote did not vary with ad exposure. There was also little evidence of priming on defense issues.

The most significant effect was defusing on the salience of the environment and the view that Bush cared about people. These matters actually became less relevant to the vote as people saw more ads. Either the overall salience of the factors decreased or the distance between the candidates was reduced to the point that voters saw no practical difference between them. Both the environment and

Figure 7-3   Defusing the Bush Vote, 1988

Impact of Each Factor on Vote
(T Values)

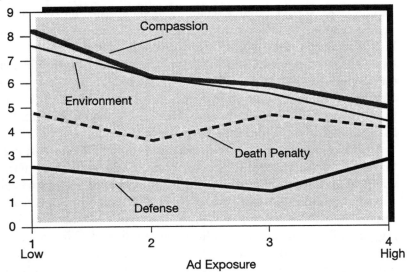

Source: October 21-24 and November 10-15, 1988 *CBS News/New York Times* surveys.

caring were potentially harmful areas to Bush. As an oil state representative, Bush had never had strong environmental credentials. Since the environment as a political issue had become very important to voters by 1988, this issue potentially was very negative for him. But the vice president was able to defuse the issue by noting his concern about the environment in ads. In one of his most famous ads, Bush also cast doubt on Dukakis's environmental credentials by arguing that the Massachusetts governor had not cleaned up Boston Harbor.

Bush defused the personality issue of caring about people by reducing its centrality to American voters. Among those who watched few ads, the matter of whether Bush cared about people was significantly linked to the vote. However, voters who saw and paid more attention to ads considered Bush's personality less relevant.

These effects were consistent with the strategic goals of Bush's campaign. They demonstrate how well-organized advertising pitches can improve a candidate's fortunes. Bush achieved defusing effects, and he was therefore able to change the standards of evaluation in ways that benefited himself.

The Gantt-Helms Senate Race in 1990

The 1990 North Carolina Senate campaign turned into one of the fiercest battles in the country. Pitting controversial Republican Helms against Gantt, a black Democratic former mayor of Charlotte, Helms started the race as a clear frontrunner. Having beaten the popular Gov. James Hunt, Jr., in 1984, the conservative Republican seemingly held a firm grip on his seat.[19] Helms appeared to be in even stronger shape after Democrats nominated Gantt, a black liberal with limited statewide name recognition.

Helms opened the contest with the same type of "liberal-bashing" that had proved successful against Hunt. Seeking to characterize Gantt as an ideological extremist, Helms portrayed him as a man outside the political mainstream of North Carolina. However, Gantt responded with an aggressive campaign accusing Helms of neglecting "pressing social needs."[20] These appeals helped Gantt surge in pre-election polls to the point where he actually led in some polls during the closing weeks of the campaign. Press accounts cited issues such as "the environment, abortion rights and education" as the crucial ones that had revived Gantt's fortunes and helped him develop key support among young people.[21]

Helms, though, came back with television commercials accusing Gantt of supporting unrestricted abortion and gay rights, opposing the death penalty, and backing racial quotas. One ad in the waning days of the campaign, Helms's infamous "White Hands" commercial, generated a national uproar by blatantly claiming that the quotas supported by Gantt would lead to the loss of jobs for whites. The spot ad showed a white man's hands crumpling what clearly was a job rejection letter. "You needed that job and you were the best qualified," the announcer says. "But they had to give it to a minority because of a racial quota. Is that really fair? Harvey Gantt says it is. Gantt supports Ted Kennedy's racial quota law that makes the color of your skin more important than your qualifications."[22]

A survey undertaken at the University of North Carolina at Chapel Hill was designed to explore the impact of ads on voters' assessments. Although the fieldwork was completed in late October, before the "White Hands" ad had aired, the polling information still can be used to see how convictions about issues ranging from off-

Figure 7-4 Priming the Helms and the Gantt Vote, 1990

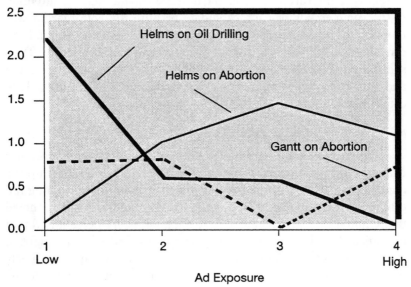

Impact of Each Factor on Vote
(T Values)

Source: October 28-31, 1990 North Carolina survey.

coast oil drilling, abortion, the role of the United States in the world, and the death penalty were affected by viewing campaign spots.[23]

Analysis reported in Chapter 5 demonstrates how effectively Helms used advertising on social issues, such as the death penalty, to boost support for his position. But priming and defusing also played a role in this election. Figure 7-4 reports how exposure to ads of both Helms and Gantt altered the standards of evaluation used by North Carolina voters. Abortion clearly was one of the major battlegrounds throughout this contest. Both candidates sought to define the controversy to their advantage. The analysis undertaken here reveals that Gantt was able through advertising to increase the salience of abortion to his vote. Even with controls included, abortion became a stronger factor in citizens' assessments as exposure to Gantt's ads increased.

Meanwhile, Helms's commercials had more of a defusing effect in regard to offshore drilling for oil and gas. In a manner reminiscent of Bush's defusing of the environment as a problematic issue, there was a strong association between seeing Helms's ads and making the offshore drilling less of a factor in vote choice.

Both priming and defusing were particularly important given the closeness of the race. The free media devoted considerable attention to the commercials of each candidate because the vote margin was thought to be so narrow. Charles Black, a leading Republican consultant to Helms, described the advertising battle this way: "You spend a million and move an inch and the other guy spends a million and a half and moves an inch back."[24] In the end, Helms was able to defeat Gantt on a surprising 52 to 48 percent vote.

Clinton and the Economy in 1992

In April 1992 Clinton advisers Carville, Stanley Greenberg, and Mandy Grunwald were worried. Their candidate had sewed up the nomination early, but they felt quite uneasy about the upcoming fall campaign. In a memo that month, Carville and Greenberg noted that Clinton's negatives had risen to a damaging 41 percent and that he trailed Bush by 24 percentage points on the crucial dimensions of trustworthiness and honesty. Focus group participants regularly complained that "no one knows why Bill Clinton wants to be president" and called him "Slick Willie."[25]

The Clinton advisers moved into action. In a top-secret memo prepared for what Grunwald euphemistically called the Manhattan Project in honor of the 1940s crash program to build a nuclear bomb, Greenberg wrote, "The campaign must move on an urgent basis before the Perot candidacy further defines us (by contrast) and the Bush-Quayle campaign defines us by malice." According to the *Newsweek* account of this plan, Clinton's problem was not so much Gennifer Flowers's accusations about adultery, avoiding the draft, or having smoked marijuana, but "the belief that Bill Clinton is a typical politician." The report noted many of the inaccurate impressions people had of Clinton: that he was rich and privileged, that he and Hillary Rodham Clinton were childless, that he could not stand up to the special interests, and that "Clinton cannot be the candidate of change." The campaign, the report said, must "take radical steps" to "depoliticize" its candidate.

Early in the summer the Clinton camp began to pretest its fall themes of a New Covenant, fighting for the forgotten middle class, and putting people first. At a series of focus groups in New Jersey, the reactions of ordinary voters were stunningly negative. One participant said the New Covenant was "just words ... glib ... insulting ... like blaming the victims." The notion of fighting for the middle class drew these comments: "baloney ... propaganda." After hearing these comments, Greenberg remarked, "They think he's so political the message stuff gets completely discounted. In fact, it makes it worse."

With the help of a coordinated research program of public opinion surveys and focus groups, the Clinton campaign embarked on an effort to redefine its candidate. At a meeting late in May, Carville suggested, "We need to mention work every 15 seconds." Grunwald agreed and said, "By the end of the convention, what do we want people to know about Clinton: that he worked his way up; that he values work; that he had moved people from welfare to work; that he has a national economic strategy to put America back to work."

The next day, they met with Bill and Hillary Clinton to lay out their plan. The proposal, as described by Greenberg, was based on the idea that "in the 1980s the few—leaders in the corporations, the Congress and the White House—neglected the many. The consequences were that work was not honored, good jobs were lost, everyone but the few felt insecure. ... The answer for the 1990s had to be a plan to do right by the American people. A plan means a contract. It's not 'Read my lips'." The campaign then sketched out a plan to coordinate paid ads on the economy in a small group of targeted states and hope for the future with a variety of media appearances on the network morning shows, "Larry King Live," and the "Arsenio Hall Show." The talk show appearances would put Clinton in more intimate settings and allow viewers to get to know him better. They also would bypass traditional reporters, who liked to ask hard-hitting questions.

This plan was remarkably successful. Because some interpretations of the 1992 elections have labeled pocketbook voting the sole reason for Clinton's victory and have asserted the absence of media effects, it is important to recognize the ways in which Clinton's media campaign encouraged economic voting. For example, Figure 7-5 demonstrates how Clinton was able through his advertising to focus public attention on the economy and his own ability to improve economic performance. Even controlling for a variety of political and demographic factors, people who had high ad exposure were more likely than those of low exposure to make the economy a factor in their votes. They were also more likely to support the view that Clinton had the ability to improve the economy.[26] At the same time,

Figure 7-5 Priming the Clinton Vote, 1992

Impact of Each Factor on Vote
(T Values)

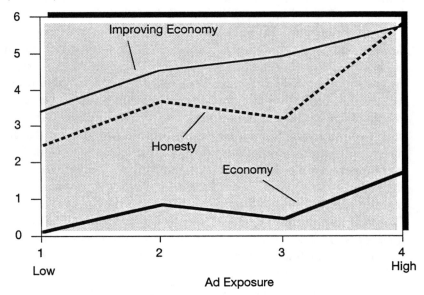

Source: October 26-31, 1992 Los Angeles survey.

Clinton was able through advertising to strengthen his own image on the trustworthiness and honesty dimension.

These results demonstrate that people's views about the economy do not merely reflect their daily experiences, but instead can be shaped by the candidates' strategies. The 1992 experience suggests that citizens' predictions for the economy can be more pessimistic than warranted on the basis of objective economic statistics. One of the reasons forecasting models based purely on economic factors failed to predict Clinton's victory was their failure to take into account the ability of candidates and the media to prime voters.[27] Clinton's advertising and the media coverage of the campaign were part of the reason why Bush got blamed for the country's poor economic performance.

Strategic Aspects of Negative Campaigning

Television can prime viewers not only through shifting the standards of evaluation but also through changing in the attribution of responsibility.[28] Voters need help in determining whom to credit and whom to blame for particular situations. It is not always apparent who is responsible for developments during the campaign. Candidates' ability to influence citizens' attributions in ways that advantage themselves can be a major strength.

In recent years, negative advertising has attracted considerable criticism. Many voters have been turned off by the nasty and personalistic tone of discourse.[29] Press reports have emphasized the negativity of political campaigns, and there have been complaints from all quarters about the poor caliber of campaigns.[30] However, there has been little study of the effects of negative campaigning in general or the strategic aspects of attributing blame in particular.[31] In their study of presidential responsibility, Iyengar and Kinder found that one of the most important ways in which television can prime voters is by prompting shifts in attributions. Stories that emphasized presidential responsibility were found to make people more likely to believe that the president was responsible for government performance and thus to blame him when things went wrong.[32] Attributions of responsibility for campaign behavior can be equally important to citizens' voting patterns.

In 1988, CBS News/*New York Times* asked voters two questions in an effort to measure attributions of responsibility for the negativity of the campaign: "Did most of Bush's [Dukakis's] T.V. commercials that you saw explain what George Bush [Michael Dukakis] stands for, or did most of the commercials attack George Bush [Michael Dukakis]?" and "Who is more responsible for the negative campaigning there has been this year, George Bush or Michael Dukakis?" These questions were repeated in surveys during the 1992 general election for Bush and Clinton.

There were interesting contrasts in people's attributions between 1988 and 1992. In 1988, Bush played the blame game quite effectively. Although he is generally acknowledged as having been the more aggressive campaigner that year, he did not reap an undue share of the blame for negativity. More people in October saw his ads as attacking the opponent (37 percent) than explaining his own views (21 percent), but the same was true for Dukakis. (34 percent thought his ads attacked and 25 percent believed they explained.) (See Table 7-1.) Not until the end of the campaign did Bush receive a disproportionate share of the blame.

TABLE 7-1

Tone of Ads and Responsibility for Negative Campaigning

1988 Campaign	October	Early November	Mid-November
Bush Ads			
Explain His Views	21%	14%	14%
Attack Opponent	37	36	43
Both	9	11	10
Don't Know/No Answer	33	39	33
Dukakis Ads			
Explain His Views	25	24	24
Attack Opponent	34	26	31
Both	9	11	8
Don't Know/No Answer	32	39	37
Responsibility for Negativity			
Bush	—	25	30
Dukakis	—	16	19
Both	—	24	24
Neither	—	3	3
Don't Know/No Answer	—	32	24

1992 Campaign	September	October	
Bush Ads			
Explain His Views	24%	16%	
Attack Opponent	46	56	
Both	16	10	
Don't Know/No Answer	14	18	
Clinton Ads			
Explain His Views	37	46	
Attack Opponent	31	24	
Both	17	12	
Don't Know/No Answer	15	18	
Responsibility for Negativity			
Bush	39	60	
Clinton	21	13	
Both	22	18	
Neither	4	3	
Don't Know/No Answer	14	6	

Sources: October 21-24, 1988, CBS News/*New York Times* Survey; November 2-4, 1988, CBS News/*New York Times* Survey; November 10-15, 1988, CBS News/*New York Times* Survey; September 28-29, 1992, Winston-Salem Survey; October 26-31, 1992, Los Angeles County Survey.

Note: Entries indicate percentages of individuals believing candidate explained or attacked, and that he was responsible for the negativity of the campaign.

— No data available.

If one compiles the ratio of attack/explain responses for Bush and Dukakis, respectively, at different points in the campaign, viewers were evenly split in their ratios between Bush (1.8) and Dukakis (1.3) in October. By November, though, Bush's attack/explain ratio was 3.1, whereas Dukakis's was only 1.3.[33] These figures were in line with reality. A study of CBS news stories involving ads during the 1988 general election reveals that 75 percent of Bush's commercials aired during the news were negative about Dukakis, while only 33 percent of Dukakis's ads were negative about Bush.

The picture in 1992 could not have been more different. In September, almost twice as many people said Bush's commercials attacked Clinton (46 percent) than said the ads explained his own views (24 percent). In contrast, more people thought Clinton's ads explained his views (37 percent) than attacked the opponent (31 percent). People also were more likely to name Bush (39 percent) than Clinton (21 percent) as being responsible for the negative campaigning. By late October, Bush was being blamed by the even larger margin of 60 to 13 percent. In 1988, 25 percent had blamed Bush and 16 percent Dukakis for campaign negativity.

To some extent Democrats anticipated Bush's 1992 attack ads and focused attention on the blame game.[34] In an effort to inoculate himself against Republican attacks, Clinton and his fellow Democrats talked about GOP tendencies to engage in attack politics as early as the Democratic convention. In his acceptance speech, Clinton warned: "To all those in this campaign season who would criticize Arkansas, come on down . . . you'll see us struggling against some of the problems we haven't solved yet. But you'll also see a lot of great people doing amazing things." A delegate from Chicago, Jonathan Quinn, was more direct about likely attacks on Clinton: "I am fearful about the attacks on Clinton's character. I don't think we've seen anything yet. I think the Republicans are going to ravage him, and I'm nervous about it. . . . I think things will get brutally ugly."[35] Clinton himself emphasized the importance of not being "Dukakisized," and repeated Bush's widely publicized comment to David Frost early in the year about Bush's willingness to "do anything" to win the election.

In a clear contrast to the high-road strategy of Dukakis, the Clinton team also responded immediately to Republican onslaughts. When Bush ran attack ads in early October accusing the Arkansas governor of raising taxes, Clinton broadcast an instant rebuttal. The spot started with a bold red headline: "GEORGE BUSH ATTACK AD." The commercial went on to say, "George Bush is running attack ads. He says all these people would have their taxes raised by Bill Clinton. Scary, huh? 'Misleading,' says the *Washington Post.* And the *Wall Street Journal* says 'Clinton has proposed to cut taxes for the sort of people featured in [Bush's] ad.' "

Bush's broadcast of an ad on the draft-evasion issue using *Time* magazine's famous cover story asking whether Clinton could be trusted also led Clinton's media advisers to test a commercial featuring editorial responses from around the country. Though the ad was never broadcast, because people in focus groups felt it was too harsh, the spot illustrates the quick-response mentality of the Clinton team: "All across America people are hurting, and what is George Bush doing? The press calls his campaign gutter politics [*St. Petersburg Times*]. Malicious and dangerous mudslinging [the *Tennessean*]. Wrong, deceitful [*Des Moines Register*]. It's sad to see a president stoop this low [*Atlanta Constitution*]. Nasty and shrill [*New York Times*]. Deplorably sordid [*Los Angeles Times*]. Lies and attempted distraction [Hutchinson, Kan., *News*]. Bush's smear . . . new low [*USA Today*]. Cheap shot, Mr. President [*Miami Herald*]. Stop sleazy tactics and talk straight [Wilmington, Del., *News Journal*]. We can't afford four more years."[36]

The same tactic was in evidence on October 7, when Bush raised the character issue in response to a question on the "Larry King Live" show. Under prodding from the host, Bush attacked Clinton for leading antiwar demonstrations while a student at Oxford University: "I cannot for the life of me understand mobilizing demonstrations and demonstrating against your own country, no matter how strongly you feel, when you are in a foreign land. Maybe I'm old fashioned, but to go to a foreign country and demonstrate against your own country when your sons and daughters are dying halfway around the world, I am sorry but I think that is wrong." When asked in the same interview about a student trip Clinton made to Moscow in 1969, Bush said: "I don't want to tell you what I really think. To go to Moscow, one year after Russia crushed Czechoslovakia, not remember who you saw there. . . ."[37]

In 1988, Bush's attacks were reported favorably by the press and Dukakis's weak rebuttals were seen as evidence of passivity. Bush's 1992 attack met a different fate. Clinton took the lead in responding. In the first presidential debate, Clinton turned to Bush and accused the president of engaging in a McCarthy-style smear on his patriotism. He also reminded Bush that in the 1950s, Bush's father, Sen. Prescott Bush, had displayed courage in standing up to McCarthy.

The press response was very sympathetic to Clinton. Bush was met with unfavorable headlines across the country. For example, the *Washington Post* headlined their stories "Clinton Denounces Attacks by Bush" and "President Drops Moscow Trip Issue: Bush Denies Attacking Foe's Patriotism." The *New York Times* ran stories entitled "Clinton Says Desperation Is Fueling Bush Criticism," "Bush Camp Pursues an Offensive By Having Others Make the Attack," and "Campaign Renews Disputes of the Vietnam War Years." The backlash against Republican attacks took their toll on President Bush. A path analysis shows how attack strategies by Bush and Clinton as well as attributions of responsibility for negative campaigning influenced the vote. Using a design similar to the paired ads design reported in previous chapters, this analysis investigates how voters responded when faced with the combination of Bush and Clinton ads. The results indicate that attacks produced a strong voter backlash. The more each candidate was seen as attacking, the more likely voters were to blame that person for negative campaigning.[38]

These attributions are important because there was an inverse correlation between blame and the vote. Voters who saw Bush as responsible for negativity were more likely to vote for Clinton. Since more people were blaming Bush than Clinton for the tone of the race, this trend clearly was a liability for Bush. Shortly after the election, Bush aide James Pinkerton was forced to admit in a campaign postmortem, "We've got to ask ourselves what would make a voter vote for a draft-dodging, womanizing, fill-in-the-blank sleazeball? What would drive them to it? This says a lot about us, doesn't it?"[39]

Ironically, in light of its moralistic protests against Bush's attacks, the Clinton camp had prepared ads for the last week of the campaign challenging Perot's suitability for the presidency. One featured people-on-the-street interviews with former Perot volunteers saying Perot lacked character. Another said, "Ross Perot's plan? It could make things worse. He wants a 50-cent gas tax, which hits middle-class families hardest. He wants to raise taxes on the middle class. And he wants to cut Medicare benefits." Each statement was footnoted with a page number from Perot's book, *United We Stand*.⁴⁰ The commercials were not broadcast when it was apparent right before the election that Perot represented no threat to Clinton.

It had become the conventional wisdom based on the 1988 experience that attack ads work. The widespread acceptance of this view, in fact, explains in part the frequency of negative campaigns. This perspective, though, ignores contrary evidence. Negative commercials are advantageous when they help candidates define the terms of debate and pinpoint liabilities of the opponent. Thus Bush was able to dominate the agenda and prime voters in the 1988 general election. Yet it also is clear from 1992 that Bush was the object of a backlash that enabled Clinton to attract voters.

From the standpoint of each candidate, one of the considerations that makes negative ads undependable as a strategic device is that it can be hard to get the benefits of attack without suffering the blame for an unpleasant campaign. Attack strategies must be used with great prudence. Simply going on the offensive is not necessarily going to be effective. If attributions of blame outweigh the benefits of controlling the agenda, attacks are likely to backfire. For negative ads to work, then, they must help candidates define the terms of debate without also making them come across as mean-spirited.

Chapter 8

Advertising and Democratic Elections

In this book, I have investigated television advertising from a number of different perspectives. What is the strategic use of political commercials? How do the media cover ads? What impact do campaign spots have on viewers? Briefly, I found that commercials influence how voters learn about the candidates (Chapter 5), what they identify as priorities (Chapter 6), and their standards of assessment and attributions of blame (Chapter 7). Ads have their strongest impact when candidates are not well known and in electoral settings of low visibility, and when media coverage reinforces the basic message of the commercial. Strategic elements within each election are also crucial, particularly those related to the timing and content of ads and to decisions on when and where to attack.

This chapter examines the implications of the results for democratic elections. Elections are crucial to democratic systems. They are a means by which citizens choose who occupies positions of formal responsibility. There is little doubt that ads have altered the way citizens make electoral decisions. Yet the research reported here has shown that not all electoral arenas face the same risk. Since the impact of an advertisement depends considerably on the campaign context, the same type of commercial can pose very different challenges in various settings. It therefore is important to determine under what conditions ads are most worrisome.

The Crucial Role of Elites

Most studies of democratic linkages have approached the subject from the standpoint of voters. Are voters knowledgeable about or interested in politics? Do they vote on the basis of issues, party

identification, or their perceptions of the candidates' personal qualities? Are voters governed by short- or long-term forces? What role
does the state of the economy play in elections? The list could go on,
for it is clear that the study of voters has been the overriding concern
of scholars for some time.[1]

Although the focus has yielded rich dividends, the preoccupation
with American voters has distracted researchers from candidates and
other political elites. Campaigners are crucial in elections. They set
the choices available to voters. They influence the rate of political
change. They establish the perimeters of the electoral arena.
Nevertheless, research on leaders has virtually disappeared from
library shelves (with the exception of biographical and journalistic
accounts). Forty years ago, scholars such as C. Wright Mills studied
the relations among leaders to see if a "power elite" governed
America. Others have explored changes in the composition of
leadership to determine whether there was a "circulation of elites."
But over the last three decades, election analysts have studied voters
to the near exclusion of candidates.[2]

Happily, this pattern is beginning to change. Work by John
Zaller demonstrates the importance of political elites in structuring
public opinion. Richard Brody has shown that citizens' responses to
the president's handling of international crises depend considerably
on the unity of elite reactions. Presidents are likely to have more
solid and long-lasting public support when elite opinion is united.
Benjamin Page and Robert Shapiro argue that the public in general
responds quickly and reasonably to elite cues.[3]

These studies demonstrate the influence of the political elite.
Thus we need to examine how candidates present themselves to the
electorate. One valuable reflection of elite behavior is political
advertising. With the exception of spots produced by independent
organizations, ads are an avenue of mass communications that is
directly under the control of candidates and their staffs—unlike news
broadcasts, where intermediaries outside the campaign act as a check
on what candidates do. Campaigners also choose when and where ad
messages are aired. As stated by media adviser John Deardourff,
"Paid advertising is the most reliable, the most effective, and the only
one of those . . . vehicles in which a candidate is able to say exactly
what he or she wants to say in the words that he or she wants to use
with the certainty of delivery of the precise message that the
candidate wants to deliver." [4]

Commercials have become one of the most valuable weapons in the arsenals of candidates. The rise of mass communication technologies at a time when the political system places great emphasis on personal popularity gives leaders a powerful means of influencing voters. The combination of new technologies, an open electoral system, and the weakening of many of the traditional anchors in American politics (such as party organizations) makes it imperative to examine the normative aspects of television advertising.

Democratic Expectations

Few aspects of democracy have been discussed over the course of American history as much as the quality of information provided during the election process. Candidates are expected to address the subjects at stake in a given election and provide some indication of where they stand in regard to those matters. In fact, this information allows voters to hold leaders accountable. Failure to provide suitable material undermines the representative basis of American democracy.[5]

As an intermediary institution, the media are expected to devote enough attention to candidates' character attributes and to the issues to help voters bridge the gaps left by candidates' communications. Not many people directly experience election campaigns. Voters are dependent on the media to help them interpret political realities. When reporters provide the type of information that educates citizens regarding the choices facing them, the election process is significantly enhanced.

However, there is disagreement over exactly how detailed information from candidates and the media should be. The classical model of democracy calls for specific, issue-oriented material.[6] Candidates are expected to have detailed positions on the major issues facing the country and to communicate these views clearly to voters. Issue-based voting models as well as textbook descriptions of American elections emphasize the policy aspects of campaigns.

Others, though, have argued that popular control can be achieved through other approaches. For example, the party responsibility model uses partisanship as the means of accountability. Parties foster representation because they encapsulate general lines of thinking about major policy positions. Therefore, voters can make substantive judgments about candidates based purely on party labels.[7] Similarly, retrospective evaluations have become widely accepted as a means of popular control. Advocates argue that the candidates' approach to issues alone is not an appropriate test because voters can be sophisticated and rational without engaging in issue-based voting. As long as leaders can be held accountable for the broad direction of government performance, democratic tenets are satisfied.[8]

Still others have argued that knowledge about the character of potential leaders is vital to democratic elections.[9] Elections are seen as a means of evaluating the judgment of leaders who will do the deliberating in a representative democracy. According to this perspective, assessments about leadership qualities and character are quite relevant to voters' decision making.

The emergence of thirty-second ads and nine-second sound bites as the primary means of political communication represents a potential challenge to each of these models.[10] Since classical democratic theory places a premium on detailed policy information, the chief danger under this model is deception and distortion by the candidates in regard to their positions on issues. Ads that mislead viewers or distort an opponent's record are particularly dangerous. Numerous campaigners have used ads to create impressions of themselves that turned out to be inaccurate (including Johnson as the peace candidate in 1964 and Bush as the "no new taxes" man of 1988). The same logic applies to models centered on leaders' judgment. The primary danger of ads in this view is their potential to manipulate views about personal traits—leadership, trustworthiness, and independence. In 1984, for example, Hart was remarkably successful at getting people to see Mondale, who had formidable Washington experience and interest group support, as just another old-style politician currying favor with special interests.

But these are not the only risks from advertisements. The party responsibility model assumes that long-term party identification will protect viewers against excesses by candidates. Yet even this model recognizes that party attachments have loosened in recent years and that new arenas based on intraparty nominating contests have arisen. These settings are precisely where ads achieve their greatest impact. The combination of unknown candidates, volatile preferences, and shared party label gives ads enormous influence. The emergence of independent candidates, such as Perot, furthermore has put the party responsibility model in danger in regard to general elections because party ties are less decisive in a three-way race. In these settings, advertising takes on great strategic significance. The ability to win with a plurality of the vote encourages candidates to use commercials to appeal to narrow pockets of voters.

The retrospective voting model also raises important normative questions. This approach appears on the surface to be the least vulnerable to ads. Since vote choice is presumed to be based on citizens' views about the economy, which are in turn rooted in people's personal experiences, ads would not seem too influential on electoral decisions. But a closer inspection reveals that even this model requires voters to assign blame for unsatisfactory performance and to assess candidates' capabilities to deal with economic matters.[11] In 1992, for example, Clinton—primarily through advertising—was able to boost public perceptions about his ability to improve the economy and to show people that he was a caring individual. At the same time, he and Perot were able to blame Bush and the Republicans for the nation's poor economic performance.

Attributions of responsibility are particularly open to media influence. Through techniques based on priming and defusing, ads can elevate or lower particular standards of evaluation. In fact, during eras of scarce resources, elections often rest on how well candidates play the blame game.[12] Therefore, although traditional voting models diagnose the problem of advertisements quite differently, each one identifies particular dangers regarding the quality of information presented to voters and the ability of citizens to engage in informed decision making.

The Risk of Manipulation

The concerns expressed about American elections did not originate with television. Writers long have complained about the dangers of outside influences on voters. Nineteenth-century reformers, for example, fought outright bribery in an era when cash payoffs to citizens in exchange for votes were quite common. The extension of voting rights in this century precipitated wild debates regarding the impact of external agents: opponents of expanded suffrage claimed that newly enfranchised women would be unduly influenced by their husbands and that Catholic immigrants would become pawns of the pope!

Several features of democratic systems have been thought to reduce the danger of external manipulation. Widespread acceptance of the democratic culture by political elites is seen in pluralist models as providing a sufficient guarantee of fair and open competition. Self-regulation, it is said, weakens the threat from candidates and helps to ensure that election appeals are made fairly. At the same time, a variety of intermediary institutions supposedly protects citizens from overly ambitious campaigners. People can express opinions and hold leaders accountable through organizations representing their political perspectives. Parties and interest groups have been seen as the most important linkages in modern theories of democracy. Because these organizations facilitate the joint activity of citizens having common points of view, they are a means of bridging the gap between citizens and leaders.

The problem with this view of democracy is that its proponents have been strangely quiet about key aspects of leadership behavior. In the rush to reconcile less than optimistic views of citizens' behavior with hopes for democracy, sight has been lost of the crucial responsibilities of candidates in the election process. Pluralist perspectives, for example, ignore the fact that elite competition can go beyond the bounds of fair play when there is no referee to penalize players for making deceptive appeals. With the powerful advertising tools at candidates' disposal, citizens are exposed to potent campaign appeals.[13]

The decline of self-regulation by candidates' organizations would not be quite so problematic if there were a universally acknowledged body to protect citizens against subtle manipulation of their standards of evaluation. Unfortunately, there is no external referee with the authority to police electoral competition. Political parties and interest groups have lost much of their grip on elections. Government agencies (such as the Federal Election Commission and the Federal Communications Commission) meanwhile have chosen not to regulate campaign appeals because political speech is constitutionally protected.

The weakness of external regulators at a time when candidates control influential communication technologies has given candidates great incentives to attempt manipulation of voters through the airwaves. The classic problem of electoral deception involves substantive manipulation, whereby leaders deceive citizens about policy matters. According to Page and Shapiro, "To the extent that the public is given false or incorrect or biased information, or is deprived of important relevant information, people may make mistaken evaluations of policy alternatives and may express support for policies harmful to their own or society's interests, or in conflict with values they cherish." [14]

If elections were primarily about public policy, substantive manipulation would remain the most dangerous threat to the political system. However, contests involve perceptions about electability and personal images as well. Many races in recent years have turned on questions of momentum, likability, and mistakes. How the game is played often has become more important than the actual task of setting the future course of government action.

The fact that elections generally involve short-term campaign phenomena creates another type of deception, which I call strategic manipulation. In this situation, efforts are made to shift impressions of the campaign in a direction favorable to particular candidates. For example, candidates often seek to influence short-term evaluations. Specifically, spot commercials can be employed to alter views about an opponent's likability; they can lead to exaggerated claims regarding a contender's electoral prospects; they can be used to change campaign dynamics and distract voters from pressing matters of the day.

Television commercials are particularly problematic because they combine audio and visual technologies. Sounds, colors, and visual presentations can be used in deceptive ways. For example, Buchanan's ad consultants in 1992 occasionally speeded up or slowed down Bush's physical movements to create unfavorable impressions of the president. Independent ad producer Floyd Brown also admitted that he had doctored an ad showing Clinton's hand raised high with Senator Kennedy's. The joint picture was faked by combining separate pictures of the men alone. [15] This type of editing poses obvious problems for viewers, who remember the visual image but are not in a position to recognize electronic chicanery.

Strategic manipulation has not attracted as much study as substantive or symbolic manipulation, but in a media era it is a serious threat. A campaign structure that is open, volatile, and heavily dependent on media coverage gives candidates clear incentives to seek advantage strategically. The rise of new technologies and the employment of professional campaign managers in the United States have broadened the range of tactics considered acceptable and given campaigners extraordinary tools for influencing voters.

Different Arenas, Different Threats

The susceptibility of voters to advertising appeals has long generated despair from political observers. McGinniss's book, *The Selling of the President,* and Spero's volume, *The Duping of the American Voter,* express common fears about the dangers of advertisements.[16] But these authors failed to recognize that not all electoral arenas are subject to the same threat. The visibility of the setting makes a big difference.

The major threat in highly visible arenas, such as presidential general election campaigns, is substantive manipulation. The 1988 general election gave a textbook illustration of this danger, as the relatively unknown Dukakis saw his entire campaign shattered by Bush's successful efforts to move the campaign from past performance to flags, furloughs, and patriotism. Bush used advertising on tax and spending matters as well as crime that year to fill in the public profile of the relatively unknown Dukakis. The vice president was able to dominate the campaign because few voters knew much about the Massachusetts governor, 1988 was a year with a fluid policy agenda, and Dukakis did not successfully defend himself. Bush painted a portrait of the Massachusetts governor that many observers considered grossly exaggerated; Bush pictured an unrepentant liberal who was soft on crime and out of touch with the American people. Combined with uncritical coverage from the media, Bush's ads in this election had consequences that were both substantial and quite disturbing.

Less visible electoral arenas, such as presidential nomination campaigns, are more vulnerable to strategic manipulation. Because they are less visible contests that are heavily influenced by campaign dynamics, they contain fewer of the countervailing forces than are present in presidential general elections. Democrats compete against Democrats and Republicans against Republicans in a sequential nominating process.[17] In this situation, party identification is not central to vote choice. The setting limits the power of long-term forces and makes it possible for short-term factors, such as advertising and media coverage, to dominate.

Senate races share some features with nominating races. These contests are susceptible to ad appeals because relatively unknown candidates compete in races that resemble roller-coaster rides. There often are wild swings in electoral fortunes during the course of the campaign. The absence of prior beliefs about the candidates makes advertising influential.[18] It is easier to create a new political profile (for yourself or the opponent) than to alter a well-defined image. Candidates who are the least known are the most able to use advertisements to influence the public. But they also are the most susceptible to having an opponent create an unfair image of themselves through television.

Slicing and Dicing the Electorate

Campaign advertisements also pose problems for democratic elections on the systemic level. Even if ads influence voting behavior only in certain circumstances, they have consequences for the way in which the campaign is viewed. Advertisements are one of the primary means of communication, and much of how people feel about the electoral system is a product of how campaign battles are contested.

In contemporary elections it is common for political consultants to divide voters into advertising segments based on public opinion polls and focus groups: the committed (those who are for you), the hopeless (those who are against you and about whom little can be done), and the undecided (those who could vote either way). The last group, of course, is the central target of campaign tactics.

Ads are developed to stir the hopes and fears of the 20 to 30 percent of the electorate that is undecided, not the 70 to 80 percent that is committed or hopeless. Narrow pockets of support are identified and targeted appeals are made. Many Americans complain that campaign discussions do not reflect their concerns. Their complaints are legitimate. With advertising appeals designed for the small group of voters who are undecided, it is little wonder many voters feel left out.

In this system of segmentation and targeted appeals, candidates have clear incentives to identify pockets of potential support and find issues that will move these voters. Whether it is the backlash against affirmative action among white rural dwellers in North Carolina (one of the winning issues for Helms in 1990) or Bush's attacks on Clinton for his 1969 antiwar demonstrations (which did not save the election for Bush), the current electoral system encourages candidates to find divisive issues that pit social group against social group.

It is not surprising in this situation that Americans feel bad at the end of election campaigns. Candidates engage in an electronic form of civil war not unlike what happens in divided societies. The battleground issues often touch on race, lifestyle, and gender, which are among the most contentious topics in America. Ads and sound bites are the weapons of choice in these confrontations.

The long-run dangers from the electronic air wars are ill feelings and loss of the sense of community. Bill Clinton addressed these fears in his nomination acceptance speech. Long before his patriotism had been challenged, Clinton warned about the danger of divisiveness and the importance of community: "The New Covenant is about more than opportunities and responsibilities for you and your families. It's also about our common community. Tonight every one of you knows deep in your heart that we are too divided. It is time to heal America. . . . Look beyond the stereotypes that blind us. We need each other . . . this is America. There is no them. There is only us." [19]

What Can Be Done?

The controversies that have arisen concerning television commercials have generated heartfelt pleas for fundamental changes in U.S. campaigns. Following the example of Australia, and until recently West Germany, some have called for an outright ban on televised campaign ads in the United States. Others have suggested the application of the rule followed in France, where ads are banned during the closing weeks of the campaign.[20] These calls undoubtedly reflect deep frustration over the uses of advertisements in the United States.[21] But it is far too simple to blame ads for electoral deficiencies. The problem of political commercials is as much a function of campaign structure and voters' reactions as of candidates' behavior. Structural and attitudinal changes have loosened the forces that used to restrain elite strategies. The rise of a mass-based campaign system at a time when candidates have powerful means of influencing viewers rewards media-centered campaigns.

At the same time, voters are vulnerable to candidates' messages because the forces that used to provide social integration have lost their influence. Intermediary organizations no longer organize political reality. Consensus has broken down on key domestic and foreign policy questions. Voters are bombarded with spot ads precisely because of their proven short-term effectiveness, as has been evident in recent races.

Recent court rulings make an outright ban on campaign commercials unlikely. Most court decisions have treated candidates' expenditures on advertisements as tantamount to free speech.[22] Since ads are a form of expression, they are subject to constitutional protection and are thereby quite difficult to restrict. Most attempts at direct regulation have been resisted as unconstitutional encroachments upon free speech.[23] Self-monitoring efforts, such as those proposed by the National Association of Political Consultants, are of limited value.

However, there is an informal mechanism in the advertising area which when combined with regulatory reform, promises more success: the media. In the case of candidates' advertising, government regulation clearly would be inadequate without direct and effective media oversight. Reporters have the power to make or break the regulation of advertising by how they cover spot commercials.

For example, follow-up reporting by the news media would enable viewers to link ad sponsorship to responsibility. Journalists who aggressively focused on negative commercials would help the public hold candidates accountable for ads that crossed the threshold of acceptability. This attention would alter the strategic environment of campaigns and create clear disincentives for the excessive or unfair use of attack ads.

Currently, advertising coverage falls far short of what would be needed to uphold democratic elections. Reporters devote plenty of attention to candidates' ads, but not necessarily in a way that furthers citizens' knowledge. They are more likely, for example, to use ads to discuss the horse race than the policy views of the candidates.

But with a different approach to ad coverage, television could become an enlightening force in American elections. Journalists in the United States have an unusually high credibility with the public. American reporters are seen as being more fair and trustworthy than in other countries. A recent comparative study of five countries illustrates this point. Whereas 69 percent of the Americans surveyed had great confidence in the media, only 41 percent of Germans and 38 percent of the British gave high ratings to journalists.[24]

What is needed in the United States is a "truth in political advertising" code which would feature a prominent oversight role for the media. Both Jamieson and David Broder have suggested that journalists should exercise their historic function of safeguarding the integrity of the election process.[25] The media could use their high public credibility to improve the functioning of the political system.

There are several tenets to this code that would improve the quality of electoral discourse. Reporters must use Ad Watches to evaluate the accuracy of candidates' claims. Candidates periodically make exaggerated claims in their efforts to win votes. Journalists need to look into their claims and report to voters on their accuracy. The 1992 race was notable because journalists made detailed assessments of candidates' claims. Newspapers routinely printed the text of commercials in Ad Watches, with sentence-by-sentence evaluations of their honesty. In addition, television reporters reviewed videos of commercials with an eye toward false claims, exaggerated promises, or unrealistic commitments.[26]

These efforts are valuable, but journalists must go beyond fact checking to true oversight. Commercials have become the major strategic tool for the contesting of American elections. Candidates devote the largest portion of their overall campaign budgets to advertising. Their ads feature their own appeals as well as comments about their opposition. Arbitrators are needed to ensure that ads are not misused and that the electronic battle is fought fairly. Almost every election now features claims and counter claims regarding the fairness of television ads. Voters are not usually in a position to assess these claims, and the Federal Election Commission has chosen not to adjudicate them.

The media are left with the responsibility to expose manipulation, distortion, and deception, not just inaccurate use of facts. Candidates who exceed the boundaries of fair play should be brought to task by reporters. Unfair tactics or misleading editing needs to be publicized. Commercials that engage in obvious appeals to racism, for example, should be condemned. Media pressure could protect the airwaves, as happened when the "Daisy" ad was condemned in 1964.

Television has a special obligation because it is the medium through which most Americans receive their political news. The Cable News Network pioneered the Ad Watch technique of broadcasting the spot in a smaller square on the side of the screen so that the ad would not overpower the analysis. This valuable innovation should become a model for the rest of the electronic media.

Aggressive Ad Watches are especially important in spots involving race, lifestyle issues, gender, or other topics with emotional overtones.[27] The danger in focusing on such commercials is that viewers will remember the candidate's message, not the critique. Since ads on "hot button" issues using well-recognized codewords are becoming quite common, reporters need to check candidates' messages to limit manipulatory appeals.

These actions will help protect the integrity of the electoral process. Reporters are the only major group with the credibility vis-à-vis the American public to arbitrate electoral advertising. In fact, a 1985 Gallup poll revealed that citizens would like the media to undertake an aggressive watchdog role.[28] Government regulators at the Federal Communications Commission or the Federal Election Commission would not be as effective in such a role. Nor would political elites be seen as credible because they are associated with partisan politics.

There is some danger for the media in openly assuming this role. Many Americans already are concerned about what they believe is excessive influence and bias on the part of the news media.[29] If journalists aggressively challenge candidates' statements, they may be viewed as part of the problem rather than the solution. There are increasing signs of a backlash against the media, and reporters could become subject to more stringent criticism regarding their overall influence and objectivity.

In 1991, for example, Louisiana gubernatorial candidate Duke tried to foster antipathy to the media through a last-minute ad directly criticizing coverage of his campaign: "Have you ever heard such weeping and gnashing of teeth? The news media have given up any pretense of fair play. The liberals have gone ballistic. The special interests have gone mad. The politicians who play up to them are lining up on cue. Principles lie abandoned and hypocrisy rules the day. I raise issues that must be discussed, and get back venom instead. Try a little experiment. Next time you hear them accuse me of intolerance and hatred, notice who is doing the shouting." [30] Bush also attempted to build support for his 1992 reelection in his slogan: "Annoy the media: re-elect Bush."

Local surveys conducted in Los Angeles during the fall 1992 race revealed that 44 percent rated the media as having done a fair or poor job of covering the presidential campaign while 54 percent thought the media had done an excellent or good job. In the fall campaign, 43 percent felt reporters had been biased against particular candidates and 49 percent said they had not been. When asked to identify which campaigner had received the most biased coverage, 43 percent named Bush, 32 percent named Clinton, 21 percent named Perot, and 4 percent cited other candidates. Content analysis from the Center for Media and Public Affairs reveals that Bush earned the highest percentage of negative comments (71 percent) from network evening newscasts, compared with Clinton (48 percent) and Perot (55 percent). The content analysis also fits with evidence that reporters were more likely to report Democratic leanings in 1992 than in earlier years.[31]

Despite the drawbacks, oversight by the media is vital enough to the political system to warrant the risk of backlash. The quality of information presented during elections is important enough to outweigh the practical difficulties facing the fourth estate. Nothing is more central to democratic elections than electoral discourse. Without informative material, voters have little means of holding leaders accountable or engaging in popular consent.[32] By encouraging candidates to address the substantive concerns of the electorate, media watchdogs will raise the caliber of the political process and help voters make meaningful choices.

The Challenge of the New Media

No discussion of media oversight can be complete without a consideration of the striking changes that are taking place in the news industry. The most crucial developments in recent years have been the explosion of new media outlets and the declining ability of the top national newspapers and television networks to dominate campaigns. In fact, in 1992 the prestige press was upstaged by the talk shows, early-morning news, entertainment shows, and the local news. In that year conventional wisdom was trounced when Perot proved that millions of people can be persuaded to watch thirty-minute infomercials.

The most prominent stories in the 1992 presidential campaign were not generated by CBS, NBC, ABC, the *New York Times,* or the *Washington Post.* Instead, they came from the *National Enquirer,* which reported Flowers's accusations against Clinton, and from Larry King, when he coaxed Perot into announcing interest in the presidency. Technological changes have made it possible to provide instant access to newsmakers. The rise of cable television, the use of satellite transmissions, and the ability of local newsgatherers to cover national stories have dramatically altered the media terrain. These changes have been compounded by the fact that the television networks have lost almost 40 percent of their audience in recent years. The result is unprecedented opportunities for alternative formats to attract audiences.

Another factor that has led to important changes is citizens' unhappiness with the job being done by the media. The emphasis on character and extended coverage of what the public views as trivial matters is bothersome to many citizens. A Boston focus group participant, for example, complained about the tendency of reporters to appoint themselves character cops: "there are ten thousand people [in the media] looking around, trying to dig something . . . you almost have to be God or Jesus Christ to make it through." [33] Another person said, "I think what happens is that the press sometimes misreads what the candidates are saying, and they try to promote certain personalities over others."

Focus groups also provide insight into the popularity of the new outlets. A North Carolina participant said, "A lot of [the candidates] have been on 'Donahue,' some of the talk shows, they're going to get coverage like that, you know, people in the audience can ask questions that they want answers to, and give their views on a lot of things that are not presented in these campaign clips." Another person chimed in with her hope: "I wish they had Barbara Walters interview all of them. She asks questions that I would ask." The popularity of the audience-questioning format of the second presidential debate in 1992 reveals further citizens' craving for direct contact with the candidates in spontaneous settings.

It remains to be seen what long-term impact these new outlets will have on presidential politics. [34] The hosts of the new outlets are known for asking "softball" questions. It is no accident that Bush used the "Larry King Live" show to make his most outrageous charges against Clinton for traveling to Moscow while a student at Oxford University. The former president recognized there would be little aggressive follow-up by the host.

The new media furthermore are problematic because their adherence to professional standards wavers. Some of the tabloids, for example, commonly flout the widely respected rule from Watergate days that two independent confirmations must be obtained from reliable sources before a story is run. Today, the *National Enquirer*'s norm on publication appears to be that one rumor from a next-door neighbor will suffice.

These tendencies illustrate the risks for campaign coverage in general and reporting on ads in particular. Campaign messages are more likely to be reported uncritically by the talk shows and the morning news shows than by the network news organizations. In 1992, when ads were aired on the morning shows, they were often broadcast full-screen and without any effort to point out excesses. The same mistakes had been made by the networks in 1988 in regard to the "Revolving Door" commercial. One of the ironies of 1992 was that at the very time the prestige press was devoting considerable energy to Ad Watches, the new media were not vigilant about deceptive or unfair attacks. This laxness puts voters at great risk from campaign appeals.

At the same time, one aspect of the new media offers great promise. That is the innovative use of infomercials demonstrated by Perot. One of the most surprising developments in 1992 was the fact that millions of Americans tuned in to watch thirty-minute ads. An audience estimated at 16 million saw Perot's first infomercial, and his segments averaged about 9 million viewers thereafter. Longer commercials do not necessarily include more substantive appeals. Almost all of Perot's early infomercials, for example, diagnosed the problem rather than proposed a solution. Some journalists also pointed out that some of Perot's "facts" were misleading or inaccurate. But few would dispute that these shows offered a great deal of valuable information.

The popularity of infomercials in 1992, though, does not guarantee their widespread use in the future. There is little evidence that candidates will forsake thirty- and sixty-second spots for infomercials. Once the novelty wears off and news coverage of the broadcasts declines, viewership levels will most likely turn down. Yet it is clear that longer segments can be employed fruitfully for specific purposes, especially when they attract news coverage. Perot very effectively used infomercials to convey his concerns about the national debt and job creation. Clinton purchased thirty minutes of air time right before the New Hampshire primary to defuse the Flowers controversy. These types of new outlets may be the most constructive legacy of the 1992 campaign.

Appendix

Survey Data

The project reported here relies upon survey data (both panel and cross-sectional) in combination with content and media measures to explore viewers' reactions to campaign advertisements on television since 1972. Twenty surveys taken from 1972 through 1992 were used to analyze advertising effects. The only presidential election during this period for which independent survey data (not connected with candidates' organizations) were unavailable was 1980.

Most of the opinion data come from sources other than the biennial National Election Study conducted at the University of Michigan. The reason is simple. Only twice in the 1952-1992 period has the National Election Study included any questions on political advertising: 1974 in regard to Senate campaigns and 1988 during the nominating stage of the presidential campaign. The 1988 data are quite limited because the question asked—"In the past week, did you see any television commercials for a presidential candidate?" (yes or no)—aggregates ad exposure for all candidates who competed in the nominating process. It is therefore impossible to compare results for individual candidates or to evaluate the strategic aspects of advertising. The question also does not separate the Republican and Democratic nominating processes.

The survey data used in this study come from several different sources. In 1972, Patterson and McClure conducted a general election panel survey in Syracuse, New York. Three sets of personal interviews were conducted prior to election day. Preelection interviews took place in September ($N = 731$), October (reinterviews with 650 people), and early November (N=650). In addition to data on exposure to advertising, a wealth of information about views of the candidates was collected. For example, questions were asked concerning recognition, favorability and electability for Nixon and McGovern, respectively. Impressions of candidate personality traits and positions on issues were compiled, as were views about the most important problems facing the country.

A 1974 National Election Study explored advertising in Senate campaigns. This survey was a post-election nationwide questionnaire of 1,575 respondents. Individuals were interviewed between November 5 and January 31 following the election. Questions were asked about ad exposure and impact in Senate races.

In 1976, Patterson conducted a larger panel study in Los Angeles, California, and Erie, Pennsylvania. These surveys were designed to investigate the nominating and general election phases of the campaign. Respondents were asked about their exposure to ads, views about the candidates, assessments of personal qualities and issue positions, views about candidates' electability, and opinions on the most important problems facing the country. Overall, 1,236 people were interviewed in this series. Major interviews were conducted in February ($N = 1,002$), April ($N = 897$ respondents, of whom 772 had been interviewed in the earlier wave), and June ($N = 907$, with 720 coming from the original panel). A general election panel took place in October. Advertising items were asked during the April, June, and October panels.

The CBS News/*New York Times* poll conducted a national pre- and post-election survey in 1984 which included relevant questions. All together 1,994 respondents were interviewed between October 31 and November 2. Of these, 1,794 were reinterviewed on November 8 to 14, after the election. Questions were asked concerning views about the campaign, candidates' issue positions, and the most important problems facing the country.

In addition, CBS News/*New York Times* conducted several polls in 1988 that included advertising items: a regional survey of Super Tuesday primary states from February 28 to March 2 ($N = 2,251$); an October 21 to 24 questionnaire ($N = 1,827$); a pre-election survey from November 2 to 4 ($N = 1,977$), and a postelection interview from November 10-15 with 1,627 of the pre-election respondents.

The 1990 Rhode Island survey was sponsored by the A. Alfred Taubman Center for Public Policy and American Institutions at

Brown University. It was designed to explore the Senate race between Pell and Schneider. The pre-election poll was a statewide probability sample of 414 likely voters aged eighteen or above. It was undertaken September 16-19, 1990. Responses were weighted by sex and age in proportion to actual census numbers. Interviews were conducted by telephone. Overall, the survey had a margin of error around ± 5 percentage points.

The 1990 North Carolina Senate election study was conducted by the School of Journalism and the Institute for Research in Social Science at the University of North Carolina at Chapel Hill. From October 28 to 31, 1990, 833 randomly selected adult residents of North Carolina households were interviewed by telephone. The data were weighted for household size to correct for the undersampling of members of large households. The expected margin of error is ± 4 percentage points.

The 1992 presidential surveys were sponsored by the National Science Foundation and the MacArthur Foundation, and developed at the A. Alfred Taubman Center for Public Policy and American Institutions at Brown University. Part of a larger project on the 1992 campaign, they were designed to explore both the nominating and general election stages. Nominating polls were taken in the Boston metropolitan area March 2-9, 1992 ($N = 590$), and another in Los Angeles County May 18-31, 1992 ($N = 484$). General election surveys were conducted in Winston Salem ($N = 616$) from September 28 to 29 and Los Angeles County ($N = 601$) from October 26 to 31. Interviews were conducted by telephone with a random sample of adults aged eighteen years or older. Overall, these surveys had a margin of error around ± 4 percentage points.

Survey Questions

1972

Political Party: A seven-point scale from (1) strong Republican to (7) strong Democrat based on: "Generally speaking, do you consider yourself a Republican, Democrat, Independent, or what? Would you call yourself a strong Republican/Democrat or a not very strong Republican/Democrat? Do you think of yourself as closer to the Republican or Democratic Party?"

Education: Coded 0 to 20 years based on: "How many grades of school did you finish?"

Age: Coded in years based on: "In what year were you born?"

Sex: Coded as (1) male or (2) female.

Ideology: A seven-point scale from (1) strong conservative to (7) strong liberal based on: "Generally speaking, do you consider yourself a liberal, conservative, or moderate, or don't you see yourself in these terms? Would you call yourself a strong liberal/conservative or not a very strong liberal/conservative? Do you think of yourself as closer to being a liberal or closer to being a conservative?"

Race: Coded as (1) white or (2) nonwhite based on: "Respondent's ethnic or racial background."

Political Interest: "In talking with people about politics, we find many people who don't pay much attention to political campaigns. How about you? Would you say that you have been (1) very much interested, (3) somewhat interested, or (5) not much interested in following the political campaign so far this year?"

Media Exposure: Coded in days based on: "During the past seven days, about how many days did you get a chance to read a newspaper?"

1974

Political Party: A seven-point scale running from (0) strong Democrat to (6) strong Republican based on: "Generally speaking, do you usually think of yourself as a Republican, a Democrat, an Independent, or what? Would you call yourself a strong Republican/Democrat or a not very strong Republican/Democrat? Do you think of yourself as closer to the Republican or Democratic Party?"

Education: Coded 1 to 10 based on: "What is the highest grade of school or year of college that you have completed?"

Age: Coded in years based on: "Respondent's age as of November 5, 1974, election day."

Sex: Coded as (1) male or (2) female.

Ideology: A seven-point scale from (1) extremely liberal to (7) extremely conservative based on: "We hear a lot of talk these days about liberals and conservatives. I'm going to show you a seven-point scale on which the political views that people might hold are arranged from extremely liberal to extremely conservative. Where would you place yourself on this scale, or haven't you thought much about this?"

Race: Coded as (1) white or (2) nonwhite based on: "Respondent's race."

Political Interest: "Some people seem to follow what's going on in government and public affairs most of the time, whether there's an election going on or not. Others aren't that interested. Would you say you follow what's going on in government and public affairs (1) most of the time, (2) some of the time, (3) only now and then, or (4) hardly at all?"

Media Exposure: "One of the things we want to know from this interview is how people get information about politics and current events. Let's start with television. I'm going to ask you how frequently you watch some TV shows. Just tell me if you watch them (1) frequently, (2) sometimes, (4) rarely, or (5) never. How often do you watch national news broadcasts in the early evening?"

1976

Political Party: A seven-point scale from (1) strong Democrat to (7) strong Republican based on: "Generally speaking, do you usually think of yourself as a Republican, a Democrat, an Independent, or what? Would you call yourself a strong Republican/Democrat or a not very strong Republican/Democrat? Do you think of yourself as closer to the Republican or Democratic Party?"

Education: Coded 1 to 8 based on: "What is the last grade that you completed in school?"

Age: Coded in years based on "In what year were you born?"

Sex: Coded as (1) female or (2) male.

Ideology: A seven-point scale from (1) extremely liberal to (7) extremely conservative based on: "There's a lot of talk these days about liberals and conservatives. Some people consider themselves extremely liberal when it comes to politics. Others consider themselves extremely conservative when it comes to politics. Most people are somewhere in between. Which number on this scale best describes you, or haven't you thought much about it?"

Race: Coded as (1) white or (2) nonwhite based on: "What is the racial background of the respondent?"

Political Interest: "Generally speaking, how often do you talk about politics with others? Would you say (1) regularly, (2) somewhat often, (3) only once in a while, or (4) almost never?"

Media Exposure: "As you may know, network news is televised each weekday evening. Network news includes the CBS Evening News with Walter Cronkite, the ABC News with Harry Reasoner, and the NBC Evening News with John Chancellor. Many people do not watch the evening news regularly because they are eating supper, not home, busy or not interested. What about you? Do you watch network news (1) regularly, (2) somewhat often, (3) only once in a while, or (4) almost never?"

1984

Political Party: A seven-point scale running from (1) strong Republican to (7) strong Democrat based on: "Generally speaking, do you usually consider yourself a Republican, a Democrat, an Independent, or what? Is that a strong Republican/Democrat or not a very strong Republican/Democrat? Do you think of yourself as closer to the Republican Party or to the Democratic Party?"

Education: Coded 1 to 4 based on: "What was the last grade in school you completed?"

Age: Coded in years based on "How old are you?"

Sex: Coded as (1) male or (2) female.

Ideology: "How would you describe your views on most political matters? Do you think of yourself as (1) liberal, (2) moderate, or (3) conservative?"

Race: Coded as (1) white or (2) nonwhite based on: "Are you white, black or some other race?"

Political Interest: "How much did you talk about the presidential election and candidates at home: (1) a lot, (2) some, or (3) hardly at all?"

Media Exposure: Not asked.

1988

Political Party: A five-point scale from (1) Republican to (5) Democrat based on: "Generally speaking, do you usually consider yourself a Republican, a Democrat, an Independent, or what? Do you think of yourself as closer to the Republican Party or to the Democratic Party?"

Education: Coded 1 to 4 based on: "What was the last grade in school you completed?"

Age: Coded in years based on: "How old are you?"

Sex: Coded as (1) male or (2) female.

Ideology: "How would you describe your views on most political matters? Do you think of yourself as (1) liberal, (2) moderate, or (3) conservative?"

Race: Coded as (1) white or (2) nonwhite based on: "Are you white, black or some other race?"

Political Interest: "In the last week, have you talked about the 1988 presidential campaign with anyone?" Coded as (1) yes or (2) no.

Media Exposure: Coded in days based on: "How many days out of the last seven days have you watched the news on television?"

1990 North Carolina

Political Party: "Generally speaking, do you think of yourself as a (1) Republican, (2) Independent, (3) Democrat, or what?"

Education: Coded 1 to 21 based on: "How many years of school have you completed?"

Age: Coded in years based on: "In which year were you born?"

Sex: Coded as (1) male or (2) female.

Ideology: "In general, when it comes to politics, do you usually think of yourself as (1) a liberal, (2) a moderate, (3) a conservative, or what?"

Race: Coded as (1) white or (2) nonwhite based on: "What race do you consider yourself?"

Political Interest: Not asked.

Media Exposure: Coded in days based on: "What about newspapers? How many days out of the last seven did you read a daily newspaper?"

1990 Rhode Island

Political Party: "Regardless of how you vote, do you usually think of yourself as a (1) Republican, (2) Independent, (3) Democrat, or something else?"

Education: A six-point scale based on: "What is the last grade of school you completed?"

Age: A six-point scale based on "Which of the following age groups are you in?"

Sex: Coded as (1) male or (2) female.

Ideology: Not asked.

Race: Not asked.

Political Interest: Not asked.

Media Exposure: Not asked.

1992

Political Party: "Regardless of how you vote, do you usually think of yourself as a (1) Republican, (2) Independent, (3) Democrat, or something else?"

Education: A six-point scale based on: "What is the last grade of school you completed?"

Age: A six-point scale based on: "Which of the following age groups are you in?"

Sex: Coded as (1) male or (2) female.

Ideology: "How would you describe your views on most political matters? Generally, do you think of yourself as a (1) liberal, (2) moderate, (3) conservative, or something else?"

Race: Coded as (1) white or (2) nonwhite based on: "Are you white, African American, Hispanic, Asian or some other race?"

Political Interest: "Some people seem to follow what's going on in government and public affairs most of the time, whether there's an election going on or not. Others aren't that interested. Would you say you follow what's going on in government and public affairs (1) most of the time, (2) some of the time, (3) only now and then, or (4) hardly at all?"

Media Exposure: "How many days in the last week have you seen anything about the upcoming presidential primary/election on national television news? (1) five days or more, (2) three or four days, (3) one or two days, or (4) not at any time?"

Best-Remembered Ads, 1984-1992

Mondale, "Future," 1984

Crosby, Stills, Nash, and Young sing portions of the lyrics from their song, "Teach Your Children," while images of missiles shooting out of underground silos are juxtaposed with closeups of children's faces. The ad concludes with a picture of a forest of trees shaking from an explosion, and a young girl's face appearing on screen. Then a globe fills the screen and the words "Mondale/ Ferraro" rotate into view.[1]

Reagan, "Bear in the Woods," 1984

(A bear lumbers through the woods.) "There's a bear in the woods. For some people the bear is easy to see; others don't see it at all. Some people say the bear is tame; others say it's vicious and dangerous. Since no one can be sure who is right, isn't it smart to be as strong as the bear—if there is a bear!"[2]

Bush, "Revolving Door," 1988

(Dissonant sounds are heard: a drum . . . music . . . metal stairs.) "As governor, Michael Dukakis vetoed mandatory sentences for drug dealers." (A guard with a rifle climbs the circular stairs of a prison watchtower. The words "The Dukakis Furlough Program" are superimposed on the bottom of the prison visual.) "He vetoed the death penalty." (A guard with a gun walks along a barbed wire fence.) "His revolving door prison policy gave weekend furloughs to first-degree murderers not eligible for parole." (A revolving door formed by bars rotates as men in prison clothing walk in and back out the door in a long line. The words "268 Escaped" are superimposed.) "While out, many committed other crimes like kidnapping and rape." (The camera comes in for a closer shot of the prisoners in slow motion revolving through the door.) "And many are still at large." (The words "And Many Are Still At Large" are superimposed.) "Now Michael Dukakis says he wants to do for America what he's done for Massachusetts." (The picture changes to a guard on a roof with a watchtower in the background.) "America can't afford that risk!" (A small color picture of Bush appears, and the words "Paid for by Bush/Quayle 88" appear in small print.) [3]

Dukakis "Family/Education," 1988

(At night a young man flips dough in a pizza parlor.) "Jimmy got accepted to college, but his family couldn't afford tuition." (Dukakis appears on the screen.) A voice-over says: "Mike Dukakis wants to help. . . . If a kid like Jimmy has the grades for college, America should find a way to send him." [4]

Clinton, "The Plan," 1992

"The people of New Hampshire know better than anyone. America is in trouble; our people are really hurting. In the '80s, the rich got richer, the middle class declined, poverty exploded. Politicians in Washington raised their pay and pointed fingers. But no one took responsibility. It's time we had a president who cares, who takes responsibility, who has a plan for change. I'm Bill Clinton and I believe you deserve more than 30-second ads or vague promises. That's why I've offered a comprehensive plan to get our economy moving again, to take care of our own people, and regain our economic leadership. It starts with a tax cut for the middle class and asks the rich to pay their fair share again. It includes national health insurance, a major investment in education, training for our workers, tough trade laws, and no more tax breaks for corporations to move our jobs overseas. Take a look at our plan and let me know what you think. I hope you'll join us in this crusade for change. Together we can put government back on the side of the forgotten middle class and restore the American Dream."[5]

Clinton, "How're You Doing?" 1992

A voice-over says: "Remember President Bush saying, 'And if you elect me President, you will be better off four years from now than you are today.'" The announcer responds: "Average family income down $1,600 in two years" (Commerce Department Bureau of Census 9/1/92). A voice-over says: "President Bush says, 'You will be better off four years from now than you are today.'" The announcer responds: "Family health care costs up $1,800 in four years" (Health Insurance Association of America, 1988; KPMG Peat Marwick 1992). A voice-over says: President Bush says, 'You will be better off in four years.'" The announcer responds: "The second biggest tax increase in history" (Congressional Budget Office Study 1/30/92; *New York Times* 8/7/92). A voice-over says: "President Bush says, 'If you elect me President, you will be better off four years from now than you are today.'" The announcer asks: Well, it's four years later. How're you doing?" [6]

Bush on Clinton Economics, 1992

An announcer says: "Bill Clinton says he'll only tax the rich to pay for his campaign promises. But here's what Clinton economics could mean to you. (Picture of male steamfitter) $1,088 more in taxes. (Picture of female scientist) $2,072 more in taxes. 100 leading economists say his plan means higher taxes and bigger deficits. (Picture of professional couple) $1,191 more in taxes. (Picture of black housing lender) $2,072 more in taxes. You can't trust Clinton economics. It's wrong for you. It's wrong for America." [7]

Perot on Job Creation, 1992

(Background of ticking clock; text scrolling up screen) "It is a time when the threat of unemployment is greater than the threat of war. It is a time that the national debt demands as much attention as the national security. It is a time when the barriers to a better life are rising and the barriers between nations are falling. The issue is the economy. And it is a time that demands a candidate who is not a business-as-usual politician, but a business leader with the know-how to balance the budget, rebuild the job base and restore the meaning of 'Made in the U.S.A.' In this election, we can choose a candidate who has made the free enterprise system work, who has created thousands of jobs by building successful businesses. The candidate is Ross Perot. The election is November 3. The choice is yours." [8]

Perot on National Debt and Children, 1992

(Background of children's faces; text scrolling up screen) "Our children dream of the world that we promised them as parents, a world of unlimited opportunity. What would they say to us if they knew that by the year 2000, we will have left them with a national debt of $8 trillion? What would they say to us if they knew that we are making them the first generation of Americans with a standard of living below the generation before them? We cannot do this to our children. In this election, we have the opportunity to choose a candidate who is not a career politician, but a proven business leader with the ability to take on the tasks at hand, to balance the budget, to expand the tax base, to give our children back their American dream. The candidate is Ross Perot. The issue is our children. The choice is yours." [9]

TABLE A-1
Ad Coefficients from Recall and Program Log Data

	Nixon: Honor Commitments		McGovern: Vietnam Withdrawal		Nixon: Electability		Agenda Setting on Foreign Affairs	
	Recall	Logs	Recall	Logs	Recall	Logs	Recall	Logs
Ads	.10 (.06)[1]	.30 (.12)[2]	.06 (.06)	.08 (.14)	.13 (.06)[1]	.48 (.14)[3]	.07 (.07)	.05 (.15)
Party	.04 (.02)[1]	.04 (.02)	-.01 (.03)	-.02 (.03)	.16 (.03)[3]	.15 (.03)[3]	.02 (.03)	.02 (.03)
Education	-.01 (.01)[1]	-.02 (.01)[2]	-.02 (.01)[3]	-.02 (.01)[3]	-.01 (.01)	-.02 (.01)[1]	-.01 (.01)	-.01 (.01)
Age	.00 (.00)	.00 (.00)	.00 (.00)	.00 (.00)	.00 (.00)	.00 (.00)	.00 (.00)	.00 (.00)
Sex	-.01 (.10)	-.01 (.10)	-.07 (.11)	-.05 (.11)	.14 (.12)	.15 (.11)	.35 (.12)[2]	.34 (.12)[2]
Ideology	-.00 (.02)	-.00 (.02)	.03 (.03)	.03 (.03)	.06 (.03)[1]	.07 (.03)[1]	.04 (.03)	.04 (.03)
Race	.68 (.28)[2]	.62 (.28)[1]	.41 (.31)	.41 (.31)	1.75 (.33)[3]	1.65 (.32)[3]	-.32 (.36)	-.30 (.36)
Political interest	.03 (.04)	.04 (.04)	.05 (.04)	.05 (.04)	.04 (.05)	.05 (.05)	.06 (.05)	.07 (.05)
Media exposure	-.05 (.02)[1]	-.04 (.02)[1]	-.06 (.03)[1]	-.06 (.03)[1]	.03 (.03)	.03 (.03)	-.01 (.03)	-.01 (.03)
Constant	1.50 (.49)	1.78 (.52)	2.10 (.56)	2.00 (.58)	-.75 (.59)	-.18 (.60)	4.53 (.63)	4.34 (.64)
N	342	345	345	348	343	346	345	350

Sources: November 1972 Patterson and McClure survey.

Note: Entries are unstandardized regression coefficients with standard errors in parentheses. Coefficients marked with superscripts were statistically significant. Estimates are based on ordinary least squares, with the exception of the agenda-setting item, which is derived from logistic regression.

[1] p < .05   [2] p < .01   [3] p < .001

TABLE A-2

Distribution of Prominent Ads Used in Content Study, 1952-1992

	Republicans	Democrats	Independents	Total
1952				
General Election	8	8	0	16
1956				
General Election	4	4	0	8
1960				
General Election	2	12	0	14
Kennedy Nomination	0	2	0	2
1964				
General Election	7	19	0	26
1968				
General Election	2	11	1	14
McCarthy Nomination	0	2	0	2
1972				
General Election	21	13	0	34
McGovern Nomination	0	1	0	1
Humphrey Nomination	0	2	0	2
Lindsay Nomination	0	1	0	1
Wallace Nomination	0	1	0	1
1976				
General Election	11	17	0	28
Ford Nomination	2	0	0	2
Carter Nomination	0	3	0	3
Udall Nomination	0	2	0	2
Bayh Nomination	0	1	0	1
1980				
General Election	32	12	0	44
Reagan Nomination	5	0	0	5
Bush Nomination	1	0	0	1
Carter Nomination	0	2	0	2
Kennedy Nomination	0	10	0	10
1984				
General Election	13	9	0	22
Hart Nomination	0	1	0	1
1988				
General Election	17	12	0	29

(Table continues)

TABLE A-2
(continued)

	Republicans	Democrats	Independents	Total
1992				
General Election	8	2	6	16
Bush Nomination	7	0	0	7
Buchanan Nomination	2	0	0	2
General Republican Nomination	3	0	0	3
Clinton Nomination	0	6	0	6
Kerrey Nomination	0	3	0	3
Tsongas Nomination	0	2	0	2
General Democratic Nomination	0	1	0	1
Proposition	0	0	5	5
General Independent	0	0	8	8
Total	145	159	20	324

Sources: For 1952-1988, Kathleen Jamieson, *Packaging the Presidency*, 2d ed. (New York: Oxford University Press, 1992); and for 1992, "CBS Evening News" tapes.

Note: Entries indicate number of prominent ads each year for Republicans, Democrats, and Independents.

T A B L E A-3
CBS Stories About Party Ads, 1972-1992

	Republican	Democrat	Both Rep. and Dem.	Independent	Total
1972	2	9	0	0	11
General Election	2	2	0	0	0
Nominating Campaign	0	7	0	0	0
1976	8	7	4	0	19
General Election	2	1	2	0	0
Nominating Campaign	6	6	2	0	0
1980	7	8	3	2	20
General Election	4	2	1	1	0
Nominating Campaign	3	6	2	1	0
1984	6	10	5	0	21
General Election	2	0	3	0	0
Nominating Campaign	4	10	2	0	0
1988	19	24	7	0	50
General Election	10	5	6	0	0
Nominating Campaign	9	19	1	0	0
1992	20	14	4	15	53
General Election	8	2	3	11	0
Nominating Campaign	12	12	1	4	0
Total	62	72	23	17	174

Sources: CBS Evening News, *Vanderbilt Television News Index and Abstracts* (for campaigns 1972-1988); and "CBS Evening News" tapes (for 1992 campaign).

Note: Entries indicate number of "CBS Evening News" stories about ads each year for Republicans, Democrats, both parties, and Independents.

Notes

Preface

1. The 1990 elections alone generated $203 million in spending on ads, according to an estimate by the Television Bureau of Advertising, a nonprofit organization representing the television industry. See Kim Foltz, "$203 Million Was Spent on Political Ads in '90," *New York Times*, February 12, 1991, D17.

2. Two notable exceptions are Kathleen Jamieson, *Packaging the Presidency*, 2d. ed. (New York: Oxford University Press, 1992); and Edwin Diamond and Stephen Bates, *The Spot* (Cambridge: MIT Press, 1984).

3. Robert Dahl, *A Preface to Democratic Theory* (Chicago: University of Chicago Press, 1957); Joseph Schumpeter, *Capitalism, Socialism and Democracy* (New York: Harper and Row, 1942); and Norman Luttbeg, ed., *Public Opinion and Public Policy*, 3d ed. (Itasca, Ill.: Peacock, 1981). But for a different interpretation, which emphasizes the ability of voters to make reasoned decisions based on small bits of information, see Samuel Popkin, *The Reasoning Voter* (Chicago: University of Chicago Press, 1991).

4. Joe McGinniss, *The Selling of the President* (New York: Simon and Schuster, 1969); and Robert Spero, *The Duping of the American Voter* (New York: Lippincott and Crowell, 1980).

5. A classic illustration of psychological reasoning is found in Linda Alwitt and Andrew Mitchell, eds., *Psychological Processes and Advertising Effects* (Hillsdale, N.J.: Erlbaum, 1985). The best application of psychological models to the evening news is Shanto Iyengar and Donald Kinder, *News That Matters* (Chicago: University of Chicago Press, 1987). For another recent example, see Diana Owen, *Media Messages in American Presidential Elections* (Westport, Conn.: Greenwood Press, 1991).

Chapter 1 - Rethinking Ads

1. The video for this ad was taken from a Public Broadcasting Service documentary, "Tongues Untied" which was subsidized by the National Endowment for the Arts. For a more extensive description, see E. J. Dionne, Jr., "Buchanan TV Spot Assails Arts Agency," *Washington Post,* February 27, 1992, A11; and Howard Kurtz, "Buchanan Ad Consultant Turns Tables on Bush," *Washington Post,* February 28, 1992, A1, A20. The response of the filmmaker, Marlon Riggs, who is also a journalism professor at the University of California at Berkeley, can be found in "Meet the New Willie Horton," *New York Times,* March 6, 1992, A33.

2. For a description of the campaign, see "How He Won," *Newsweek,* November/December 1992 (special issue).

3. "How Bush Won," *Newsweek,* November 21, 1988, 117. Also see Paul Taylor and David Broder, "Early Volley of Bush Ads Exceeded Expectations," *Washington Post,* October 28, 1988, A1. Floyd Brown, the producer of an independently run ad showing Horton's picture in 1988, was criticized in 1992 for running an independent ad claiming Clinton would name Gov. Mario Cuomo (N.Y.) to the Supreme Court and put Sen. Edward Kennedy (Mass.) "behind the wheel at the Department of Transportation, overseeing roads . . . and bridges." For a critique of this ad, see Michael Robinson, "Clinton Camp Denounces TV Ad," *Providence Journal,* October 24, 1992, A1.

4. Kathleen Jamieson, *Packaging the Presidency,* 2d ed. (New York: Oxford University Press, 1992), 6-7.

5. See Carl Hovland, Arthur Lumsdaine, and Fred Sheffield, *Experiments on Mass Communications* (Princeton: Princeton University Press, 1949); Edward Shils and Morris Janowitz, "Impact of Allied Propaganda on Wehrmacht Solidarity in World War II," *Public Opinion Quarterly* 12 (1948): 300-304, 308-315; and William Kornhauser, *The Politics of Mass Society* (New York: Free Press, 1959).

6. Paul Lazarsfeld, Bernard Berelson, and Hazel Gaudet, *The People's Choice* (New York: Columbia Press, 1948); and Bernard Berelson, Paul Lazarsfeld, and William McPhee, *Voting* (Chicago: University of Chicago Press, 1954). A review of this literature is provided in Joseph Klapper, *The Effects of Mass Communication* (New York: Free Press, 1960).

7. Shanto Iyengar and Donald Kinder, *News That Matters* (Chicago: University of Chicago Press, 1987).

8. Shanto Iyengar, "Framing Responsibility for Political Issues," *Political Behavior* 12 (1990): 19-40; and Shanto Iyengar, *Is Anyone Responsible?* (Chicago: University of Chicago Press, 1991).

9. John Zaller, *The Nature and Origins of Mass Opinion* (New York: Cambridge University Press, 1992); Richard Brody, *Assessing the President: The Media, Elite Opinion, and Public Support* (Stanford:

Stanford University Press, 1991); and Benjamin Page and Robert Shapiro, *The Rational Public* (Chicago: University of Chicago Press, 1992).

10. Raymond Williams, *Television: Technology and Cultural Form* (New York: Schocken Books, 1974); Kathleen Hall Jamieson, "Context and the Creation of Meaning in the Advertising of the 1988 Presidential Campaign," *American Behavioral Scientist* 32 (1989): 415-424; and Ariel Sabar, "Suggestions for Further Media Research" (Unpublished paper, Brown University, 1992). For an engaging application of this notion to Perot's 1992 campaign, see Elizabeth Kolbert, "Perot Spending More on Ads Than Any Candidate Before," *New York Times,* October 28, 1992, A1.

11. William Gamson, *Talking Politics* (New York: Cambridge University Press, 1992); William Gamson, "A Constructionist Approach to Mass Media and Public Opinion," *Symbolic Interaction* 7, no. 2 (1988): 161-174; and Russell Neuman, Marion Just, and Ann Crigler, *Common Knowledge: News and the Construction of Political Meaning* (Chicago: University of Chicago Press, 1992).

12. Darrell M. West, Montague Kern, and Dean Alger, "Political Advertising and Ad Watches in the 1992 Presidential Nominating Campaign" (Paper delivered at the Annual Meeting of the American Political Science Association, Chicago, September 1992). Also see Dean Alger, "Constructing Campaign Messages and Public Understanding: The 1990 Wellstone-Boschwitz Senate Race in Minnesota," in *Political Communications and Constructing Public Understanding,* ed. Ann Crigler (Unpublished manuscript, Moorhead State University).

13. John Sprague defines a contextual effect as "variation in political behavior that depends, systematically, on properties of the environment within which that behavior is embedded." See his chapter, "Is There a Micro Theory Consistent with Contextual Analysis?" in *Strategies of Political Inquiry,* ed. Elinor Ostrom (Beverly Hills, Calif.: Sage, 1982), 99.

14. Lynda Kaid also discusses the differential effects of advertising at various levels of elections in "Political Advertising," in *Handbook of Political Communication,* ed. Dan Nimmo and Keith Sanders (Beverly Hills, Calif.: Sage, 1981), 249-271.

15. Stephen Ansolabehere and Shanto Iyengar point out the importance of the interactions of candidates and ads in a California governor's race. See their paper, "The Electoral Effects of Issues and Attacks in Campaign Advertising" (Paper delivered at the Annual Meeting of the American Political Science Association, Washington, D.C., August 1991).

16. Samuel Kernell, *Going Public: New Strategies of Presidential Leadership,* 2d ed. (Washington, D.C.: CQ Press, 1993), 9-52. Also see Martin Wattenberg, *The Rise of Candidate-Centered Politics* (Cambridge, Mass.: Harvard University Press, 1991).

17. It is hardly surprising, given these changes, that over the past two

decades we have seen a series of dark horse candidates do unexpectedly well in nomination politics. See Darrell M. West, *Making Campaigns Count* (Westport, Conn.: Greenwood Press, 1984), and James Ceaser, *Presidential Selection* (Princeton: Princeton University Press, 1979).

18. The Tsongas quote comes from Karen DeWitt, "Tsongas Pitches Economic Austerity Mixed with Patriotism," *New York Times,* January 1, 1992, 10. Finance figures between 1952 and 1980 were taken from Herbert Alexander, *Financing Politics* (Washington, D.C.: CQ Press, 1984), 4-12. The 1984 figures were supplied by Alexander and are cited in Stephen Wayne, *The Road to the White House,* 3d ed. (New York: St. Martin's Press, 1988), 28-31. The 1988 figures come from L. Patrick Devlin, "Contrasts in Presidential Campaign Commercials of 1988," *American Behavioral Scientist* 32 (1989): 389-414. The 1992 figures come from Elizabeth Kolbert, "Perot to Launch a Big Ad Pitch, but Will It Sell?" *New York Times,* October 3, 1992, 1; Elizabeth Kolbert, "Perot Spending More on Ads Than Any Candidate Before," *New York Times,* October 28, 1992, A1; and "How He Won," *Newsweek,* November/December 1992 (special issue).

19. Quoted in John Foley, Dennis Britton, and Eugene Everett, Jr., eds., *Nominating a President: The Process and the Press* (New York: Praeger, 1980), 43.

20. Quoted in Jonathan Moore, ed., *Campaign for President: 1980 in Retrospect* (Cambridge: Ballinger, 1981), 235.

21. Seymour Martin Lipset and William Schneider, *The Confidence Gap* (New York: Free Press, 1983), 17. The 1990 figure is cited in Robin Toner, "Poll Finds Postwar Glow Dimmed by the Economy," *New York Times,* March 8, 1991, A14. Changes in party identification are summarized in Paul Abramson, John Aldrich, and David Rohde, *Change and Continuity in the 1988 Elections* (Washington, D.C.: CQ Press, 1990).

22. Alexis de Tocqueville, *Democracy in America,* trans. George Lawrence (Garden City, N.J.: Doubleday, 1969), 198.

23. Other discussions of television can be found in James Carlson, *Prime Time Law Enforcement* (New York: Praeger, 1985); Thomas Volgy, ed., *Exploring Relationships between Mass Media and Political Culture* (Tucson: University of Arizona Institute of Government Research, 1975); Dean Alger, *The Media and Politics* (Englewood Cliffs, N.J.: Prentice Hall, 1989); Lance Bennett, *News* (New York: Longman, 1983); Mary Stuckey, *Playing the Game* (New York: Praeger, 1990); and Robert Denton, Jr., and Gary Woodward, *Political Communication in America* (New York: Praeger, 1985).

24. Classic studies of political marketing include Stanley Kelley's *Professional Public Relations and Political Power* (Baltimore: Johns Hopkins University Press, 1956); Dan Nimmo's *The Political Persuaders* (Englewood Cliffs, N.J.: Prentice-Hall, 1970); McGinniss's popular account, *The Selling of the President* (New York: Simon and Schuster, 1969); and Gary Jacobson, "The Impact of Broadcast Campaigning on

Electoral Outcomes," *Journal of Politics* 37 (1975): 769-793.

25. Gary Jacobson and Samuel Kernell, *Strategy and Choice in Congressional Elections,* 2d ed. (New Haven: Yale University Press, 1983).

26. Kim Kahn and John Geer, "Political Advertising: Putting First Things First" (Paper delivered at the Annual Meeting of the Midwest Political Science Association, Chicago, April 1991).

27. Gary Jacobson, *Money in Congressional Elections* (New Haven: Yale University Press, 1980); Edie Goldenberg and Michael Traugott, *Campaigning for Congress* (Washington, D.C.: CQ Press, 1984); and Henry Brady and Richard Johnston, "What's the Primary Message: Horse Race or Issue Journalism?" in *Media and Momentum,* ed. Gary Orren and Nelson Polsby (Chatham, N.J.: Chatham House, 1987).

28. Thomas Patterson and Robert McClure, *The Unseeing Eye* (New York: Putnam's, 1976).

29. Richard Joslyn, *Mass Media and Elections* (Reading, Mass.: Addison-Wesley, 1984), 195-203.

30. The Harold Mendelsohn and Irving Crespi quote comes from their book, *Polls, Television, and the New Politics* (Scranton: Chandler, 1970), 248.

31. Montague Kern, *30-Second Politics: Political Advertising in the Eighties* (New York: Praeger, 1989); Richard F. Fenno Jr., *Home Style* (Boston: Little, Brown, 1978); and Larry Sabato, *The Rise of Political Consultants* (New York: Basic Books, 1981). An example of this in regard to the Perot campaign is found in Kevin Sack, "For TV, Perot Spends Heavily on Wart Removal," *New York Times,* October 25, 1992, 28.

32. Donald Cundy, "Political Commercials and Candidate Image," in *New Perspectives on Political Advertising,* ed. Lynda Lee Kaid, Dan Nimmo, and Keith Sanders (Carbondale: Southern Illinois University Press, 1986), 210-234. Also see Michael Pfau and Henry Kenski, *Attack Politics* (New York: Praeger, 1990). A critical theory perspective on the media can be found in Timothy Luke, *Screens of Power* (Champaign: University of Illinois Press, 1989).

33. Paul Taylor and David Broder, "Early Volley of Bush Ads Exceeded Expectations," *Washington Post,* October 28, 1988, A1; "How Bush Won," *Newsweek,* November 21, 1988, 117; Paul Taylor, *See How They Run* (New York: Knopf, 1990); and Elizabeth Kolbert, "Test-Marketing a President: How Focus Groups Pervade Campaign Politics," *New York Times Magazine,* August 30, 1992, 18-21, 60, 68, 72.

34. Anthony DePalma, "For Florio and Courtner, Crucial TV Battle Turns Nasty," *New York Times,* October 2, 1989, B1; Peter Kerr, "New Jersey Election Bogs Down in Mud," *New York Times,* October 16, 1989, B1; Michael Oreskes, "Attack Politics, Rift in Big '88 Race, Comes into Its Own for Lesser Stakes," *New York Times,* October 24, 1989, A24; Michael Oreskes, "What Poison Politics Has

Done to America," *New York Times,* October 29, 1989, E1; and Robin Toner, " 'Wars' Wound Candidates and the Process," *New York Times,* March 19, 1990, 1. A discussion of how the dynamics of attack politics varies between two- and three-way races is found in Elizabeth Kolbert, "Bush Campaign Settles on a Sustained Message," *New York Times,* October 26, 1992, A14.

35. In 1992, Jerry Brown made novel use of an old-fashioned advertising technique. One of his supporters put a sideboard on his pet dog proclaiming that "Bush makes breaks for Fat Cats: Brown is on our side." A picture of this ad appeared in the *Washington Post,* March 16, 1992, A11.

36. Quoted in John Foley, Dennis Britton, and Eugene Everett, Jr., eds., *Nominating a President: The Process and the Press,* 79.

37. William McGuire, "Persuasion, Resistance, and Attitude Change," in *Handbook of Communication,* ed. Ithiel de Sola Pool (Chicago: Rand McNally, 1973), 216-252; and "The Nature of Attitudes and Attitude Change," in *Handbook of Social Psychology,* 2d ed., ed. Gardner Lindzey and Elliot Aronson (Reading, Mass.: Addison-Wesley, 1969), vol. 3, 136-314.

38. Quote taken from David Runkel, ed., *Campaign for President: The Managers Look at '88* (Dover, Mass.: Auburn House, 1989), 142.

39. See Roper Organization, *Trends in Attitudes Toward Television and Other Media: A Twenty-Four Year Review* (New York: Television Information Office, 1983).

40. Michael Robinson, "Public Affairs Television and the Growth of Political Malaise," *American Political Science Review* 70 (1976): 409-432.

41. For a discussion of the role of information in different elections, see Barbara Hinckley, Richard Hofstetter, and John Kessel, "Information and the Vote: A Comparative Election Study," *American Politics Quarterly* 2 (1974): 131-158.

42. There is some disagreement over when the first television ad aired. Stephen Wood cites the 1952 presidential campaign as the starting point in his "Television's First Political Spot Ad Campaign: Eisenhower Answers America," *Presidential Studies Quarterly,* 20 (1990): 265-283. But Jamieson claims that the first televised spot campaign came in the 1950 statewide races.

43. Iyengar and Kinder, *News That Matters.* Also see Marilyn Roberts, "The Agenda Setting Power of Political Advertising" (Ph. D. diss., University of Texas, 1990).

Chapter 2 - The Study of Campaign Ads

1. Quoted in Joe McGinniss, *The Selling of the President* (New York: Simon and Schuster, 1969), 27.
2. One sign of increasing similarity, though, is the tendency of product ads to pinpoint differences with competing products. The conventional wisdom was to refrain from mentioning the name of another company. However, as negative political advertising has demonstrated the power to win support by defining the opposition, product ads have become more likely to note differences with the competition. Hence, it is no longer uncommon to see ads contrasting McDonald's and Burger King or Coke and Pepsi.
3. Figures taken from Nicholas O'Shaughnessy, *The Phenomenon of Political Marketing* (New York: St. Martin's Press, 1990), 61. For a similar point, see Thomas Patterson and Robert McClure, *The Unseeing Eye* (New York: Putnam's, 1976), 110.
4. For example, Kathleen Jamieson presents little evidence on the impact of ads on voters in *Packaging the Presidency*, 2d ed. (New York: Oxford University Press, 1992). Patterson and McClure's *The Unseeing Eye* looks just at the 1972 presidential general election.
5. Surveys included presidential general election studies in 1972, 1976, 1984, 1988, and 1992; presidential nominating polls in 1976, 1988, and 1992; and Senate election studies in 1974, 1990, and 1992. The *New York Times* and *Washington Post* were chosen as newspapers of record because of their national prominence and oft-cited ability to set the agenda of news coverage. CBS was selected to aid comparability with past studies, many of which have used it as the network of record. For a discussion of biases that may result from relying on a single network, see Ann Crigler, Marion Just, and Tim Cook, "Local News, Network News and the 1992 Presidential Campaign" (Paper delivered at the Annual Meeting of the American Political Science Association, Chicago, September 1992).
6. Ernest May and Janet Fraser, eds., *Campaign '72, The Managers Speak* (Cambridge: Harvard University Press, 1973); Jonathan Moore and Janet Fraser, eds., *Campaign for President: The Managers Look at '76* (Cambridge: Ballinger, 1977); Jonathan Moore, ed., *Campaign for President: 1980 in Retrospect* (Cambridge: Ballinger, 1981); John Foley, Dennis Britton, and Eugene Everett, Jr., eds., *Nominating a President: The Process and the Press* (New York: Praeger, 1980); Jonathan Moore, ed., *Campaign for President: The Managers Look at '84* (Dover, Mass.: Auburn House, 1986); Marvin Kalb and Hendrik Hertzberg, *Candidates '88* (Dover, Mass.: Auburn House, 1988); and David Runkel, ed., *Campaign for President: The Managers Look at '88* (Dover, Mass.: Auburn House, 1989). In 1992, I conducted interviews with key journalists listed in the preface at various points during the campaign.
7. For an illustration of this approach, see Samuel Patterson and Thomas

Kephart, "The Case of the Wayfaring Challenger: The 1988 Senate Election in Ohio," *Congress and the Presidency* 18 (1991): 105-120.

8. Two types of regression analyses were used in this study. Depending on whether the object of study was categorical or continuous in measurement, the statistical analysis was based on either ordinary least squares regression (continuous dependent variables) or logistic regression (categorical dependent variables). See George Bohrnstedt and David Knoke, *Statistics for Social Data Analysis,* 2d ed. (Itasca, Ill.: Peacock, 1988); and John Aldrich and Forrest Nelson, *Linear Probability, Logit, and Probit Models* (Beverly Hills, Calif.: Sage, 1984).

9. My study treats the control factors as external to the analysis of advertising. It is possible, of course, that attitudes and background characteristics dictate ad exposure. To make sure this was not the case, I reran this model with party, education, age, sex, ideology, and race treated as exogenous to advertising. The regression estimates for these predictors ranged from .03 to .07, and explained only 2 percent of the overall variation in exposure to campaign advertisements.

10. Some researchers suggest controlling for conversations with friends and family members on the grounds that this is another source of information for people. However, Paul Allen Beck demonstrates that media appeals have a significant impact on conversations about the campaign. This result suggests that conversations are not an independent information source but a factor that is mediated by patterns of media coverage. See Beck, "Voters' Intermediation Environments in the 1988 Presidential Campaign," *Public Opinion Quarterly* 55 (1991), 371-394.

11. These are the races for which appropriate survey questions on ads were asked by independent polling organizations not associated with particular candidates.

12. Roy Behr and Shanto Iyengar, "Television News, Real-World Cues, and Changes in the Public Agenda," *Public Opinion Quarterly* 49 (1985): 38-57. Also see Shanto Iyengar and Donald Kinder, *News That Matters* (Chicago: University of Chicago Press, 1987), 139-140.

13. Herbert Asher discusses path analysis in *Causal Modeling* (Beverly Hills, Calif.: Sage, 1976).

14. The 1972 scale was a combination of exposure and frequency of viewing: "How often have you heard about the presidential campaign from the following source? Television advertisements: many times, several times, one or a few times, or not at any time?" The 1976 items consisted of "Do you remember seeing any television commercials for a presidential candidate?" (yes or no) and "At this particular time, how much attention are you paying to the presidential election campaign—a lot of attention, some attention, or not much attention?" The 1984 items were based on "Both presidential candidates had a lot of television commercials during this campaign. Was there any one commercial that made a strong impression on you?" and "How much attention have you been able to pay to the 1984 presidential cam-

paign—a lot, some, or not much so far?" In 1988 the questions included: "In the past week, have you seen any commercials on television for George Bush [Michael Dukakis]?" (yes or no) and "How much attention have you paid to these commercials for George Bush [Michael Dukakis]—a lot, some, not much, or no attention so far?" The 1990 items for the Rhode Island Senate race consisted of the following: "In the past month, have you seen any commercials on television for Claiborne Pell [Claudine Schneider]?" (yes or no) and "How much attention have you paid to these commercials for Claiborne Pell [Claudine Schneider]—a lot, some, not much, or no attention so far?" The 1990 North Carolina Senate question was as follows: "How many advertisements for the Gantt [Helms] campaign have you seen on TV all together—many, some, a few, or none?" The 1992 results were based on "How many days in the last week have you seen presidential campaign ads on television for [name of candidate]: five days or more, three or four days, one or two days, or not at any time?"

15. Vincent Price and John Zaller, "Measuring Individual Differences in Likelihood of News Reception" (Paper delivered at the Annual Meeting of the American Political Science Association, San Francisco, August 1990).

16. Patterson and McClure, *The Unseeing Eye,* 110.

17. Ibid., appendix, esp. 193-195.

18. The question wording for the dependent variables in this table were as follows: "Richard Nixon favors honoring our commitments to other nations: 1) extremely likely, 2) quite likely, 3) slightly likely, 4) not sure, 5) slightly unlikely, 6) quite unlikely, 7) extremely unlikely"; "George McGovern favors an immediate pull-out of all U.S. troops from Vietnam: 1) extremely likely, 2) quite likely, 3) slightly likely, 4) not sure, 5) slightly unlikely, 6) quite unlikely, 7) extremely unlikely"; "Richard Nixon will win the presidential election: 1) extremely likely, 2) quite likely, 3) slightly likely, 4) not sure, 5) slightly unlikely, 6) quite unlikely, 7) extremely unlikely"; and "There are many problems of concern to people today. Based on your own everyday experiences, what one political problem matters most to you personally?" (open-ended responses coded 1 for mention of foreign affairs and 0 for other topics). The question wording for the control variables included here is given in the Appendix.

19. The model also shows that Republicans, conservatives, and whites were likely to see Nixon as electable; and the people likely to see Nixon as honoring commitments were Republicans, the well-educated, whites, and those with high newspaper exposure. Individuals most likely to believe McGovern favored withdrawal from Vietnam were the well-educated and those with high newspaper exposure. Most of the respondents who thought foreign affairs was the most important problem facing the country were women.

Chapter 3 - The Strategic Use of Commercials

1. The contemporary era is considered to have a monopoly on costly races, but examples from the past demonstrate that this is not the case. George Washington's first campaign featured extensive efforts at mobilizing support: "When he ran for the Virginia House of Burgesses from Fairfax County in 1757, he provided his friends with the 'customary means of winning votes': namely 28 gallons of rum, 50 gallons of rum punch, 34 gallons of wine, 46 gallons of beer, and 2 gallons of cider royal. Even in those days this was considered a large campaign expenditure, because there were only 391 voters in his district, for an average outlay of more than a quart and a half per person." This quote is cited by George Thayer, *Who Shakes the Money Tree?* (New York: Simon and Schuster, 1973), 25.

2. Kathleen Jamieson, *Packaging the Presidency*, 2d ed. (New York: Oxford University Press, 1992), 50. Jamieson (pp. 6-7) points out that scurrilous attacks on political opponents have been characteristic of American campaigns from the beginning.

3. Quoted in ibid., 195. For a description of Johnson's strategy, see Edwin Diamond and Stephen Bates, *The Spot* (Cambridge: MIT Press, 1984), 127-140.

4. One notable exception is Jamieson, *Packaging the Presidency*.

5. Elizabeth Kolbert, "Secrecy over TV Ads, or, The Peculiar Logic of Political Combat," *New York Times,* September 17, 1992, A21.

6. Jules Witcover describes the detailed planning documents prepared by Carter advisers in his book, *Marathon* (New York: Viking Press, 1977).

7. This quote is taken from Jonathan Moore, ed., *Campaign for President: The Managers Look at '84* (Dover, Mass.: Auburn House, 1986), 206. An example regarding the use of focus groups to influence Mondale's advertising themes against Hart is found on 78-79.

8. Anthony Downs, *An Economic Theory of Democracy* (New York: Harper, 1957).

9. Benjamin Page, *Choices and Echoes in Presidential Elections* (Chicago: University of Chicago Press, 1978), chapter 2.

10. This quote comes from Joe McGinniss, *The Selling of the President* (New York: Simon and Schuster, 1969), 34.

11. Robert Spero, *The Duping of the American Voter* (New York: Lippincott and Crowell, 1980). Also see Lawrence Grossman, "Reflections on Television's Role in American Presidential Elections" (Discussion Paper D-3, the Joan Shorenstein Barone Center on the Press, Politics and Public Policy, Harvard University, January 1990).

12. The 1988 results were taken from the October 21-24 CBS News/*New York Times* poll. This survey was a national random sample of 1,287 registered voters. The 1992 figures come from a poll of southern states undertaken by the *Atlanta Journal-Constitution,* October 24-27 with 976 likely voters. Pama Mitchell, polling director at the newspaper,

kindly made the data available to me.

13. See Leonard Shyles, "Defining 'Images' of Presidential Candidates from Televised Political Spot Advertisements," *Political Behavior* 6, 1984: 171-181; and "Defining the Issues of a Presidential Election from Televised Political Spot Advertisements," *Journal of Broadcasting* 27 (1983): 333-343.

14. Richard Joslyn, "The Content of Political Spot Ads," *Journalism Quarterly* 57 (1980): 97. Also see Margaret Latimer, "Political Advertising for Federal and State Elections: Images or Substance?" *Journalism Quarterly* 62 (1985): 861-868.

15. See C. Richard Hofstetter and Cliff Zukin, "TV Network News and Advertising in the Nixon and McGovern Campaigns," *Journalism Quarterly* 56 (1979), 106-115, 152; Thomas Patterson and Robert McClure, *The Unseeing Eye* (New York: Putnam's, 1976); and Michael Robinson and Margaret Sheehan, *Over the Wire and on TV* (New York: Russell Sage, 1983), 144-147.

16. Samuel Popkin argues that voters can take cues about more general matters from small bites of information. See Popkin, *The Reasoning Voter* (Chicago: University of Chicago Press, 1991). A similar argument appears in Thomas Byrne Edsall, "Willie Horton's Message," *New York Review of Books,* February 13, 1992, 7-11.

17. However, campaign commercials that receive the most attention are not always the most aired. For example, the "Daisy" ad in 1964 and Humphrey's poverty and war commercial in 1968 were not aired frequently, but they achieved notoriety.

18. A third complication pointed out by Jamieson is that not all ads are aired equally. One of the most obvious ways in which the strategic behavior of campaigns is manifest in the advertising arena is through what are called "time buys," the amount of air time actually purchased for particular ads. A complete analysis obviously would need to incorporate information on these time buys. Unfortunately, though, it is very difficult to reconstruct accurate time buy information for all ads from 1952 to 1992.

19. There is some variation in the completeness of the archives holdings by year, campaign stage, and type of ad. The archive is less comprehensive for the 1950s and 1960s than for the 1970s, 1980s, and 1990s. It is more complete for general election than for nomination advertisements. Holdings furthermore are uneven for radio and newspaper commercials, non-English ads, those aired by independent groups, and commercials that were produced but not aired. Since the archive does not have complete listings for Senate ads, I limited my analysis to presidential contests. Ten ads from the general election and two from the nomination stage were drawn for each presidential nominee from 1972 to 1988. Lists were provided by the archive, and ads for each candidate were randomly selected. Typical ads for 1992 were drawn randomly from tapes made available by consultants to the major candidates.

20. Jamieson, *Packaging the Presidency.* Presentations of more than five minutes were not included due to the multiple nature of the messages presented. Jamieson's book does not cover 1992, so prominent ads for that year were identified as those mentioned during the CBS Evening News.
21. For example, 1960 is underrepresented by Jamieson. Only two Republican spot ads during that general election were mentioned by her, compared to twelve for Kennedy in the fall. In general, though, it still is preferable to rely on ad historians in 1960 than a list of ads discussed in newspapers and on television. As shown in Chapter 4, there has been a dramatic increase in news coverage of advertising since that time, which obviously would bias a newspaper or television list quite seriously.
22. Jamieson, *Packaging the Presidency,* 83.
23. The patterns were different for typical ads. Twenty-three percent of appeals in 1984 were specific, 21 percent were in 1988, and 26 percent were in 1992.
24. Angus Campbell, Philip Converse, Warren Miller, and Donald Stokes, *The American Voter* (New York: Wiley, 1960).
25. Jamieson, *Packaging the Presidency,* 115.
26. Norman Nie, Sidney Verba, and John Petrocik, *The Changing American Voter,* enl. ed. (Cambridge: Harvard University Press, 1979).
27. Jamieson, *Packaging the Presidency,* 242.
28. However, the prominent ad listing underrepresents commercials on women's issues because, according to Jamieson, a long historical section dealing with the subject in her book, *Packaging the Presidency,* was cut from the final manuscript. Among the ads not described in her book that did appeal to social issues were Ellen McCormick's ads on abortion in 1976, Mondale on Jerry Falwell in 1984, the Roslyn Carter ad in 1980, and several 1972 Florida primary ads on busing.
29. Ibid., 411.
30. Wilder's strategy is described in Michael Oreskes, "Virginia Campaign Watched as Test on Abortion Rights," *New York Times,* October 29, 1989, A1; and Robin Toner, "The Selling of the First Black Governor, in the Seat of the Old Confederacy," *New York Times,* November 10, 1989, A10. The 1992 congressional advertising involving abortion is discussed by Keith Glover in "Campaigning Crusaders Air Graphic Anti-Abortion Ads," *Congressional Quarterly Weekly Report,* September 26, 1992, 2970-2972.
31. The quotes come from Jamieson, *Packaging the Presidency,* 342, 384. Diamond and Bates describe Carter's strategy in their book, *The Spot.*
32. Jamieson, *Packaging the Presidency,* 338, 386.
33. See David Gopoian, "Issue Preferences and Candidate Choice in Presidential Primaries," *American Journal of Political Science* 26 (1982): 523-546, and Larry Bartels, "Issue Voting Under Uncertainty," *American Journal of Political Science* 30 (1986): 709-728.

34. Jamieson, *Packaging the Presidency,* 338, 386, 395.
35. Larry Sabato, *The 1988 Elections in America* (Glenview, Ill.: Scott, Foresman, 1989), 24. The 1989 New Jersey elections also elicited considerable press coverage about negative advertising. See Anthony DePalma, "For Florio and Courtner, Crucial TV Battle Turns Nasty," *New York Times,* October 2, 1989, B1; Peter Kerr, "New Jersey Election Bogs Down in Mud," *New York Times,* October 16, 1989, B1; Michael Oreskes, "Attack Politics, Rift in Big '88 Race, Comes into Its Own for Lesser Stakes," *New York Times,* October 24, 1989, A24; Michael Oreskes, "What Poison Politics Has Done to America," *New York Times,* October 29, 1989, E1; and Robin Toner, " 'Wars' Wound Candidates and the Process," *New York Times,* March 19, 1990, 1. A more general discussion of negative ads can be found in Joseph Napolitan, "Negative Campaigning" (Paper delivered at the Annual Conference of the International Association of Political Consultants, Nice, France, October 1989).
36. L. Patrick Devlin, "Contrasts in Presidential Campaign Commercials of 1988," *American Behavioral Scientist* 32 (1989): 401.
37. This quote comes from the "CBS Evening News," February 26, 1992.
38. Quoted in Robert Lineberry with George Edwards, *Government in America,* 4th ed. (Glenview, Ill.: Scott, Foresman, 1989), 153.
39. William Riker, "Why Negative Campaigning is Rational: The Rhetoric of the Ratification Campaign of 1787-1788" (Paper delivered at the Annual Meeting of the American Political Science Association, Atlanta, August 1989).
40. Jamieson finds lower levels of "opposition" ads from 1952 to 1988. But she restricts her analysis to presidential general elections and adopts a different definition from mine. According to her formulation, the ad is oppositional "if more than 50 percent of the ad focuses on the record of the opponent without providing comparative information about what the sponsoring candidate would have done or germane information about the sponsoring candidate's record." My formulation classifies an ad as negative if unflattering, threatening, or pejorative statements are made, regardless of whether comparative information is provided. Often, candidates attack without telling what they would do about a particular problem. For information on Jamieson's approach, see her book, *Dirty Politics: Deception, Distraction, and Democracy* (New York: Oxford University Press, 1992), 270 (chart 4-3).
41. Jamieson, *Packaging the Presidency,* 197.
42. Ibid., 232.
43. Diamond and Bates, *The Spot,* 179.
44. Jamieson, *Packaging the Presidency,* 245.
45. Ibid., 407. Also see L. Patrick Devlin, "Contrasts in Presidential Campaign Commercials of 1980," *Political Communications Review,* 7 (1982): 11-12.
46. L. Patrick Devlin, "Contrasts in Presidential Campaign Commercials of 1984," *Political Communications Review* 12 (1987): 26.

47. L. Patrick Devlin, "Contrasts in Presidential Campaign Commercials of 1988," *American Behavioral Scientist* 32 (1989): 390.

48. The comparable figures for negativity in typical ads were the campaign (67 percent), foreign policy (64 percent), international affairs (53 percent), domestic performance (44 percent), domestic policy (37 percent), personal qualities (31 percent), and party (25 percent). For a similar interpretation, see Renee Loth, "The Word Is In: Negative Is Positive," *Boston Globe*, March 30, 1992, 8.

49. Devlin, "Contrasts in Presidential Campaign Commercials of 1988," 389.

50. Michael Oreskes, "TV Is a Player in Crucial Race for California," *New York Times*, April 29, 1990, 22. Also see M. Charles Bakst, "Sundlun, Paolino Television Commercials Take Negative Turn," *Providence Journal*, June 10, 1990, D1.

51. See Karen Johnson-Cartee and Gary Copeland, "Southern Voters' Reaction to Negative Political Ads in 1986 Election," *Journalism Quarterly* 66 (1989): 888-893, 986. Also see Brian Roddy and Gina Garramone, "Appeals and Strategies of Negative Political Advertising," *Journal of Broadcasting and Electronic Media* 32 (1988): 415-427; Gina Garramone, "Voter Responses to Negative Political Ads," *Journalism Quarterly* 61 (1984): 250-259; and Gina Garramone, "Effects of Negative Political Advertising," *Journal of Broadcasting and Electronic Media* 29 (1985): 147-159.

Chapter 4 - Media Coverage of Ads

1. For a review, see Doris Graber, *Mass Media and American Politics*, 3d ed. (Washington, D.C.: CQ Press, 1989); Michael Baruch Grossman and Martha Joynt Kumar, *Portraying the President: The White House and the News Media* (Baltimore: Johns Hopkins University Press, 1981); and Dorothy Davidson Nesbit, *Videostyle in Senate Campaigns* (Knoxville: University of Tennessee Press, 1988).

2. Michael Robinson and Margaret Sheehan, *Over the Wire and on TV* (New York: Russell Sage, 1983), 149. Also see Edie Goldenberg and Michael Traugott, *Campaigning for Congress* (Washington, D.C.: CQ Press, 1984); Peter Clarke and Susan Evans, *Covering Campaigns: Journalism in Congressional Elections* (Stanford: Stanford University Press, 1983); F. Christopher Arterton, "Campaign Organizations Confront the Media-Political Environment," in *Race for the Presidency*, ed. James David Barber (Englewood Cliffs, N.J.: Prentice Hall, 1978), 3-24; and Donald Matthews, "Winnowing," in *Race for the Presidency*, 55-78.

3. Nelson Polsby discusses the faddishness of press coverage in "The News Media as an Alternative to Party in the Presidential Selection Process," in *Political Parties in the Eighties*, Robert Goldwin ed. (Washington, D.C.: American Enterprise Institute, 1980), 50-66.

4. For an engaging analysis of expectations, see Larry Bartels, *Presidential Primaries and the Dynamics of Public Choice* (Princeton: Princeton University Press, 1988).

5. For a discussion of Vietnam, see Kathleen Turner, *Lyndon Johnson's Dual War: Vietnam and the Press* (Chicago: University of Chicago Press, 1985); Peter Braestrup, *Big Story: How the American Press and Television Reported and Interpreted the Crisis of Tet 1968 in Vietnam and Washington* (Boulder, Colo.: Westview Press, 1977); and Daniel Hallin, "The Media, the War in Vietnam and Political Support," *Journal of Politics* 46 (1984): 2-24. Gladys and Kurt Lang analyze media coverage of Watergate in their book, *The Battle for Public Opinion: The President, the Press, and the Polls During Watergate* (New York: Columbia University Press, 1983).

6. Herbert Gans discusses newsgathering techniques in his book, *Deciding What's News: A Study of CBS Evening News, NBC Nightly News, Newsweek and Time* (New York: Vintage, 1979). Also see Stephen Hess, *The Washington Reporters* (Washington, D.C.: Brookings Institution, 1981); and Leon Sigal, *Reporters and Officials: The Organization and Politics of Newsmaking* (Lexington, Mass.: D.C. Heath, 1973).

7. One illustration of this insider approach is a book by Timothy Crouse, *The Boys on the Bus* (New York: Ballantine, 1973).

8. See Theodore White, *The Making of the President 1960* (New York: Atheneum, 1961), for an early example of White's style of analysis. For example, White shows how Nixon's paranoia about the press pervaded his entire staff. One aide said in June 1960: "Stuff the bastards. They're all against Dick anyway. Make them work—we aren't going to hand out prepared remarks; let them get their pencils out and listen and take notes," p. 366.

9. There are a number of excellent reviews of changes in the presidential nominating process. See John Kessel, *Presidential Campaign Politics* (Homewood, Ill.: Dorsey Press, 1980); James Ceaser, *Presidential Selection* (Princeton: Princeton University Press, 1979); Byron Shafer, *Quiet Revolution: The Struggle for the Democratic Party and the Shaping of Post-Reform Politics* (New York: Russell Sage, 1983); and Martin Wattenberg, *The Rise of Candidate-Centered Politics* (Cambridge: Harvard University Press, 1991).

10. Henry Brady and Richard Johnston, "What's the Primary Message: Horse Race or Issue Journalism?" in *Media and Momentum*, ed. Gary Orren and Nelson Polsby (Chatham, N.J.: Chatham House, 1987), 162; and Graber, *Mass Media and American Politics*, 190. Also see Matthew Kerbel, "Coverage of the 1992 Primaries on Network and Cable Television through 'Super Tuesday'" (Paper delivered at the Annual Meeting of the Midwest Political Science Association, Chicago, April 1992).

11. Robinson and Sheehan, *Over the Wire and on TV*, 149.

12. Bernard Berelson, Paul Lazarsfeld, and William McPhee, *Voting*

(Chicago: University of Chicago Press, 1954), 106. Also quoted in Thomas Patterson, *The Mass Media Election* (New York: Praeger, 1980), 105.

13. Patterson, *The Mass Media Election,* 105.

14. Hugh Winebrenner discusses how Iowa was turned into a "media event" in his book, *The Iowa Precinct Caucuses* (Ames: Iowa State University Press, 1987).

15. Research assistants went through the *Times* and *Post* indexes of presidential election years and located stories about advertising. Press coverage was divided between the nominating period, which was defined as January 1 to the time of the California primary in each election year, and the general election, which ran from September 1 to election day. Articles were reviewed to determine the nature of the coverage. The study of television news proceeded along similar lines. Using the *Vanderbilt Television News Index and Abstracts,* which summarizes news stories for each network, reviewers tabulated the number and content of stories about political commercials that appeared Monday through Friday for the nominating process (January 1 until the California primary in June) and general election (September 1 to election day) each presidential year. The CBS analysis starts in 1972 because that was the first full presidential election year for which the abstracting service at Vanderbilt University compiled transcripts for the network evening news. CBS is used as the network of record in order to maintain comparability with past studies.

16. Appendix Table A-3 presents a breakdown of the CBS stories about paid ads by party, campaign stage, and election year. There were interesting partisan differences in ad coverage by campaign stage. More Democratic ads ($N = 60$) were discussed during the nominating process than Republican ones ($N = 34$). This was undoubtedly due to the larger number of competitive Democratic than Republican primaries between 1972 and 1992. Democrats had competitive races in every election year during this period, whereas Republicans had nomination battles only in 1976, 1980, 1988, and 1992. However, during the general election, the opposite was true. More Republican commercials ($N = 28$) received free CBS air time in fall campaigns than Democratic ads ($N = 12$). This was especially the case in 1988, when there were ten stories about Bush ads, but only five about those of Dukakis (there also were six joint stories about their ads). Apparently, the well-publicized confrontation between Bush and CBS anchorman Dan Rather at the time of the New Hampshire primary did not reduce Bush's air time.

17. For similar results on the general election from 1972 to 1988 based on all three networks, see Lynda Lee Kaid, Rob Gobetz, Jane Garner, Chris Leland, and David Scott, "Television News and Presidential Campaigns: The Legitimization of Televised Political Advertising," *Social Science Quarterly* (in press).

18. The early 1960s, though, were an exception to the pattern just

described. There was little coverage of ads during the close campaign of 1960 and during those of earlier years. Remember that advertising was in its infancy at that time. There was little attention paid to television advertising or to the way in which the media could alter campaign dynamics. Johnson's 1964 landslide, though, generated eighteen articles on advertising from September through election day. There was unusual interest in advertising that year as a result of the controversial "Daisy" ad, which provoked several stories itself. Furthermore, 1964 was when it became apparent that advertising was dominating the campaign and helping to define candidates' images. After that race and the subsequent publication of Joe McGinniss's book on Nixon's 1968 advertising campaign (*The Selling of the President* [New York: Simon and Schuster, 1969]), awareness of television advertising became much higher among reporters.

19. Robinson and Sheehan, *Over the Wire and on TV*. This tendency in news coverage was less likely to be the case for ads for Republicans (61 percent) than for Democrats (68 percent).

20. Quote cited in David Runkel, ed., *Campaign for President: The Managers Look at '88*, (Dover, Mass.: Auburn House, 1989), 136.

21. Kathleen Jamieson, *Packaging the Presidency*, 2d ed. (New York: Oxford University Press, 1992), 198.

22. Ibid., 200-201.

23. See Kiku Adatto, "Sound Bite Democracy: Network Evening News Presidential Campaign Coverage, 1968 and 1988" (Research Paper R-2, Joan Shorenstein Barone Center for Press, Politics, and Public Policy, June 1990); and Kiku Adatto, "The Incredible Shrinking Sound Bite," *New Republic*, May 29, 1990, 20-23. Jack White discusses Horton in "Bush's Most Valuable Player," *Time*, November 14, 1988, 20-21.

24. Kathleen Jamieson described the development of Ad Watches in a telephone conversation with me on January 30, 1992.

25. I spoke by telephone with Howard Kurtz on April 8, 1992, with Mara Liasson on April 27, 1992, and with Renee Loth on April 27, 1992.

26. Quoted in Howard Kurtz, "In Advertising Give and Take, Clinton Camp Took and Responded," *Washington Post*, November 6, 1992, A10.

27. The question was: "How helpful to viewers would you say these stories about campaign ads have been? 1) very helpful, 2) somewhat helpful, or 3) not very helpful."

28. E. J. Dionne, Jr., "Buchanan TV Spot Assails Arts Agency," *Washington Post*, February 27, 1992, A11.

29. The Ad Watch column by Howard Kurtz is found in the *Washington Post*, February 28, 1992, A20, and by Renee Loth in the *Boston Globe*, February 28, 1992, 12. Also see Howard Kurtz, "Buchanan Ad Consultant Turns Tables on Bush," *Washington Post*, February 28, 1992, A1, A20, and the response of Marlon Riggs, a journalism professor at the University of California at Berkeley, in "Meet the

New Willie Horton," *New York Times,* March 6, 1992, A33.

30. See Robin Toner, "Moving Toward a Crucial Round, Presidential Contest Turns Rough," *New York Times,* February 28, 1992, A1, A17; Elizabeth Kolbert, "Bitter G.O.P. Air War Reflects Competitiveness of Georgia Race," *New York Times,* February 28, 1992, A16; and Alessandra Stanley, "Gay Groups React Coolly to Buchanan Commercials," *New York Times,* March 8, 1992, 26.

31. See Ad Watch column by Howard Kurtz in the *Washington Post,* February 28, 1992, A20, and Kurtz, "Buchanan Ad Consultant Turns Tables on Bush."

32. Renee Loth, Ad Watch, *Boston Globe,* February 28, 1992, 12.

33. Radio ironically may be the most effective medium for Ad Watches because of its ability to replay commercials without the video. However, as pointed out by Mara Liasson, radio has a far smaller audience than television news or newspapers.

34. For a review of CNN's coverage, see Jerry Hagstrom, "Ad Attack," *National Journal,* May 4, 1992, 810-815. Brooks Jackson's analysis was given in a telephone interview with me on July 20, 1992. Jackson also cited focus group research by Jamieson showing that 67 percent of Georgia Republicans who saw Buchanan's ad thought it was unfair.

35. For extended reviews of radio ads, see Kolbert, "Fueled by Words Alone, Radio Ads Are Nastier," *New York Times,* October 5, 1992, A17; Kolbert, "Bush and Clinton Customize Their TV and Radio Ads in the Swing States," *New York Times,* October 22, 1992, A20; and Kolbert, "For the Most Negative Ads, Turn on the Nearest Radio," *New York Times,* October 30, 1992, A19.

36. Quoted in Darrell West, Montague Kern, and Dean Alger, "Political Advertising and Ad Watches in the 1992 Presidential Nominating Campaign" (Paper delivered at the Annual Meeting of the American Political Science Association, Chicago, September 1992). Several networks in 1992 also used focus groups after debates to evaluate candidates' performances.

37. I spoke by telephone with Mara Liasson on April 27, 1992.

Chapter 5 - Learning About the Candidates

1. Thomas Patterson and Robert McClure, *The Unseeing Eye* (New York: Putnam's, 1976). Also see Robert Meadow and Lee Sigelman, "Some Effects and Noneffects of Campaign Commercials," *Political Behavior* 4 (1982): 163-174, and, for a more extended review of past media studies, Harold Mendelsohn and Irving Crespi, *Polls, Television, and the New Politics* (Scranton: Chandler, 1970). However, for a different interpretation, see Donald Cundy, "Political Commercials and Candidate Image," in *New Perspectives on Political Advertising,* ed. Lynda Lee Kaid, Dan Nimmo, and Keith Sanders (Carbondale: Southern Illinois University Press, 1986), 210-234.

2. Prominent studies include Gina Garramone, "Issue Versus Image Orientation and Effects of Political Advertising," *Communication Research* 10 (1983): 59-76; and Charles Atkin and Gary Heald, "Effects of Political Advertising," *Public Opinion Quarterly* 40 (1976): 216-228.

3. Kathleen Jamieson, *Packaging the Presidency*, 2d ed. (New York: Oxford University Press, 1992); Edwin Diamond and Stephen Bates, *The Spot* (Cambridge: MIT Press, 1984); L. Patrick Devlin, "Contrasts in Presidential Campaign Commercials of 1988," *American Behavioral Scientist* 32 (1989): 389-414.

4. William McGuire, "Persuasion, Resistance, and Attitude Change," in *Handbook of Communication*, ed. Ithiel de Sola Pool (Chicago: Rand McNally, 1973), 216-252; Kaid, Nimmo, and Sanders, *New Perspectives on Political Advertising;* and Lynda Lee Kaid, "Political Advertising," in *Handbook of Political Communication*, ed. Dan Nimmo and Keith Sanders (Beverly Hills, Calif.: Sage, 1981), 249-271.

5. Patterson and McClure, *The Unseeing Eye.*

6. Gina Garramone, "Issue versus Image Orientation"; Ronald Mulder, "The Effects of Televised Political Ads in the 1975 Chicago Mayoral Election," *Journalism Quarterly* 56 (1979): 25-36; Atkin and Heald, "Effects of Political Advertising"; and Charles Atkin, Lawrence Bowen, Oguz Nayman, and Kenneth Sheinkopf, "Quality versus Quantity in Televised Political Ads," *Public Opinion Quarterly* 37 (1973): 209-224.

7. Alan Abramowitz, "Viability, Electability, and Candidate Choice in a Presidential Primary Election," *Journal of Politics* 51 (1989): 977-992, and David Gopoian, "Issue Preferences and Candidate Choice in Presidential Primaries," *American Journal of Political Science* 26 (1982): 523-546.

8. Larry Bartels, *Presidential Primaries and the Dynamics of Public Choice* (Princeton: Princeton University Press, 1988), and Edie Goldenberg and Michael Traugott, *Campaigning for Congress* (Washington, D.C.: CQ Press, 1984), 85-91.

9. See Stanley Kelley, Jr., and Thad Mirer, "The Simple Act of Voting," *American Political Science Review* 68 (1974): 572-591. However, National Election Study coding of likes and dislikes allows for issue-oriented material as well as affective qualities.

10. Quoted in Patterson and McClure, *The Unseeing Eye*, 130.

11. John Kessel, *Presidential Campaign Politics* (Homewood, Ill.: Dorsey Press, 1980).

12. J. Gregory Payne, John Marlier, and Robert Baukus, "Polispots in the 1988 Presidential Primaries," *American Behavioral Scientist* 32 (1989): 365-381. Also see Richard F. Fenno, Jr., *The United States Senate: A Bicameral Perspective* (Washington, D.C.: American Enterprise Institute, 1982).

13. Upon hearing this story at a postelection campaign seminar, John Anderson quipped that Dole's fourteen seconds consisted of a news

report about his car breaking down in New Hampshire. Both stories are taken from Jonathan Moore, ed., *Campaign for President: 1980 in Retrospect* (Cambridge: Ballinger, 1981), 129-130.

14. The 1990 Rhode Island Senate race again was an exception as both incumbents were very well liked. In September Pell had a 75 percent favorability rating, while Schneider had a 66 percent rating.

15. In the 1974 National Election Study, candidate recognition was a dichotomous variable (heard coded 1/not heard coded 5) based on "Now let's talk about the campaign for Senator. Do you remember what the candidates' names were?" The 1976 Patterson survey used "I am going to read the names of people who have been mentioned as possible candidates for the Democratic and Republican presidential nominations. As I read each name tell me if you have: 1) never heard the name before, 2) if you have heard the name, but really don't know anything about him, or 3) if you know something about him. First, how about [candidate]?" In the 1984 and 1988 CBS, 1990 Rhode Island, and 1992 surveys, candidate recognition was based on: "Is your opinion of [candidate] favorable, not favorable, undecided, or haven't you heard enough about [candidate] yet to have an opinion?" Recognition was a two-category variable in which those saying they were favorable or unfavorable were coded 0 as recognizing the candidate, and those who were undecided or said they hadn't heard enough were classified 1 as not recognizing the candidate. The North Carolina question gauged citizen familiarity with the Senate race: "How much do you think you know about the Gantt-Helms Senate race—1) a lot, 2) some, 3) only a little, or 4) nothing at all?" The 1972 Patterson and McClure survey did not include a recognition question.

16. The favorability item in the 1974 National Election Study was based on: "Was there anything in particular about the Democratic/Republican candidate for Senator that made you want to vote for him?" (coded 0 if yes and 1 if no). The 1976 Patterson survey used: "Now I'd like to get your feelings on those candidates whom you know something about. Please look at Card 2. You can use this scale to give us an indication of your feelings toward the candidates. If you feel extremely favorable toward a candidate, you would give him the number 1. If you feel fairly favorable, you would give him the number 2. If you feel only slightly favorable, you would give him a 3. If your feelings are mixed between favorable and unfavorable, you would give him a 4. Suppose, however, that you feel unfavorable toward a candidate. You would give him a 7 if you feel extremely unfavorable, a 6 if fairly unfavorable, and a 5 if only slightly unfavorable. Which number on the scale best describes your feelings about [candidate]?" In the 1984 and 1988 CBS, 1990 Rhode Island, and 1992 surveys, candidate favorability was based on: "Is your opinion of [candidate] favorable, not favorable, undecided, or haven't you heard enough about [candidate] yet to have an opinion?" Favorability was measured as a three-category item (1 favorable, 2 undecided, 3 not favorable). The

1972 Patterson and McClure and 1990 North Carolina Senate surveys did not include questions on favorability.

17. Quoted in "How He Won," *Newsweek,* November/December 1992 (special issue), 64.

18. The question wording for electability in the 1972 Patterson and McClure study was: "Richard Nixon will win the presidential election: 1) extremely likely, 2) quite likely, 3) slightly likely, 4) not sure, 5) slightly unlikely, 6) quite unlikely, 7) extremely unlikely." The 1976 Patterson survey used: "Let's consider the Democratic/Republican candidates whom you know something about. We'd like to know what chance you think each candidate has of becoming his party's nominee for President. Look at Card 3. This scale is similar to the one we just worked with. If you think it likely that a candidate will get his party's nomination you would select a 1, 2, or 3; if unlikely, then a 5, 6, or 7. Select a 4 if you feel it is as likely to happen as not to happen. It is important to base your opinions only on whether you think a candidate will be the nominee, and not on whether you want him to be the nominee. Which number on the card best describes the likelihood that [candidate] will be the Democratic/Republican presidential nominee?" Electability in the 1988 CBS, 1990 Rhode Island, and 1992 surveys was measured as a dichotomous variable (1 if electable, 0 if not electable) by the question: "Regardless of which candidate you support [for the nomination], which of these (Democratic/Republican) candidates do you think would have the best chance of winning the election in November [if he were nominated]?" No electability item was asked in the 1974 National Election Study, the 1984 CBS survey, or the 1990 North Carolina survey.

19. The question wordings in the 1972 Patterson and McClure study were: "Richard Nixon favors honoring our commitments to other nations: 1) extremely likely, 2) quite likely, 3) slightly likely, 4) not sure, 5) slightly unlikely, 6) quite unlikely, 7) extremely unlikely"; "George McGovern favors an immediate pull-out of all U.S. troops from Vietnam: 1) extremely likely, 2) quite likely, 3) slightly likely, 4) not sure, 5) slightly unlikely, 6) quite unlikely, 7) extremely unlikely," and "Richard Nixon/George McGovern is experienced in government: 1) extremely likely, 2) quite likely, 3) slightly likely, 4) not sure, 5) slightly unlikely, 6) quite unlikely, 7) extremely unlikely."

20. The 1976 Patterson survey used scales of 1 through 7 for candidates' positions and character traits: "There is a lot of talk these days about the level of spending by the federal government for social welfare programs. Some people feel that the current level of social welfare spending is necessary because almost everyone receiving this government help really needs it. Others feel a great deal of this social welfare spending is wasted because a lot of people receiving this government help don't deserve it. Where would you place [candidate] on this scale or don't you know about his position? 1 is current level of social welfare is necessary and 7 is a great deal of current social welfare

spending is wasted"; "Some people think our military strength has diminished in comparison to Russia and that much more must be spent on planes, ships, and weapons to build a stronger defense. Others feel that our military defense is adequate and that no increase in military spending is currently necessary. Where would you place [candidate] on this scale, or don't you know about his position? 1 is spend much more on military defense and 7 is no increase in military defense spending"; "Now, we'd like to discuss a few of the presidential candidates with you. People have different opinions about the specific qualities of individual candidates. Look at Card 4. Some people think that a certain candidate is very trustworthy, that is, they feel he is completely sincere, truthful, straightforward, and honest. Others might think that the same candidate is very untrustworthy. Which number best describes your feeling about [candidate] or don't you know how trustworthy or untrustworthy he is? 1 is very trustworthy and 7 is very untrustworthy"; and "Next, whether or not a candidate has a great deal of ability, that is, competent, capable, and skillful. Which number best describes your feeling about [candidate] or don't you know about him? 1 is great deal of ability and 7 is almost no ability."

21. Questions in the 1988 CBS nominating study included: "Right now, would you say the United States is 1) superior in military strength to the Soviet Union, 2) is about equal in strength, or 3) is not as strong as the Soviet Union?" "Are imports of Japanese goods 1) creating unfair competition for U.S. industries, or 2) are Japanese imports really being blamed for U.S. industrial problems?" "In order to reduce the size of the federal budget deficit, would you be 1) willing, or 2) not willing to pay more in federal taxes?" "Do you think that [candidate] 1) says what he really believes most of the time, or 2) says what he thinks people want to hear?" "Regardless of which candidate you support for the nomination, which of these Democratic/Republican candidates do you think cares the most about the needs and problems of people like yourself?" (coded 1 for mention of each candidate and 0 if not), and "Do you think that [candidate] has strong qualities of leadership?" (coded 1 if yes and 2 if no).

22. Michael Kelly, "Clinton, After Raising Hopes, Tries to Lower Expectations," *New York Times,* November 9, 1992, A1.

23. The 1992 nominating questions were based on: "Regardless of which candidate you support for the nomination, which of these candidates do you think cares the most about the needs and problems of people like yourself?" (coded 1 for mention of each candidate and 0 if not); "Which of these candidates do you think can best handle the economy?" (coded 1 for mention of each candidate and 0 if not); and "We'd like to know your impressions of the candidates. Please tell us whether you 1) strongly agree, 2) agree, 3) disagree, or 4) strongly disagree with the following statement: [candidate] is honest and trustworthy." The 1992 general election questions included: "Now we would like to know something about the feelings you have toward

[candidate]. Has [candidate]—because of the kind of person he is, or because of something he has done—ever made you feel hopeful/disgusted/excited? (yes or no)"; "If [candidate] were elected President, would he make the U.S. economy get better, get worse, or stay about the same?"; and "If [candidate] were elected President, would he improve America's standing in the world? (yes or no)."

24. The multivariate model for the 1990 Rhode Island Senate race controlled for party identification, education, age, and sex only. The 1990 North Carolina poll did not include a measure for political interest. The 1988 CBS Super Tuesday nominating study did not include a question on free media exposure.

25. This quote comes from an interview with the author conducted July 20, 1992.

26. "How He Won," 40.

27. Quotes taken from Darrell West, Montague Kern, and Dean Alger, "Political Advertising and Ad Watches in the 1992 Presidential Nominating Campaign" (Paper delivered at the Annual Meeting of the American Political Science Association, Chicago, September 1992), 15-16. A more detailed account of advertising in the 1992 primaries can be found in this paper.

28. Jamieson, *Packaging the Presidency,* and Devlin, "Contrasts in Presidential Campaign Commercials of 1988."

29. See a discussion of Kerrey's appeals to electability in the *New York Times,* February 14, 1992, A18. Clinton had a similar ad, which is described in the *Washington Post,* February 6, 1992, A16.

30. This analysis is based on a review of television news coverage, as summarized by the *Vanderbilt Television News Index and Abstracts.*

31. The model for Carter's electability shows that seeing ads and watching the television news were associated with believing Carter was likely to become his party's nominee. For Dukakis, seeing ads, watching television news, and having low education were linked to the view that he would have the best chance of winning the November election. The factors most strongly linked to the impression that Buchanan was electable included seeing ads, being poorly educated, being younger, and not being a strong Republican. Bush's electoral prospects were associated with seeing ads, being well-educated, older, and a strong Republican, and having high exposure to television news. The view that Clinton was electable was associated with seeing ads and being a strong Democrat, nonwhite, and interested in politics. Nixon's electability effect was limited to those seeing ads, Republicans, conservatives, and whites.

32. Group variations in advertising also are important, as television does not influence all people in the same way. For example, Frank Fahrenkopf, chairman of the Republican National Committee, described how in 1983 his party tried to defuse the inflation issue for Reagan by emphasizing the economic recovery: "We ... did some targeted advertising on the inflation issue aimed at women voters,

particularly those over 45 who were working women, outside-of-the-home working women, where we felt there was some softness. That was very calculatedly done to lead us into the beginning of 1984." In fact, so pervasive have targeting strategies become in the commercial world that tobacco companies have come under fire for targeting smoking products at blacks, women, and children in their advertising campaigns. The Fahrenkopf quote is taken from Jonathan Moore, ed., *Campaign for President: The Managers Look at '84* (Dover, Mass.: Auburn House, 1986), 108.

33. Jack Germond and Jules Witcover, *Whose Broad Stripes and Bright Stars?* (New York: Warner, 1989), 283-286.

34. Ibid., 290.

35. This quote is taken from Herbert Asher, *Causal Modeling* (Beverly Hills, Calif.: Sage, 1976), 29. Another review of path analysis can be found in George Bohrnstedt and David Knoke, *Statistics for Social Data Analysis,* 2d ed., (Itasca, Ill.: Peacock, 1988), 431-465.

36. Roy Behr and Shanto Iyengar, "Television News, Real-World Cues, and Changes in the Public Agenda," *Public Opinion Quarterly* 49 (1985): 38-57. Also see Shanto Iyengar and Donald Kinder, *News That Matters* (Chicago: University of Chicago Press, 1987), 139-140.

37. Another example of two-stage models can be found in Benjamin Page and Calvin Jones, "Reciprocal Effects of Policy Preferences, Party Loyalties and the Vote," *American Political Science Review* 73 (1979): 1071-1089.

38. The direct effect of electability on the vote in this two-stage analysis was .47 ($p < .001$). Other coefficients that were significant included race (.13; $p < .001$), party identification (-.05; $p < .01$), and sex (-.11; $p < .01$).

39. The best predictors of views regarding electability were exposure to Dukakis ads (.18; $p < .01$) and party (.06; $p < .01$). The significant relationship for advertisements remains even after preferred candidate choice is included in the model as a control factor.

40. The direct effect of electability on the vote in this two-stage analysis was .47 ($p < .001$). The effect on electability from exposure to Dukakis ads was .20 ($p < .001$) and from exposure to Gore ads was .06 (not significant). The following variables were included as control variables: party identification, education, age, sex, race, ideology, political interest, and media exposure.

41. This quote and those that follow come from an interview with the author conducted May 13, 1992. Bob Woodward documents the massive bureaucratic in-fighting that preceded the insertion of the "read my lips" line in Bush's 1988 convention speech in "Origin of the Tax Pledge," *Washington Post,* October 4, 1992, A1.

42. The direct effect of electability on the vote in this two-stage analysis was .40 ($p < .001$). People who saw Bush ads were less likely to say they would vote for him (-.02; $p < .05$). Exposure to Buchanan ads had no significant impact on the vote. The effect on electability from

exposure to Bush ads was -.02 ($p < .10$) and from exposure to Buchanan ads was .01 (not significant). The following variables were included in the analysis as control variables: party identification, education, age, sex, race, ideology, political interest, and media exposure.

43. This information on Bush's ads comes from an interview of Montague Kern with Robin Roberts on April 10, 1992.

Chapter 6 - Agenda Setting

1. The classics in this area are E. E. Schattschneider, *The Semisovereign People* (Hinsdale, Ill.: Dryden Press, 1960); Roger Cobb and Charles Elder, *Participation in American Politics: The Dynamics of Agenda-Building*, 2d ed. (Baltimore: Johns Hopkins University Press, 1983); and John Kingdon, *Agendas, Alternatives, and Public Policies* (Boston: Little, Brown, 1984).

2. Good examples include Maxwell McCombs and Donald Shaw, "The Agenda-Setting Function of Mass Media," *Public Opinion Quarterly* 36 (1972): 176-187; Ray Funkhouser, "The Issues of the Sixties: An Exploratory Study in the Dynamics of Public Opinion," *Public Opinion Quarterly* 37 (1973): 62-75; Jack McLeod, Lee Becker, and James Byrnes, "Another Look at the Agenda-Setting Function of the Press," *Communication Research* 1 (1974): 131-166; Lutz Erbring, Edie Goldenberg, and Arthur Miller, "Front-Page News and Real-World Cues: A New Look at Agenda-Setting by the Media," *American Journal of Political Science* 24 (1980): 16-49; and David Weaver, *Media Agenda-Setting in a Presidential Election* (New York: Praeger, 1981).

3. Shanto Iyengar and Donald Kinder, *News That Matters* (Chicago: University of Chicago Press, 1987), 112; and Samuel Kernell, *Going Public*, 2d ed. (Washington, D.C.: CQ Press, 1993). Also see Benjamin Page, Robert Shapiro, and Glenn Dempsey, "What Moves Public Opinion?" *American Political Science Review* 81 (1987): 23-44.

4. Stanley Feldman, "Economic Self-Interest and Political Behavior," *American Journal of Political Science* 26 (1982): 446-466. Also see Euel Elliott, *Issues and Elections* (Boulder, Colo.: Westview Press, 1989).

5. Paul Light, *The President's Agenda* (Baltimore: Johns Hopkins University Press, 1982).

6. Cobb and Elder, *Participation in American Politics*, 91-92. Also see Arthur Miller, Edie Goldenberg, and Lutz Erbring, "Type-set Politics: Impact of Newspapers on Public Confidence," *American Political Science Review* 73 (1979): 67-84; Michael MacKuen, "Exposure to Information, Belief Integration, and Individual Responsiveness to Agenda Change," *American Political Science Review* 78 (1984): 372-391; and Michael MacKuen, "Political Drama, Economic Conditions,

and the Dynamics of Presidential Popularity," *American Journal of Political Science* 27 (1983): 165-192.

7. Good examples include Maxwell McCombs and Donald Shaw, "The Agenda-Setting Function of Mass Media"; and McLeod, Becker, and Byrnes, "Another Look at the Agenda-Setting Function of the Press."

8. Gladys and Kurt Lang, *The Battle for Public Opinion* (New York: Columbia University Press, 1983).

9. Kingdon, *Agendas, Alternatives, and Public Policies,* 61-64.

10. Ibid., 63.

11. Light, *The President's Agenda,* 96. For congressional studies, see Barbara Sinclair, "The Role of Committees in Agenda Setting in the U.S. Congress," *Legislative Studies Quarterly* 11 (1986): 35-45; Roberta Herzberg and Rick Wilson, "Results on Sophisticated Voting in an Experimental Setting," *Journal of Politics* 50 (1988): 471-486; and Darrell M. West, *Congress and Economic Policymaking* (Pittsburgh: University of Pittsburgh Press, 1987).

12. Charles Atkin and Gary Heald, "Effects of Political Advertising," *Public Opinion Quarterly* 40 (1976): 216-228.

13. Thomas Bowers, "Issue and Personality Information in Newspaper Political Advertising," *Journalism Quarterly* 49 (1972): 446-452; and Bowers, "Newspaper Political Advertising and the Agenda-Setting Function," *Journalism Quarterly* 50 (1973): 552-556.

14. For a review of the character issue, see Peter Goldman, Tom Mathews, and Tony Fuller, *The Quest for the Presidency 1988* (New York: Simon and Schuster, 1989); and Jack Germond and Jules Witcover, *Whose Broad Stripes and Bright Stars?* (New York: Warner, 1989).

15. Nelson Polsby discusses this quality of press coverage in "The News Media as an Alternative to Party in the Presidential Selection Process," in *Political Parties in the Eighties,* ed. Robert Goldwin (Washington, D.C.: American Enterprise Institute, 1980), 50-66.

16. Each of these open-ended questions was coded 1 for mention of a particular problem and 0 if no mention. The 1972 Patterson and McClure survey question was: "There are many problems of concern to people today. Based on your own everyday experiences, what one political problem matters most to you personally?" The 1974 National Election Study used: "Tell me the letter of the issue which is most important to you" (from ten cards provided). The 1976 Patterson survey was based on: "Please think for a moment of the problems that face this country today. In your mind, what do you feel is the one most important problem that the national government in Washington should do something about?" and "So far during the presidential campaign, what do you think is the one most important thing that has happened?" In 1984, the CBS News/*New York Times* poll asked: "What is the single most important thing you would like to see Ronald Reagan accomplish in the next four years as President?" and "What was the best/worst thing Ronald Reagan/Walter Mondale did in this campaign?" The 1988 CBS News/*New York Times* poll asked: "As far as

you are concerned, what should be the single most important issue in this election?" and "What is the best/worst thing George Bush/Michael Dukakis did in this campaign?" The 1990 Rhode Island survey asked: "As far as you are concerned, what is the single most important policy issue in the Senate election?" and "What is the most important event that has occurred in the Senate campaign?" The 1992 surveys asked: "As far as you are concerned, what is the most important problem facing the country today?" and "What do you think is the most important event that has happened so far in this presidential campaign?" The 1990 North Carolina survey did not ask about the most important problem facing the state.

17. For the text of this speech, see "Bush's Presidential Nomination Acceptance Address," *Congressional Quarterly Weekly Report* 46 (1988), 2353-2356.

18. See Eric Uslaner and Margaret Conway, "The Responsible Electorate: Watergate, The Economy, and Vote Choice in 1974," *American Political Science Review* 79 (1985): 788-803.

19. The 1984 and 1988 CBS News/*New York Times* post-general election surveys did not include measures for free media exposure.

20. The 1984 analysis of individual ads does not include a measure of media exposure; the October 1988 CBS News/*New York Times* survey regarding Bush's "Revolving Door" and Dukakis's family/education commercials does incorporate media exposure as a control factor.

21. There often has been confusion between the Bush-produced "Revolving Door" ad, which did not mention Horton directly by name, and the Horton ad aired by an independent political action committee, which used his name and picture. It is not clear whether viewers actually distinguished the two, since both dealt with crime.

22. Marjorie Hershey, "The Campaign and the Media," in *The Election of 1988,* ed. Gerald M. Pomper (Chatham, N.J.: Chatham House, 1989), 95-96.

23. Criticisms about Dukakis's failure to respond to Bush, however, were influenced by personal circumstances. People in the Northeast, those above forty-five years of age, and women were most likely after viewing Dukakis advertising to conclude Dukakis had erred in not responding to Bush's attacks. For more general discussions of the impact of personal predicaments, see Lutz Erbring, Edie Goldenberg, and Arthur Miller, "Front-Page News and Real-World Cues: A New Look at Agenda-Setting by the Media," *American Journal of Political Science* 24 (1980): 16-49; Tom Tyler, "Impact of Directly and Indirectly Experienced Events: The Origins of Crime-Related Judgments and Behaviors," *Journal of Personality and Social Psychology* 39 (1980): 13-28; and David Sears, Tom Tyler, T. Citrin, and Donald Kinder, "Political System Support and Public Response to the Energy Crisis," *American Journal of Political Science* 22 (1978): 56-82.

24. "How He Won," *Newsweek,* November/December 1992 (special issue), 78.

25. I also confirmed this result through a logistic regression analysis which included an interaction term for gender and exposure to Bush's "Revolving Door" ad. The coefficient for the interaction term was 1.39 with a standard error of .62 ($p < .05$), indicating a strong relationship in the expected direction.

26. Quote taken from David Runkel, ed., *Campaign for President: The Managers Look at '88* (Dover, Mass.: Auburn House, 1989), 113-114.

27. For a related argument, see Darrell M. West, "Television and Presidential Popularity in America," *British Journal of Political Science* 21 (1991): 199-214.

28. Stephen Ansolabehere and Shanto Iyengar, "The Electoral Effects of Issues and Attacks in Campaign Advertising" (Paper delivered at the Annual Meeting of the American Political Science Association, Washington, D.C., August 1991).

29. Quote taken from Runkel, *Campaign for President: The Managers Look at '88*, 110. In anticipation of similar treatment, Bill Clinton in 1992 hired someone to do opposition research on himself. See Sonni Efron and David Lauter, "Spy vs. Spy: Campaign Dirt Game," *Los Angeles Times,* March 28, 1992, 1.

30. After the election, Atwater claimed that it was Gore, during the Democratic nominating process, who first criticized Dukakis on the Horton furlough issue. See Runkel, *Campaign for President: The Managers Look at '88,* 115.

31. Ibid., 221.

32. Ibid., 9.

33. In this two-stage analysis of the 1988 CBS News/*New York Times* survey data, the direct effect on the vote of citing crime as the most important problem was .70 ($p < .05$). People who saw Bush's "Revolving Door" ad were more likely to cite crime (.10; $p < .01$), while those who saw Dukakis's family education ad were less likely to name crime (-.06; $p < .05$). The following variables were included in the analysis as control variables: party identification, education, age, sex, race, ideology, political interest, and media exposure. Neither ad had a direct effect on the vote, so those linkages were removed from the path model. Other agenda items displaying significant correlations with the vote included social welfare problems and jobs.

34. Quote taken from Runkel, *Campaign for President: The Managers Look at '88,* 9.

35. See Kiku Adatto, "Sound Bite Democracy: Network Evening News Presidential Campaign Coverage, 1968 and 1988" (Research Paper R-2, Joan Shorenstein Barone Center for Press, Politics and Public Policy, June 1990), 9, 26-27. On October 25, 1988, CBS reporter Lesley Stahl corrected the Revolving Door claim that "268 escaped" by pointing out that four first-degree murderers escaped while on parole. Other reporting on the furlough ad can be found on ABC on September 22, CBS on October 28, "Meet the Press" and "Face the Nation" the last weekend in October, and "Good Morning America"

in early October.

36. "How He Won," 84.
37. Richard Berke, "The Ad Campaign: Mixing Harshness with Warmth," *New York Times,* October 22, 1992, A20; and Leslie Phillips, "Bush Ads Revive 'Man on the Street,'" *USA Today,* October 23, 1992, A2.
38. Robin Toner, "Clinton Retains Significant Lead in Latest Survey," *New York Times,* September 16, 1992, A1.
39. Toner, "Clinton Fending off Assaults, Retains Sizable Lead, Poll Finds," *New York Times,* October 15, 1992, A1.
40. "How He Won," 81.
41. Toner, "Clinton Fending Off Assaults." After the election, it was revealed that searches had been made of Perot's passport file, too.
42. Quoted in Howard Kurtz, "In Advertising Give and Take, Clinton Camp Took and Responded," *Washington Post,* November 6, 1992, A10.
43. "How He Won," 84.

Chapter 7 - Priming, Defusing, and the Blame Game

1. See Herbert Simon, *Models of Thought* (New Haven: Yale University Press, 1979); S. E. Asch, "Forming Impressions of Personality," *Journal of Abnormal and Social Psychology* 41 (1946): 258-290; and B. Fischhoff, P. Slovic, and S. Lichtenstein, "Knowing What You Want," in *Cognitive Processes in Choice and Decision Behavior,* ed. T. Wallsten (Hillsdale, N.J.: Erlbaum, 1980).
2. A number of studies have investigated this relationship. See George Bishop, Robert Oldendick, and Alfred Tuchfarber, "Political Information Processing: Question Order and Context Effects," *Political Behavior* 4 (1982): 177-200; C. Turner and E. Krauss, "Fallible Indicators of the Subjective State of the Nation," *American Psychologist* 33 (1978): 456-470; and Amos Tversky and Daniel Kahneman, "The Framing of Decisions and the Psychology of Choice," *Science* 211 (1981): 453-458.
3. Peter Goldman, Tom Mathews, and Tony Fuller, *The Quest for the Presidency, 1988* (New York: Simon and Schuster, 1989); Jack Germond and Jules Witcover, *Whose Broad Stripes and Bright Stars?* (New York: Warner, 1989).
4. Daniel Kahneman, Paul Slovic, and Amos Tversky, *Judgment Under Uncertainty: Heuristics and Biases* (New York: Cambridge University Press, 1982).
5. Goldman, Mathews, and Fuller, *The Quest for the Presidency, 1988;* and Germond and Witcover, *Whose Broad Stripes and Bright Stars?*
6. Shanto Iyengar and Donald Kinder, *News That Matters* (Chicago: University of Chicago Press, 1987), 63-64. Also see Jon Krosnick and Donald Kinder, "Altering the Foundations of Popular Support for the

President Through Priming: Reagan and the Iran-Contra Affair," *American Political Science Review* 84 (1990): 497-512.

7. Iyengar and Kinder, *News That Matters,* 63.
8. Krosnick and Kinder, "Altering the Foundations of Popular Support."
9. Lawrence Jacobs and Robert Shapiro, "Issues, Candidate Image, and Priming: The Use of Private Polls in Kennedy's 1960 Presidential Campaign" (Unpublished paper, Columbia University, 1992).
10. Michael Robinson and Margaret Sheehan, *Over the Wire and on TV* (New York: Russell Sage, 1983); and F. Christopher Arterton, "Campaign Organizations Confront the Media-Political Environment," in *Race for the Presidency,* ed. James David Barber (Englewood Cliffs, N.J.: Prentice Hall, 1978), 3-24.
11. Richard Brody and Catherine Shapiro, "Policy Failure and Public Support," *Political Behavior* 11 (1989): 353-369. A more general discussion of this argument can be found in Richard Brody, *Assessing the President: The Media, Elite Opinion, and Public Support* (Stanford, Calif.: Stanford University Press, 1991).
12. Jeff Fishel, *Presidents and Promises* (Washington, D.C.: CQ Press, 1985); and Gerald Pomper with Susan Lederman, *Elections in America,* 2d ed. (New York: Longman, 1980).
13. Iyengar and Kinder, *News That Matters,* 66-68.
14. Krosnick and Kinder, "Altering the Foundations of Popular Support."
15. Descriptions of the 1972 presidential campaign can be found in Thomas Patterson and Robert McClure, *The Unseeing Eye* (New York: Putnam's, 1976); and Warren Miller and J. Merrill Shanks, "Policy Directions and Presidential Leadership: Alternative Interpretations of the 1980 Presidential Election," *British Journal of Political Science* 12 (1982): 299-356.
16. Theodore White, *The Making of the President, 1972* (New York: Atheneum, 1973).
17. Goldman, Mathews, and Fuller, *The Quest for the Presidency, 1988;* and Germond and Witcover, *Whose Broad Stripes and Bright Stars?*
18. The questions used in this analysis were based on an October 1988 CBS News/*New York Times* survey. The items used were: "If George Bush were elected President, do you think he would make U.S. defenses stronger, make them weaker, or would he keep defenses at the present level?" "Regardless of who you intend to vote for, do you think 1) George Bush or 2) Michael Dukakis would do a better job of protecting the environment?" "Regardless of who you intend to vote for, do you think 1) George Bush or 2) Michael Dukakis cares more about the needs and problems of people like yourself?" and [The death penalty for people convicted of controlling large drug dealing operations]: "Does George Bush agree with your position on this issue, or doesn't he? (1) yes or (2) no."
19. Dave Kaplan, "Early Readings on '90 Elections," *Congressional Quarterly Weekly Report,* February 17, 1990, 488-489. A discussion of the 1990 contest can be found in Montague Kern and Marion Just,

"Constructing Candidate Images: Focus Group Discourse about Campaign News and Advertising" (Paper delivered at the Annual Meeting of the New England Political Science Association, Providence, April 1992).

20. Bob Benenson, "Republicans' Net Loss: One Seat and Many Expectations," *Congressional Quarterly Weekly Report,* November 10, 1990, 3824-3829.

21. Thomas Edsall, "Carolina Senate Contest Shows Voters' Age Gap," *Washington Post,* November 4, 1990, A16.

22. Edsall, "Helms Makes Race an Issue," *Washington Post,* November 1, 1990, A1, 6.

23. These questions were asked in the following way: "Do you 1) support or 2) oppose drilling for gas and oil off the coast of North Carolina?" "Do you think abortions should 1) be legal under any circumstances, 2) legal only under certain circumstances, or 3) never legal under any circumstances?" "Do you think it will be best for the future of this country 1) if we take an active part in world affairs, or 2) if we stay out of world affairs?" and "Do you 1) favor or 2) oppose the death penalty for persons convicted of murder?"

24. Robin Toner, "An Underdog Forces Helms into a Surprisingly Tight Race," *New York Times,* October 31, 1990, A1, D25.

25. This and the following description of the Clinton strategy can be found in "How He Won," *Newsweek,* November/December 1992 (special issue), 40-56. Also see Michael Kelly, "The Making of a First Family: A Blueprint," *New York Times,* November 14, 1992, 1.

26. This analysis was based on the questions: "As far as you are concerned, what is the most important problem facing the country today?" (open-ended responses coded for mentioning or not mentioning the economy); "If Bill Clinton were elected president, would he make the U.S. economy get better, get worse, or stay about the same?"; and "Bill Clinton is honest and trustworthy: strongly agree, agree, disagree, or strongly disagree." The vote was support or nonsupport for Clinton. Controls were included for party identification, education, age, sex, race, ideology, political interest, and media exposure.

27. For example, Yale economist Ray Fair's model, based on national economic growth, boldly predicted a big Bush reelection. What it failed to recognize, though, was the cumulative nature of economic fears and the ability of candidates to influence attributions of responsibility. A discussion of 1992 forecasting models is found in Richard Morin, "For Political Forecasters, Key Variable Is the Winner," *Washington Post,* September 5, 1992, A1. Only two of the five forecasters cited in this article anticipated a Clinton victory.

28. A discussion of presidential attributions can be found in Iyengar and Kinder, *News That Matters,* 82-89.

29. Larry Sabato summarizes the public disgust with negative campaigning in *The 1988 Elections in America* (Glenview, Ill.: Scott, Foresman, 1989), 24.

30. L. Patrick Devlin, "Contrasts in Presidential Campaign Commercials of 1988," *American Behavioral Scientist* 32 (1989): 401.

31. For an exception, see Michael Pfau and Henry Kenski, *Attack Politics* (New York: Praeger, 1990).

32. Iyengar and Kinder, *News That Matters*, 82-89.

33. Panel data from before and after the election show 58 percent felt in both the pre- and postelection surveys that Bush was responsible for negative campaigning. Among low ad viewers, 46 percent consistently cited Bush as the culprit, while among high viewers, 67 percent named him.

34. Discussions of voter backlash against Bush can be found in Howard Kurtz, "Bush's Negative Ads Appear to Be Backfiring," *Washington Post*, October 10, 1992, A12; Renee Loth, "Ads Afford View of Camps' Strong, Weak Spots," *Boston Globe*, October 22, 1992, 19; Howard Kurtz, "Negative Ads Appear to Lose Potency," *Washington Post*, October 26, 1992, A1; Howard Kurtz, "Perot Escalates Costly TV Ad Blitz Targeting Media, Parties, Pundits," *Washington Post*, October 27, 1992, A1; and Leslie Phillips, "Hopefuls May Spend Record $300 Million," *USA Today*, October 23-25, 1992, A1.

35. The Clinton quote comes from the text of his acceptance speech printed in *Congressional Quarterly Weekly Report*, July 18, 1992, 2130. Quinn's quote is cited in Phil Duncan, "Unease about Party's Chances Underlies Week of Glitz," *Congressional Quarterly Weekly Report*, July 18, 1992, 2091.

36. Text shown in Howard Kurtz, "In Advertising Give and Take, Clinton Camp Took and Responded," *Washington Post*, November 6, 1992, A10.

37. The first quote comes from Michael Kelly with David Johnston, "Campaign Renews Disputes of the Vietnam War Years," *New York Times*, October 9, 1992, 1. The second quote is taken from Michael Isikoff, "Clinton Denounces Attacks by Bush," *Washington Post*, October 9, 1992, A1.

38. In this two-stage analysis of the September 1992 Winston-Salem, N.C., data, the direct effect on the vote of attributions of responsibility for negative campaigning was -.24 ($p < .001$). People who saw Bush as attacking were more likely to attribute responsibility to him (.31; $p < .001$), while those who saw Dukakis as attacking were more likely to attribute responsibility to him (.32; $p < .001$). The following variables were included in the analysis as control variables: party identification, education, age, sex, race, ideology, political interest, and media exposure.

39. Quote cited in David Hilzenrath, "GOP Aide Slams Administration," *Washington Post*, November 6, 1992, A18.

40. See Kurtz, "Advertising Give and Take," A10; and Ross Perot, *United We Stand* (New York: Hyperion, 1992).

Chapter 8 - Advertising and Democratic Elections

1. For a summary of this literature, see Eric R.A.N. Smith, *The Unchanging American Voter* (Berkeley: University of California Press, 1989); Michael Margolis and Gary Mauser, eds., *Manipulating Public Opinion* (Pacific Grove, Calif.: Brooks/Cole, 1989); and Paul Abramson, John Aldrich, and David Rohde, *Change and Continuity in the 1988 Elections* (Washington, D.C.: CQ Press, 1990).

2. C. Wright Mills, *The Power Elite* (New York: Oxford University Press, 1956). Some scholars have looked at candidates. For example, work by Fenno demonstrates the importance of candidate "home style" in congressional elections. At the presidential level, Page and West make the simple but important point that people do not vote in a vacuum; rather they make decisions within the options that candidates present them. Hershey has examined how elites construct interpretations of election outcomes. See Richard F. Fenno, Jr., *Home Style* (Boston: Little, Brown, 1978); Benjamin Page, *Choices and Echoes in Presidential Elections* (Chicago: University of Chicago Press, 1978); Darrell West, *Making Campaigns Count* (Westport, Conn.: Greenwood Press, 1984); and Marjorie Randon Hershey, "The Constructed Explanation: Interpreting Election Results in the 1984 Presidential Race," *Journal of Politics* 54 (1992): 943-976.

3. John Zaller, *The Nature and Origins of Mass Opinion* (New York: Cambridge University Press, 1992); Richard Brody, *Assessing the President: The Media, Elite Opinion, and Public Support* (Stanford Calif.: Stanford University Press, 1991); and Benjamin Page and Robert Shapiro, *The Rational Public* (Chicago: University of Chicago Press, 1992).

4. Quoted in John Foley, Dennis Britton, and Eugene Everett, Jr., eds., *Nominating a President: The Process and the Press* (New York: Praeger, 1980), 58.

5. John Dryzek, *Discursive Democracy* (Cambridge, England: Cambridge University Press, 1990); Christopher Arterton, *Teledemocracy: Can Technology Protect Democracy?* (Newbury Park, Calif.: Sage, 1987); Jeffrey Abramson, Christopher Arterton, and Gary Orren, *The Electronic Commonwealth: The Impact of New Media Technologies on Democratic Politics* (New York: Basic Books, 1988); and Robert Entman, *Democracy Without Citizens* (New York: Oxford University Press, 1989). General analyses of the impact of the media can be found in W. Russell Neuman, *The Paradox of Mass Politics* (Cambridge: Harvard University Press, 1986); and Theodore Lowi, *The Personal President* (Ithaca, N.Y.: Cornell University Press, 1985).

6. Joseph Schumpeter, *Capitalism, Socialism and Democracy* (New York: Harper and Row, 1942), 250-268.

7. Nelson Polsby, *Consequences of Party Reform* (New York: Oxford University Press, 1983).

8. Morris Fiorina, *Retrospective Evaluations in American National*

Elections (New Haven, Conn.: Yale University Press, 1981).

9. Richard Merelman, *Making Something of Ourselves: On Culture and Politics in the United States* (Berkeley: University of California Press, 1984). Nancy Rosenblum also has made this point in a personal communication to me.

10. Benjamin Barber has made a very useful distinction between strong and thin democracy in *Strong Democracy: Participatory Politics for a New Age* (Berkeley: University of California Press, 1984). Thin democracy makes relatively few demands of the electorate. This formulation sees the major activity of citizens as choosing leaders. Candidates are expected to facilitate voters' decisions by avoiding information that is misleading or incorrect. This view of democracy obviously places little emphasis on the general civic education of voters (other than that required for electoral choice), and therefore requires that little detailed information be presented in campaign ads. Strong democracy, on the other hand, rests on a more fully involved electorate. Not only are candidates expected to avoid misinformation, they face the positive requirement of transmitting material to the electorate that will aid voters' judgments as well as facilitate political education beyond the immediate choice between candidates. This formulation clearly places a much heavier burden on campaign advertising than does thin democracy.

11. Diana Mutz, "Mass Media and the Depoliticization of Personal Experience," *American Journal of Political Science* 36 (1992): 483-508.

12. The emphasis placed on brevity today often leads consultants to advise candidates not to communicate an idea that is too lengthy to fit on a bumper sticker! This bumper sticker standard is illustrated in Paul Magnusson, "Bush Just Might Buy This Plan—If No One Calls It 'Industrial Policy,'" *Business Week,* April 1, 1991, 27.

13. Barbara Hinckley, Richard Hofstetter, and John Kessel, "Information and the Vote: A Comparative Election Study," *American Politics Quarterly* 2 (1974): 131-158; Kim Kahn, "Senate Elections in the News," *Legislative Studies Quarterly* 16 (1991): 349-374; and Kim Kahn, "Does Being Male Help? An Investigation of the Effects of Candidate Gender and Campaign Coverage on Evaluations of U.S. Senate Candidates," *Journal of Politics* 54 (1992): 497-517.

14. Benjamin Page and Robert Shapiro, "Educating and Manipulating the Public," in *Manipulating Public Opinion,* ed. Margolis and Mauser, 307-308. Also see Page, *Choices and Echoes in Presidential Elections,* 266-277; Schumpeter, *Capitalism, Socialism and Democracy,* 250-268, and Kathleen Jamieson, *Dirty Politics: Deception, Distraction, and Democracy* (New York: Oxford University Press, 1992).

15. Floyd Brown's fakery is described in Mike Robinson, "Clinton Camp Denounces TV Ad," *Providence Journal,* October 24, 1992, A1.

16. Joe McGinniss, *The Selling of the President* (New York: Simon and Schuster, 1969); and Robert Spero, *The Duping of the American Voter*

(New York: Lippincott and Crowell, 1980).

17. J. Gregory Payne, John Marlier, and Robert Baukus, "Polispots in the 1988 Presidential Primaries," *American Behavioral Scientist* 32 (1989): 375.

18. Where strong prior beliefs are present, the danger of advertising goes down dramatically. But, of course, in a rapidly changing world where traditional moorings are disappearing—witness the collapse of communism on the world scene—even prior assumptions are being challenged. For a discussion of constraints on ad influence, see Elizabeth Kolbert, "Ad Effect on Vote Slipping," *New York Times,* March 22, 1992, "Week in Review," 4.

19. The Clinton quote comes from the text of his acceptance speech as printed in *Congressional Quarterly Weekly Report,* July 18, 1992, 2130.

20. Klaus Schoenbach, "The Role of Mass Media in West German Election Campaigns," *Legislative Studies Quarterly* 12 (1987): 373-394. For a review of the experience of other countries, see Howard Penniman and Austin Ranney, "The Regulation of Televised Political Advertising in Six Selected Democracies" (Paper prepared for the Committee for the Study of the American Electorate, Washington, D.C., undated).

21. Critics have also complained about the effectiveness of ad targeting on underage youths by tobacco companies. Research reported in the December 11, 1991, issue of the *Journal of the American Medical Association* has shown that the cartoon figure Old Joe Camel, used to advertise Camel cigarettes, has been a huge hit among youths aged twelve to nineteen years. Compared with adults in general, students were much more likely to indicate that they recognized Old Joe, liked him as a friend, and thought the ads looked cool. See Walecia Konrad, "I'd Toddle a Mile for a Camel," *Business Week,* December 23, 1991, 34.

22. The classic Supreme Court ruling in the campaign area was *Buckley v. Valeo* in 1976. This case struck down a number of finance regulations as unconstitutional encroachments. See Clarke Caywood and Ivan Preston, "The Continuing Debate on Political Advertising: Toward a Jeopardy Theory of Political Advertising as Regulated Speech," *Journal of Public Policy and Marketing* 8 (1989): 204-226. For other reviews of newly emerging technologies, see Jeffrey Abramson, Christopher Arterton, and Gary Orren, *The Electronic Commonwealth;* (New York: Basic Books, 1988), and Erwin Krasnow, Lawrence Longley, and Herbert Terry, *The Politics of Broadcast Regulation,* 3d ed. (New York: St. Martin's, 1982).

23. A more extended discussion of reform proposals can be found in Darrell West, "Reforming Campaign Ads," *PS: Political Science and Politics* 24 (1992): 74-77.

24. Laurence Parisot, "Attitudes about the Media: A Five-Country Comparison," *Public Opinion* 10 (1988): 18-19, 60. However, viewers

do see differences in the helpfulness of television and newspapers. A May 1992 survey of Los Angeles residents revealed that those who followed Ad Watches in newspapers were much more likely (35 percent) to see them as being very helpful than those who relied on television (16 percent).

25. Kathleen Hall Jamieson, "For Televised Mendacity, This Year Is the Worst Ever," *Washington Post,* October 30, 1988, C1; and David Broder, "Five Ways to Put Some Sanity Back in Elections," *Washington Post,* January 14, 1990, B1.

26. Media scholar Jamieson has been instrumental in encouraging these Ad Watch efforts. According to personal correspondence from her, forty-two campaigns in 1990 were subjected to detailed critiques. For example, television stations airing discussions of particular ads included WFAA in Dallas, KVUE in Austin, WCVB in Boston, KRON in San Francisco, WBBM in Chicago, and WCCO in Minneapolis. Newspapers that followed ad campaigns closely were the *New York Times, Washington Post, Los Angeles Times, Chicago Sun-Times, Dallas Morning News, Houston Chronicle, Cleveland Plain-Dealer, Akron Beacon-Journal,* and *Louisville Courier-Journal.*

27. Race, of course, has been a controversial subject in many areas of American life. For a discussion of controversial rapper Ice Cube, see Craig McCoy, "Korean-American Merchants Claim Victory against Rapper Ice Cube," *Boston Globe,* November 28, 1991, A35. Also see Edward Carmines and James Stimson, *Issue Evolution: Race and the Transformation of American Politics* (Princeton: Princeton University Press, 1989).

28. Quoted by Kathleen Jamieson and Karlyn Kohrs Campbell in *The Interplay of Influence,* 2d ed. (Belmont, Calif.: Wadsworth, 1988), 55.

29. For an example of this thinking, see L. Brent Bozell and Brent Baker, eds., *And That's the Way It Isn't* (Alexandria, Va.: Media Research Center, 1990). Also see Lynda Lee Kaid, Rob Gobetz, Jane Garner, Chris Leland, and David Scott, "Television News and Presidential Campaigns: The Legitimization of Televised Political Advertising," *Social Science Quarterly* (forthcoming), and Elizabeth Kolbert, "As Political Campaigns Turn Negative, the Press Is Given a Negative Rating," *New York Times,* May 1, 1992, A18.

30. Text is quoted from Roberto Suro, "In Louisiana, Both Edwards and Duke Are Sending a Message of Fear," *New York Times,* November 15, 1991, A20.

31. The media rating was in response to an October 1992 question in our Los Angeles County survey: "So far this year, would you say the news media have done an excellent, good, fair, or poor job of covering this presidential campaign?" The press bias question also was asked in the October survey: "In your opinion, has news coverage of this year's fall presidential campaign been biased against any individual candidate? If so, which candidate received the most biased coverage?" The figures on television coverage come from Howard Kurtz, "Networks Stressed the

Negative in Comments about Bush, Study Finds," *Washington Post,* November 15, 1992, A7. The longitudinal evidence on the party leanings of reporters is discussed by William Glaberson in "More Reporters Leaning Democratic, Study Says," *New York Times,* November 18, 1992, A20. Also see Elizabeth Kolbert, "Maybe the Media Did Treat Bush a Bit Harshly," *New York Times,* November 22, 1992, "Week in Review," 3.

32. Jeffrey Tulis, *The Rhetorical Presidency* (Princeton: Princeton University Press, 1987).

33. These and following quotes are taken from Darrell West, Montague Kern, and Dean Alger, "Political Advertising and Ad Watches in the 1992 Presidential Nominating Campaign" (Paper delivered at the Annual Meeting of the American Political Science Association, Chicago, September 1992), 24.

34. After the election, Clinton used call-in radio and TV shows, radio addresses, and an 800 telephone number that people could call with suggestions. See Richard Berke, "Clinton Plans Call-in Shows and Other Outreach Efforts," *New York Times,* November 21, 1992, 8.

Appendix

1. L. Patrick Devlin, "Contrasts in Presidential Campaign Commercials of 1984," *Political Communications Review* 12 (1987): 26.

2. Ibid.

3. L. Patrick Devlin, "Contrasts in Presidential Campaign Commercials of 1988," *American Behavioral Scientist* 32 (1989): 390.

4. Ed McCabe, "The Campaign You Never Saw," *New York Times,* December 12, 1988, 32.

5. Author's transcription from 1992 Clinton primary ad tapes.

6. Author's transcription from 1992 general election ad tapes.

7. Ibid.

8. Ibid.

9. Ibid.

Index